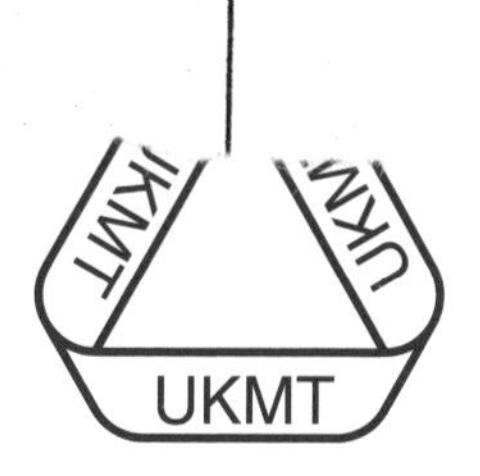

The UK Mathematics Trust

Yearbook

2013 – 2014

This book contains an account of UKMT activities from 1st September 2013 to 31st August 2014. It contains all question papers, solutions and results as well as a variety of other information.

Published by the United Kingdom Mathematics Trust.
School of Mathematics, The University of Leeds, Leeds LS2 9JT
Telephone: 0113 343 2339
E-mail: enquiry@ukmt.org.uk
Website: http://www.ukmt.org.uk

Cover design: – The backdrop is a Penrose tiling whose complexity reflects the activities of the UKMT.

The photographs are

Front Cover:

JMC 2014 certificate winners, Durham Johnston School

Back Cover:

Scottish dancing at the AKSF 2013 meeting

UK team at the Balkans Mathematical Olympiad 2014

ISBN 978-1-906001-23-0

Printed and bound in Great Britain by
H. Charlesworth & Co. Ltd, Wakefield

Contents

The year 2013/14 has been another busy and successful one for UKMT, and you can read about many of the Trust's activities in this Yearbook.

In particular I am very happy to report that the total number of entries to the Maths Challenges reached its highest ever level this year, overtaking the previous record in 2008/9. Entry numbers for the Junior Challenge rose from 284,070 in 2012/13 to 290,820 and the number of participating schools also increased from 3,849 to 3,909. For the Intermediate Challenge, numbers of entries and participating schools increased from 245,760 entries and 3,097 schools in 2012/13 to 254,130 entries and 3,147 schools in 2013/14. Likewise numbers for the Senior Challenge rose again from 98,560 entries and 2,037 schools in 2012/13 to 104,360 entries and 2,113 schools this year. In addition entries for the Team Challenge and for the Senior Team Challenge (the latter run in collaboration with the Further Maths Support Programme) both rose again this year to 1,730 and 1,147 teams respectively.

There was an almost fivefold increase in the number of entries to the Mathematical Olympiad for Girls (MOG) last September. The team sent to the European Girls' Mathematical Olympiad in Turkey in the spring claimed two silver medals and finished in 8th place out of 29 teams, its highest position yet.

All the members of this year's IMO team, recently back from the International Olympiad competition in South Africa, were awarded medals (four silver and two bronze) and the UK finished 20th out of 101 participating countries. Our congratulations go to them and also to Geoff Smith, who was elected as IMO Chair. The other big news for UKMT from the IMO competition was that the jury approved the UK's bid to host the competition in 2019, which will be the 60th anniversary of the IMO.

This year UKMT was host to KSF2013; the annual meeting of the Association Kangourou sans Frontières took place in Edinburgh from Tuesday 29th October – Sunday 3rd November 2013 and was very successful.

A recent venture for UKMT has been the introduction of two–day non-residential 'Mathematical Circles'. The number of these has been increased using a two-year grant from the Department for Education. This grant also allowed us to run two summer schools in Oxford in August 2013, and again in August 2014, in addition to the two National Mathematics Summer Schools, which moved to Bradford in 2013 as the usual Birmingham venue was undergoing refurbishment. A new Summer

School for Girls took place in Oxford in August 2013 and will continue to run, funded by donations including from the Clay Mathematics Institute.

All these activities, and the Trust's many other activities too numerous to mention here, could not take place without the enormous commitment and dedication of many UKMT volunteers around the country. I would like to finish by expressing huge thanks to them all, as well as to the Director, Rachel Greenhalgh, and her small but dedicated band of UKMT staff in Leeds!

Frances Kirwan
Balliol College, Oxford
August 2014

Introduction

Foundation of the Trust

National mathematics competitions have existed in the UK for several decades. Up until 1987 the total annual participation was something like 8,000. Then there was an enormous growth, from 24,000 in 1988 to around a quarter of a million in 1995 – without doubt due to the drive, energy and leadership of Dr Tony Gardiner. By the end of this period there were some nine or ten competitions for United Kingdom schools and their students organised by three different bodies: the British Mathematical Olympiad Committee, the National Committee for Mathematical Contests and the UK Mathematics Foundation. During 1995 discussions took place between interested parties which led to agreement to seek a way of setting up a single body to continue and develop these competitions and related activities. This led to the formation of the United Kingdom Mathematics Trust, which was incorporated as a company limited by guarantee in October 1996 and registered with the Charity Commission.

Throughout its existence, the UKMT has continued to nurture and expand the number of competitions. As a result, over six hundred thousand students throughout the UK now participate in the challenges alone, and their teachers (as well as others) not only provide much valued help and encouragement, but also take advantage of the support offered to them by the Trust.

The Royal Institution of Great Britain is the Trust's Patron, and it and the Mathematical Association are Participating Bodies. The Association of Teachers of Mathematics, the Edinburgh Mathematical Society, the Institute of Mathematics and Its Applications, the London Mathematical Society and the Royal Society are all Supporting Bodies.

Aims and Activities of the Trust

According to its constitution, the Trust has a very wide brief, namely "to advance the education of children and young people in mathematics". To attain this, it is empowered to engage in activities ranging from teaching to publishing and lobbying. But its focal point is the organisation of mathematical competitions, from popular mass "challenges" to the selection and training of the British team for the annual International Mathematical Olympiad (IMO).

There are three main challenges, the UK Junior, Intermediate and Senior Mathematical Challenges. The number of challenge entries in 2013-2014 totalled 649,310, an increase of over 20,000 on last year. The challenges were organised by the Challenges Subtrust (CS). The Challenges are open to all pupils of the appropriate age. Certificates are awarded for the best performances and the most successful participants are encouraged to enter follow-up competitions.

At the junior and intermediate levels, a total of around 11000 pupils enter the follow-up competitions. These consist of the Junior Mathematical Olympiad and a suite of papers forming the Intermediate Mathematical Olympiad and Kangaroo under the auspices of the Challenges Subtrust.

The British Mathematical Olympiad Committee Subtrust (BMOS) organises two rounds of the British Mathematical Olympiad. Usually about 800 students who have distinguished themselves in the Senior Mathematical Challenge are invited to enter Round 1, leading to about 100 in Round 2. From the latter, around twenty are invited to a training weekend at Trinity College, Cambridge. Additionally, an elite squad, identified largely by performances in the UKMT competitions, is trained at camps and by correspondence courses throughout the year. The UK team is then selected for the annual International Mathematical Olympiad (IMO) which usually takes place in July. Recent IMOs were held as follows: USA (2001), UK (2002), Japan (2003), Athens (2004), Mexico (2005), Slovenia (2006), Vietnam (2007), Madrid (2008), Bremen (2009), Kazakhstan (2010), Amsterdam (2011), Argentina (2012), Colombia (2013) and South Africa in 2014. The BMOS also runs a mentoring scheme for high achievers at senior, intermediate and junior levels.

Structure and Membership of the Trust

The governing body of the Trust is its Council. The events have been organised by three Subtrusts who report directly to the Council. The work of the Trust in setting question papers, marking scripts, monitoring competitions, mentoring students and helping in many other ways depends critically on a host of volunteers. A complete list of members of the Trust, its Subtrusts and other volunteers appears at the end of this publication.

Challenges Office Staff

Rachel Greenhalgh continues in her role as Director of the Trust, ably supported by the Maths Challenges Office staff of Nicky Bray, Janet Clark, Gerard Cummings, Heather Macklin, Shona Raffle-Edwards and Jo Williams. Beverley Detoeuf continues as Packing Office Manager and leads the packing and processing team of Claire Hall, Gwyneth Hartley, Piatta Hellevaara, Rachael Raby-Cox, Stewart Ramsay and Alison Steggall, ably assisted by Mary Roberts, Packing Office Supervisor.

An outline of the events

This is a brief description of the challenges, their follow-up competitions and other activities. Much fuller information can be found later in the book.

Junior competitions

The UK Junior Mathematical Challenge, typically held on the last Thursday in April, is a one hour, 25 question, multiple choice paper for pupils up to and including:

Y8 in England and Wales; S2 in Scotland, and Y9 in Northern Ireland.

Pupils enter their personal details and answers on a special answer sheet for machine reading. The questions are set so that the first 15 should be accessible to all participants whereas the remaining 10 are more testing.

Five marks are awarded for each correct answer to the first 15 questions and six marks are awarded for each correct answer to the rest. Each incorrect answer to questions 16–20 loses 1 mark and each incorrect answer to questions 21–25 loses 2 marks. Penalty marking is used to discourage guessing.

Certificates are awarded on a proportional basis:– Gold about 6%, Silver about 14% and Bronze about 20% of all entrants. Each centre also receives one 'Best in School Certificate'. A 'Best in Year Certificate' is awarded to the highest scoring candidate in each year group, in each school.

The Junior Mathematical Olympiad is the follow-up competition to the JMC. It is normally held six weeks after the JMC and between 1000 and 1200 high scorers in the JMC are invited to take part. It is a two-hour paper which has two sections. Section A contains ten questions and pupils are required to give the answer only. Section B contains six questions for which full written answers are required. It is made clear to candidates that they are not expected to complete all of Section B and that little credit will be given to fragmentary answers. Gold, silver and bronze medals are awarded to very good candidates. In 2014 a total of 263 medals was awarded. The top 25% candidates got Certificates of Distinction. Of the rest, those who had qualified for the JMO automatically via the JMC received a Certificate of Participation. In addition, the top 50 students were given book prizes.

Intermediate competitions

The UK Intermediate Mathematical Challenge is organised in a very similar way to the Junior Challenge. One difference is that the age range goes up to Y11 in England and Wales, to S4 in Scotland and Y12 in

Northern Ireland. The other difference is the timing; the IMC is held on the first Thursday in February. All other arrangements are as in the JMC.

There are five follow-up competitions under the overall title 'Intermediate Mathematical Olympiad and Kangaroo' (IMOK). Between 400 and 550 in each of Years 9, 10 and 11 (English style) sit an Olympiad paper (Cayley, Hamilton and Maclaurin respectively). In 2014, each of these was a two-hour paper and contained six questions all requiring full written solutions. A total of around 8000 pupils from the three year groups took part in a Kangaroo paper. In the European Kangaroo papers, which last an hour, there are 25 multiple-choice questions. The last ten questions are more testing than the first fifteen and correct answers gain six marks as opposed to five. Penalty marking is not applied. The same Kangaroo paper (designated 'Pink') was taken by pupils in Years 10 and 11 and a different one, 'Grey', by pupils in Year 9. In 2014, the Olympiads and Kangaroos were sat on Thursday 20th March. In the Olympiads, the top 25% of candidates got Certificates of Distinction. Most of the rest receive a Merit and of the rest, those who had qualified for the Olympiad automatically via the IMC received a Certificate of Participation. In the Kangaroos, the top 25% got a Merit and the rest a Participation. All Olympiad and Kangaroo candidates received a 'Kangaroo gift'; a specially designed UKMT key fob. In addition, the top 50 students in each year group in the Olympiad papers were given a book. Performance in the Olympiad papers and the IMC was a major factor in determining pupils to be invited to one of the UKMT summer schools early in July.

Senior competitions

In 2013, the UK Senior Mathematical Challenge was held on Thursday 7th November. Like the other Challenges, it is a 25 question, multiple choice paper marked in the same way as the Junior and Intermediate Challenges. However, it lasts 1½ hours. Certificates (including Best in School) are awarded as with the other Challenges. The follow-up competitions are organised by the British Mathematical Olympiad Subtrust.

The first is BMO1, which was held on Friday 29th November 2013. About 800 are usually invited to take part. The paper lasted 3½ hours and contained six questions to which full written solutions are required.

About 100 high scorers are then invited to sit BMO2, which was held on Thursday 30th January 2014. It also lasted 3½ hours but contained four, very demanding, questions.

The results of BMO2 are used to select a group of students to attend a Training Session at Trinity College, Cambridge at Easter. As well as being taught more mathematics and trying numerous challenging problems, this group sits a 4½ hour 'mock' Olympiad paper. On the basis of this and all other relevant information, a group of about eight is selected to take part in correspondence courses and assignments which eventually produce the UK Olympiad Team of six to go forward to the International Mathematical Olympiad in July. In 2013, the Senior Kangaroo paper, for pupils who were close to being eligible for BMO1, was held on the same day, with the number of participants increased from around 2900 to 3500.

The growth of the Challenges

In the 2005 UKMT Yearbook, we showed the growth of the Challenges since UKMT was established and this has now been updated. The graphs below show two easily identifiable quantities, the number of schools and the number of entries. In each case, the lines, from top to bottom, represent the Junior, Intermediate and Senior Challenges. As those involved in the UKMT firmly believe that the Challenges are a very worthwhile endeavour, we hope that the upward trends are continued.

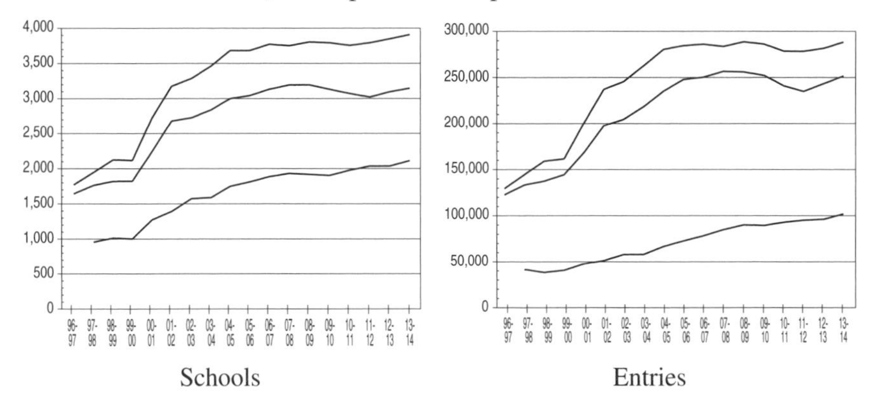

Schools

Entries

Team Maths Challenges

This event is the successor of the Enterprising Mathematics UK which was run in conjunction with the IMO in 2002. A team consists of four pupils who are in Year 9 (English style) or below with at most two members being in Year 9. In 2014, almost 1600 teams took part in Regional Finals and 80 schools competed in the National Final held in the grand surroundings of the Lindley Hall, part of the prestigious Royal Horticultural Halls in Westminster, London, on Monday 23rd June.

In addition, 1147 schools took part in the Senior Team Maths Challenges which is aimed at pupils studying maths beyond GCSE. The final, which involved over 60 teams, was held in the Camden Centre on Tuesday 4th February 2014.

Report from the Director

Thank you for helping to make 2013/14 another very successful year for the Trust, in particular it was great to see so many of you participate in the Maths Challenges. In many areas of the UK, problem-solving is a big focus within schools, and notoriously tricky to teach and assess. We hope that the Challenges, the detailed individual school feedback, and the extension materials you receive after the events, all help you with this. Please continue to spread the word so that more students can benefit from our activities and materials.

One of the highlights of my year was attending the international Kangaroo problem setting conference, organised by the Trust. In October 2013, we welcomed over 150 delegates from more than 50 countries worldwide to Edinburgh, where we set the 2014 Kangaroo question papers, which were then taken by 6 million students throughout the world.

Another highlight was fulfilment of a long-term ambition to expand the number of UKMT Summer Schools, providing the opportunity for many more students to experience a week-long residential course with like-minded peers, engaging in a mathematically demanding programme. Thanks to a grant from the DfE and support from Oxford colleges (Balliol, Christ Church, Somerville and St Anne's), we were able to run three additional summer schools in 2013/14. A report on these can be found later in the Yearbook.

Our thanks go to our other supporters and donors, in particular to the Institute and Faculty of Actuaries which continues to support the Challenges, and our new sponsor, Oxford Asset Management which supports our mentoring schemes and IMO team. We were very pleased to receive a grant from Garfield Weston Foundation to help us to increase the number of Challenge entries. We were also fortunate and grateful to receive donations large and small via www.donate.ukmt.org.uk.

As our activities and events increase, we have to take care not to overburden our volunteers. Once again, I personally would like to thank all our volunteers for their hard work and dedication throughout the year. This extraordinary group of people do so much to enable us to organise and run our events, from setting problems, to running Team Challenge events, to organising Mathematical Circles, to marking Olympiad scripts, to writing this Yearbook. The list goes on! If you would like to join this remarkable group, please contact us via enquiry@ukmt.org.uk. We would love to have you on board!

Rachel Greenhalgh

Profile

The Institute and Faculty of Actuaries (IFoA) is the UK's only chartered professional body dedicated to educating, developing and regulating actuaries based both in the UK and internationally.

What is an actuary?

Actuaries are experts in risk management. They use their mathematical skills to help measure the probability and risk of future events. This information is useful to many industries, including healthcare, pensions, insurance, banking and investments, where a single decision can have a major financial impact.

It is a global profession with internationally-recognised qualifications. It is also very highly regarded, in the way that medicine and law are, and an actuarial career can be one of the most diverse, exciting and rewarding in the world. In fact, due to the difficult exams and the expertise required, being an actuary carries quite a reputation.

Training and development

To qualify as an actuary you need to complete the IFoA's exams. Most actuarial trainees take the exams whilst working for an actuarial employer. Exemptions from some of the exams may be awarded to students who have studied to an appropriate standard in a relevant degree, or have studied actuarial science at Postgraduate level. Qualification typically takes three to six years. Those on a graduate actuarial trainee programme can expect to earn £25,000-£35,000 a year. This increases to well over £100,000 as you gain more experience and seniority.

International outlook

The IFoA qualification is already highly valued throughout the world, with 40% of its members based outside the UK. Mutual recognition agreements with other international actuarial bodies facilitate the ability for actuaries to move and work in other parts of the world and create a truly global profession.

For more information on the qualifications and career path visit our website

http://www.actuaries.org.uk/becoming-actuary

or join us on Facebook

www.be-an-actuary.co.uk

About Us

OxFORD Asset Management is an investment management company with a quantitative focus, based in Oxford, England. We invest and trade financial instruments world-wide, 24 hours a day. Most of our trading is done automatically by our own algorithms and using software built in-house. Our team of mathematicians, scientists and software engineers work with the latest technologies to develop these algorithms and tools to navigate a wide range of financial markets. There are 70 team members, including Researchers who identify opportunities and build our quantitative models and strategies, Software Engineers who design the software that drives our investment strategies, and IT Infrastructure Specialists who design and support our infrastructure.

OxFORD Careers for Mathematicians

We are always on the look-out for outstanding Researchers to work on quantitative financial models, with projects covering initial idea generation through to implementation and execution, tackling challenges such as prediction, optimisation and data analysis. The research often involves large and complex data sets as well as a range of analysis packages.

What do we look for in candidates?

If you are looking at a future career using your Mathematical skills, then the UKMT Challenges are a great place to start! We look for candidates to have a variety of attributes including; a strong academic background (most team members here having advanced degrees across the STEM subjects), an ability to work effectively within a team, an aptitude for mental flexibility and innovative thinking, as well as a passion for problem solving.

For more information on a career at OxFORD Asset Management, please visit:

www.oxam.com/vacancies

The Junior Mathematical Challenge and Olympiad

The Junior Mathematical Challenge was held on Thursday 1st May 2014 and over 247,000 pupils took part. Approximately 1000 pupils were invited to take part in the Junior Mathematical Olympiad which was held on Thursday 12th June. In the following pages, we shall show the question paper and solutions leaflet for both the JMC and JMO.

We start with the JMC paper, the front of which is shown below in a slightly reduced format.

UK JUNIOR MATHEMATICAL CHALLENGE

THURSDAY 1st MAY 2014

Organised by the **United Kingdom Mathematics Trust from the School of Mathematics, University of Leeds**

RULES AND GUIDELINES (to be read before starting)

1. Do not open the paper until the Invigilator tells you to do so.
2. Time allowed: **1 hour**.
   No answers, or personal details, may be entered after the allowed hour is over.
3. The use of rough paper is allowed; **calculators** and measuring instruments are **forbidden**.
4. Candidates in England and Wales must be in School Year 8 or below.
   Candidates in Scotland must be in S2 or below.
   Candidates in Northern Ireland must be in School Year 9 or below.
5. **Use B or HB pencil only**. Mark *at most one* of the options A, B, C, D, E on the Answer Sheet for each question. Do not mark more than one option.
6. *Do not expect to finish the whole paper in 1 hour.* Concentrate first on Questions 1-15. When you have checked your answers to these, have a go at some of the later questions.
7. Five marks are awarded for each correct answer to Questions 1-15.
   Six marks are awarded for each correct answer to Questions 16-25.
   Each incorrect answer to Questions 16-20 loses 1 mark.
   Each incorrect answer to Questions 21-25 loses 2 marks.
8. Your Answer Sheet will be read only by a *dumb machine*. **Do not write or doodle on the sheet except to mark your chosen options**. The machine 'sees' all black pencil markings even if they are in the wrong places. If you mark the sheet in the wrong place, or leave bits of rubber stuck to the page, the machine will 'see' a mark and interpret this mark in its own way.
9. The questions on this paper challenge you to **think**, not to guess. You get more marks, and more satisfaction, by doing one question carefully than by guessing lots of answers. The UK JMC is about solving interesting problems, not about lucky guessing.

The UKMT is a registered charity

http://www.ukmt.org.uk

1. What is $(999 - 99 + 9) \div 9$?

A 91 B 99 C 100 D 101 E 109

2. How many minutes are there in $\frac{1}{12}$ of a day?

A 240 B 120 C 60 D 30 E 15

3. In my row in the theatre the seats are numbered consecutively from T1 to T50. I am sitting in seat T17 and you are sitting in seat T39. How many seats are there between us?

A 23 B 22 C 21 D 20 E 19

4. The number 987 654 321 is multiplied by 9. How many times does the digit 8 occur in the result?

A 1 B 2 C 3 D 4 E 9

5. What is the difference between the smallest 4-digit number and the largest 3-digit number?

A 1 B 10 C 100 D 1000 E 9899

6. The diagram shows a square divided into strips of equal width. Three strips are black and two are grey. What fraction of the perimeter of the square is grey?

A $\frac{1}{5}$ B $\frac{1}{4}$ C $\frac{4}{25}$ D $\frac{1}{3}$ E $\frac{2}{5}$

7. What is $2014 - 4102$?

A -2012 B -2088 C -2092 D -2098 E -2112

8. How many prime numbers are there in the list

1, 12, 123, 1234, 12 345, 123 456 ?

A 0 B 1 C 2 D 3 E 4

9. Triangles XYZ and PQR are drawn on a square grid. What fraction of the area of triangle XYZ is the area of triangle PQR?

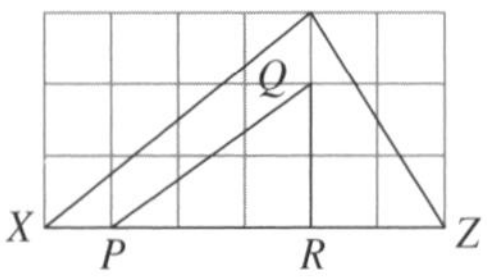

A $\frac{1}{4}$ B $\frac{7}{18}$ C $\frac{1}{2}$ D $\frac{5}{18}$ E $\frac{1}{3}$

Y Q X P R Z

10. An equilateral triangle is surrounded by three squares, as shown. What is the value of x?

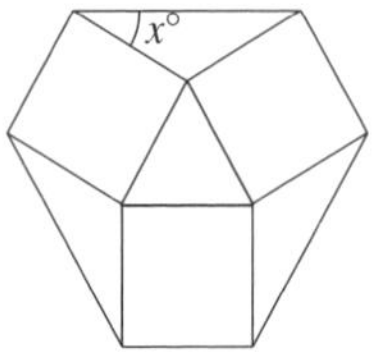

A 15 B 18 C 24 D 30 E 36

$x°$

11. The first two terms of a sequence are 1 and 2. Each of the following terms in the sequence is the sum of all the terms which come before it in the sequence.
Which of these is *not* a term in the sequence?

A 6 B 24 C 48 D 72 E 96

12. In this subtraction, P, Q, R, S and T represent single digits.

$$\begin{array}{rccccc} & 7 & Q & 2 & S & T \\ - & P & 3 & R & 9 & 6 \\ \hline & 2 & 2 & 2 & 2 & 2 \\ \hline \end{array}$$

What is the value of $P + Q + R + S + T$?

A 30 B 29 C 28 D 27 E 26

13. A rectangle is split into triangles by drawing in its diagonals.
What is the ratio of the area of triangle P to the area of triangle Q?

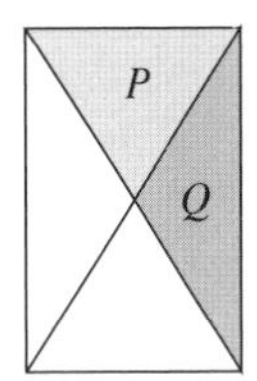

A 1 : 1 B 1 : 2 C 2 : 1 D 2 : 3

E the ratio depends on the lengths of the sides of the rectangle

14. Which of these is equal to one million millimetres?

A 1 metre B 10 metres C 100 metres D 1 kilometre E 10 kilometres

15. The diagram shows a rectangular envelope made by folding (and gluing) a single piece of paper.
What could the original unfolded piece of paper look like?
(The dashed lines are the fold lines.)

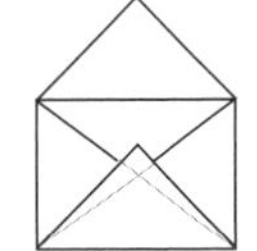

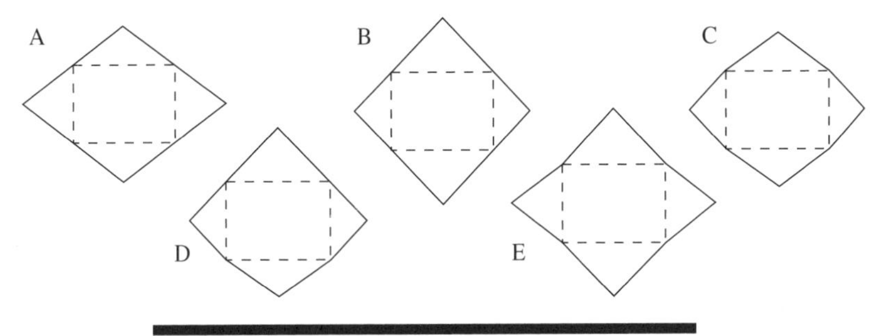

16. Only one of the following statements is true. Which one?

A 'B is true' B 'E is false' C 'Statements A to E are true'
D 'Statements A to E are false' E 'A is false'

17. The diagram is a 'map' of Jo's local rail network, where the dots represent stations and the lines are routes. Jo wants to visit all the stations, travelling only by train, starting at any station and ending at any station, with no restrictions on which routes are taken.
What is the smallest number of stations that Jo must go to more than once?

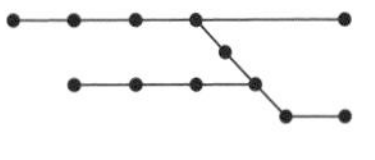

A 1 B 2 C 3 D 4 E 5

18. Which of these statements is true?

A $15\,614 = 1 + 5^6 - 1 \times 4$ B $15\,615 = 1 + 5^6 - 1 \times 5$ C $15\,616 = 1 + 5^6 - 1 \times 6$

D $15\,617 = 1 + 5^6 - 1 \times 7$ E $15\,618 = 1 + 5^6 - 1 \times 8$

19. Jack and Jill played a game for two people. In each game, the winner was awarded 2 points and the loser 1 point. No games were drawn. Jack won exactly 4 games and Jill had a final score of 10 points. How many games did they play?

A 5 B 6 C 7 D 8 E impossible to determine

20. Box P has p chocolates and box Q has q chocolates, where p and q are both odd and $p > q$. What is the smallest number of chocolates which would have to be moved from box P to box Q so that box Q has more chocolates than box P?

A $\frac{q-p+2}{2}$ B $\frac{p-q+2}{2}$ C $\frac{q+p-2}{2}$ D $\frac{p-q-2}{2}$ E $\frac{q+p+2}{2}$

---

21. Pablo's teacher has given him 27 identical white cubes. She asks him to paint some of the faces of these cubes grey and then stack the cubes so that they appear as shown. What is the largest possible number of the individual white cubes which Pablo can leave with no faces painted grey?

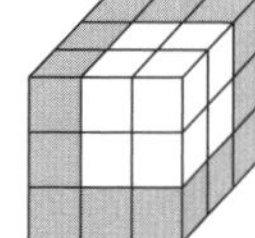
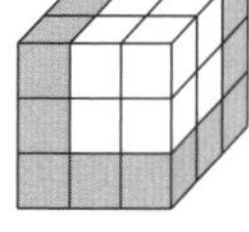

A 8 B 12 C 14 D 15 E 16

22. In the division calculation $952\,473 \div 18$, which two adjacent digits should be swapped in order to increase the result by 100?

A 9 and 5 B 5 and 2 C 2 and 4 D 4 and 7 E 7 and 3

23. Sam wants to complete the diagram so that each of the nine circles contains one of the digits from 1 to 9 inclusive and each contains a different digit. Also, the digits in each of the three lines of four circles must have the same total. What is this total?

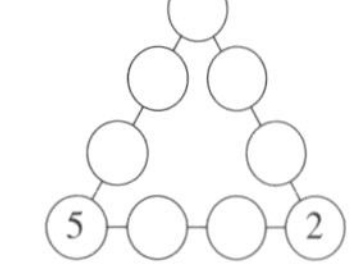

A 17 B 18 C 19 D 20 E 21

24. The diagram shows a regular octagon with sides of length 1. The octagon is divided into regions by four diagonals.

What is the difference between the area of the hatched region and the area of the region shaded grey?

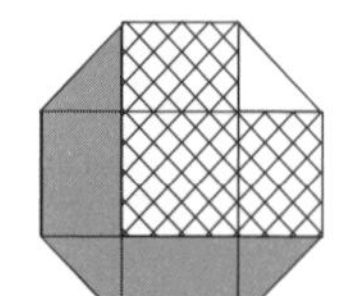

A 0 B $\frac{1}{8}$ C $\frac{1}{4}$ D $\frac{1}{2}$ E 1

25. A die has the shape of a regular tetrahedron, with the four faces having 1, 2, 3 and 4 pips. The die is placed with 4 pips 'face down' in one corner of the triangular grid shown, so that the face with 4 pips precisely covers the triangle marked with 4 pips. The die is now 'rolled', by rotating about an edge without slipping, so that 1 pip is face down. It is rolled again, so that 2 pips are face down, as indicated. The rolling continues until the die rests on the shaded triangle in the opposite corner of the grid. How many pips are now face down?

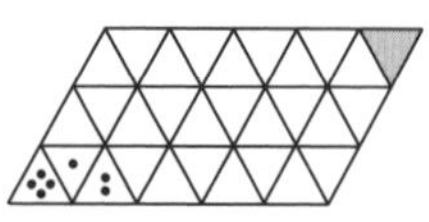

A 1 B 2 C 3 D 4 E it depends on the route taken

The JMC solutions

The usual solutions leaflet was issued.

UK JUNIOR MATHEMATICAL CHALLENGE

THURSDAY 1st MAY 2014

Organised by the **United Kingdom Mathematics Trust from the School of Mathematics, University of Leeds**

http://www.ukmt.org.uk

SOLUTIONS LEAFLET

This solutions leaflet for the JMC is sent in the hope that it might provide all concerned with some alternative solutions to the ones they have obtained. It is not intended to be definitive. The organisers would be very pleased to receive alternatives created by candidates.

The UKMT is a registered charity

1. **D** $(999 - 99 + 9) \div 9 = (900 + 9) \div 9 = 909 \div 9 = 101$.

2. **B** There are 24 hours in one day, so $\frac{1}{12}$ of a day is 2 hours. Therefore the number of minutes in $\frac{1}{12}$ of a day is $2 \times 60 = 120$.

3. **C** The seats between us are T18 to T38 *inclusive*, that is, all the seats before seat 39 except for seats 1 to 17. So the number of seats is $38 - 17 = 21$.

4. **E** $987\,654\,321 \times 9 = 8\,888\,888\,889$.

5. **A** The smallest 4-digit number is 1000 and the largest 3-digit number is 999. They differ by 1.

6. **A** Let the width of each strip be 1. Then the square has side 5 and perimeter 20. The grey strips contribute 4 to the perimeter, so the fraction of the perimeter which is grey is $\frac{4}{20} = \frac{1}{5}$.

7. **B** $2002 - 4102 = -2100$. So $2014 - 4102 = -2100 + 12 = -2088$.

8. **A** Prime numbers have exactly two distinct factors, so 1 is not a prime number as it has exactly one factor. Of the others, 12, 1234 and 123 456 are all even numbers, so are not prime as the only even prime is 2. Also, $123 = 3 \times 41$ and 12 345 is clearly a multiple of 5, so neither of these is prime. Therefore none of the numbers in the list is prime.

9. **E** The area of a triangle = $\frac{1}{2} \times$ base $\times$ height. If we let the length of the sides of each square in the grid be 1, then the area of triangle PQR is $\frac{1}{2} \times 3 \times 2 = 3$. The area of triangle XYZ is $\frac{1}{2} \times 6 \times 3 = 9$. So the required fraction is $\frac{3}{9} = \frac{1}{3}$.

10. **D** The angles at a point sum to 360°, so the largest angle in the triangle which includes the angle marked $x°$ is equal to $(360 - 90 - 90 - 60)° = 120°$. This triangle is isosceles as the sides of the three squares in the figure are equal to the sides of the equilateral triangle. So the triangle has angles 120°, $x°$ and $x°$. Therefore $x = \frac{1}{2}(180 - 120) = 30$.

11. **D** The third term of the sequence equals $1 + 2 = 3$. Now consider the fourth term: it is the sum of the first three terms. However, as the first two terms sum to the third term, the sum of the first three terms is twice the third term, i.e. $2 \times 3 = 6$. So the fourth term is twice the third term. Similar reasoning applies to each subsequent term, i.e. each term after the third term is equal to twice the term which precedes it. Therefore the sequence is 1, 2, 3, 6, 12, 24, 48, 96, ….

12. **B** As $7Q2ST - P3R96 = 22222$, it follows that $7Q2ST = P3R96 + 22222$. Looking at the units column: $2 + 6 = T$, so $T = 8$. Looking at the tens column, as $2 + 9 = 11$, we deduce that $S = 1$ and that 1 is carried to the hundreds column. Looking at the hundreds column: the carry of $1 + 2 + R$ must equal 12 since the sum has 2 in the hundreds column. So $R = 9$ and there is a carry of 1 to the thousands column. Looking at this column: the carry of $1 + 2 + 3 = Q$, so $Q = 6$. Finally, since there is no carry to the next column, $2 + P = 7$, so $P = 5$. Therefore the calculation is $76218 - 53996 = 22222$ and $P + Q + R + S + T = 5 + 6 + 9 + 1 + 8 = 29$.

13. **A** The diagram shows part of the given diagram after a rotation so that the diagonal shown is horizontal. The perpendicular height of triangle P is shown and it can be seen that this is also the perpendicular height of triangle Q. The diagonals of a rectangle bisect each other, so triangles P and Q have bases of equal length and the same perpendicular height. Therefore their areas are equal.

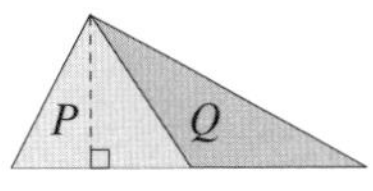

14. **D** One million millimetres is $(1\,000\,000 \div 1000)$ m $=$ 1000 m $=$ 1 km.

15. **E** Consider, for example, the bottom left-hand corner of the envelope (see Figure 1). The two flaps overlap, so that the sum of the angles marked x and y is greater than 90°.
So when the flaps are unfolded, as in Figure 2, the angle marked z is less than 180°.
Therefore the correct answer is E.

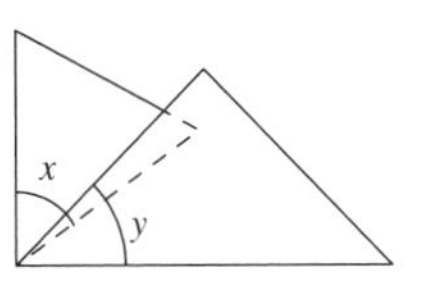

Figure 1

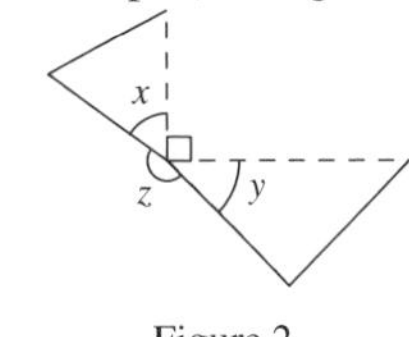

Figure 2

16. **E** If A is true then B is true which cannot be so since we are told only one statement is true. Hence A is false which is what E says. So E is the one true statement. [For completeness, we note that C and D must be false because we are told that exactly one statement is true; and B is false because A is false.]

17. **C** Whichever route is chosen, it must include section BD. We will divide the route into two sections. The first will include stations A, B, C and will finish at D. The second will start at D and include stations E, F, and G.

A B C
D
E
F G

Clearly the first section cannot be traversed without visiting at least one station more than once and the route $A - B - C - B - D$ visits only B more than once so it is an optimal solution. Also, traversing the second section involves visiting D more than once as two branches lead from it. If $D - E - D$ is part of the route then two stations are visited more than once. However, if $D - G - D$ is part of the route then only F is visited more than once. So to traverse the second section, it is necessary to visit at least two stations (one of which is D) more than once. Therefore, the complete route must involve visiting at least 3 stations more than once. An example of an optimum route is $A - B - C - B - D - F - G - F - D - E$. The stations visited twice are B, D, and F.

18. **E** The units digit of any power of 5 is 5 so the units digit of $1 + 5^6$ is 6. Therefore the units digits of the calculations in the 5 options are 2, 1, 0, 9, 8 in that order. So the only calculation which could be correct is E. Checking this gives $1 + 5^6 - 8 = 1 + 15\,625 - 8 = 15\,626 - 8 = 15\,618$.

19. **C** Since Jack won 4 games, Jill lost 4 games for which she was awarded 4 points. So the number of games she won is $(10 - 4) \div 2 = 3$. Therefore, they played 7 games in total.

20. **B** Let the smallest number of chocolates required be n. Then $q + n > p - n$, that is $2n > p - q$. Therefore $n > \frac{1}{2}(p - q)$. Since $p > q$ and p and q are both odd, $\frac{1}{2}(p - q)$ is a positive integer. So the smallest possible value of n is $\frac{1}{2}(p - q) + 1 = \frac{1}{2}(p - q + 2)$.

21. **D** Both the top and bottom layers of 9 cubes can be seen to contain 5 cubes with at least one face printed grey. The bottom layer could contain more than 5. In the middle layer, two cubes with grey faces are visible and there could be more. Therefore at least 12 cubes must have at least one face painted grey, which means that the largest number of cubes which Pablo can leave with no faces painted grey is $27 - 12 = 15$.

22. **C** In order to increase the result of the calculation (the quotient) by 100, the number to be divided (the dividend) must be increased by 100×18, that is 1800. So the new dividend needs to be 952 473 + 1800, that is 954 273. So the two digits which need to be swapped are 2 and 4.

23. **D** Note first that the sum of the first 9 positive integers is 45. Therefore, when the four numbers in each of the three lines are added together the total is 45 plus the sum of the numbers in the three corner circles, each of which contributes to the sum of two lines of circles. So if the number in the top circle is x, the total of all 3 lines is $45 + 2 + 5 + x = 52 + x$. As all three lines of circles must have the same total, $52 + x$ must be a multiple of 3. The possible values of x are 2, 5 and 8 but 2 and 5 have already been assigned. So $x = 8$ and the sum of each line is $60 \div 3 = 20$. The diagram shows one way of completing the task.

24. **C** Note that rectangles B, C, E and G are all congruent. Two of these are shaded grey and two are hatched, so the difference between the area of the hatched region and the area shaded grey is the difference between the area of square D of side 1 and the sum of the areas of triangles A, F and H. These are all isosceles right-angled triangles with hypotenuse 1 and the lower diagram shows how a square of side 1 may be divided into 4 such triangles. So the required difference in area is $1 - \frac{3}{4} = \frac{1}{4}$.

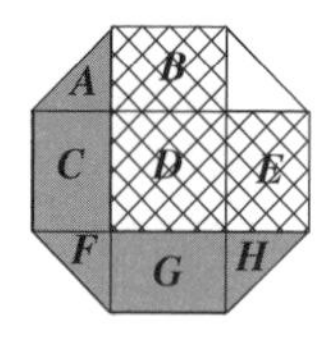

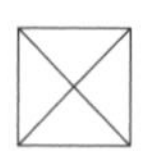

25. **A** If the die is rolled around a single vertex it covers, in turn, 6 small triangles making up a regular hexagon. It uses three different faces, repeated twice. An example is shown on the right. However, if it is rolled out from that hexagon in any direction, that will use the fourth face. The face that ends up covering each small triangle in the grid is always the same, regardless of the path taken to reach that triangle. Using these facts, it is easy to complete the diagram as shown. So, whichever route through the grid is taken, the '1' is face down when it reaches the shaded triangle.

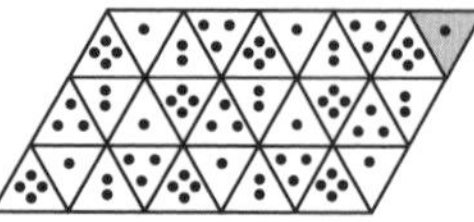

The JMC answers

The table below shows the proportion of pupils' choices. The correct answer is shown in bold. [The percentages are rounded to the nearest whole number.]

Qn	A	B	C	D	E	Blank
1	2	7	2	**86**	2	1
2	4	**80**	10	4	1	2
3	1	65	**27**	4	1	1
4	14	12	9	8	**54**	3
5	**87**	1	3	3	4	2
6	**19**	6	12	4	56	2
7	12	**51**	6	5	23	2
8	**25**	26	27	17	3	3
9	6	13	14	13	**47**	6
10	5	5	10	**62**	12	6
11	19	11	8	**51**	6	5
12	7	**59**	10	10	9	5
13	**40**	16	9	8	22	5
14	2	7	19	**49**	21	2
15	7	25	1	2	**62**	2
16	17	12	9	16	**17**	29
17	2	14	**37**	23	11	14
18	4	8	5	5	**27**	51
19	3	4	**40**	4	28	20
20	6	**16**	9	5	7	58
21	25	14	5	**9**	7	39
22	3	5	**15**	14	3	60
23	6	9	8	**13**	4	60
24	3	10	**16**	12	3	55
25	**4**	2	5	4	20	65

JMC 2014: Some comments on the pupils' choices of answers as expressed in the feedback letter to schools

The overall mean score of 46 was about the same as last year. This is a little disappointing as the 2013 mean was significantly lower than that in 2012. There were a number of questions that the Problems Group thought would be easy but which defeated the majority of the candidates. You can see from your results sheets whether your pupils found these questions difficult. If so, we would welcome your feedback on where the difficulty lies.

The biggest surprise was the response to Question 8. We know that, because of careless definitions in some books, quite a lot of people think that 1 is a prime number. (The extended solutions on our website explain why mathematicians do not count 1 as a prime number.) So it was not a surprise that a quarter of the candidates said that there is one prime number in the given list. Why, however, did over 40% think that there were 2, 3 or even 4 prime numbers in this list? If your pupils answered this question badly, please try and find out why, and let us know.

Question 3 was another disappointment. The answer does not depend on any knowledge other than the ability to count up to 39. Well over half the candidates seem to have just subtracted 17 from 39 to get 22, but a moment's thought shows that the answer is 21. Pupils often jump too quickly to the wrong conclusion on questions of this type. If your pupils come into this category, we hope you will have the time to explain where they went wrong.

Question 6 was the other question that we thought would be easy, but which few pupils answered correctly. Again, the reason why so many went wrong is not clear, and we would welcome your comments about this.

On the day of the Challenge we received a number of queries about which were 'the following statements' referred to in Question 16. The reference was, of course, to the statements given in the optional answers. It is quite common for us to use a reference to the answers in a question in this way. We hope that, if your students were puzzled by this, you have already found time to explain this when going through the questions with them.

As usual, it was good to see the number of pupils who achieved very high scores. They deserve our congratulations. These pupils were invited to take part in the Junior Mathematical Olympiad (JMO) follow up competition. This requires them not to just give the right answers, but also to explain how they found them. Writing clear mathematical explanations is not easy, but it is an essential skill for those who wish to progress to the highest levels in mathematics. So we hope that pupils who received an invitation to take part in the JMO accepted it.

The profile of marks obtained is shown below.

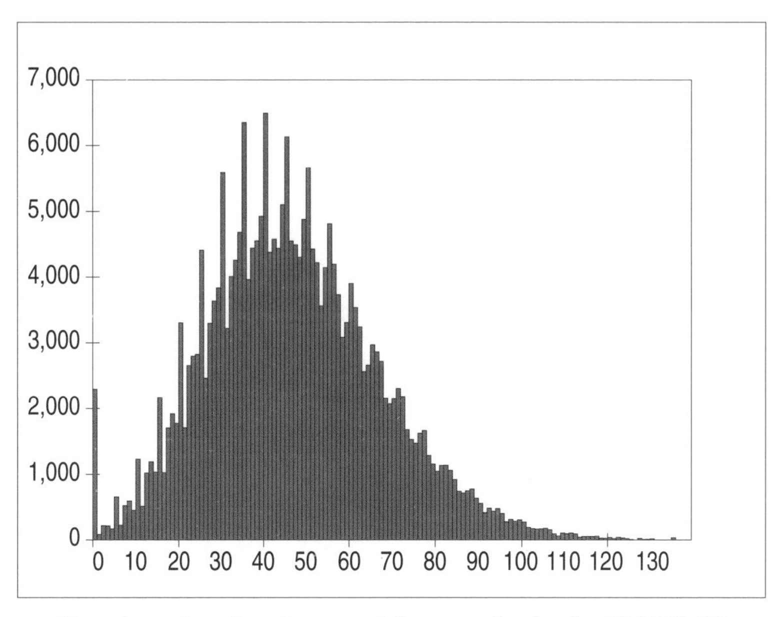

Bar chart showing the actual frequencies in the 2014 JMC

On the basis of the standard proportions used by the UKMT, the cut-off marks were set at

GOLD – 79 or over SILVER – 63 to 78 BRONZE – 50 to 62

A sample of one of the certificates is shown on the next page.

The Junior Mathematical Olympiad is the follow-up competition to the Challenge. It was decided that candidates who obtained a JMC score of 108 or over were eligible to take part in the JMO. This resulted in 1058 candidates being invited. In line with other follow-on events, schools were allowed to enter 'unqualified' candidates on payment of an appropriate fee. The number who were entered by this route was 142.

THE UNITED KINGDOM JUNIOR MATHEMATICAL CHALLENGE

The Junior Mathematical Challenge (JMC) is run by the UK Mathematics Trust. The JMC encourages mathematical reasoning, precision of thought, and fluency in using basic mathematical techniques to solve interesting problems. It is aimed at the top third of pupils in years 7 and 8 in England and Wales, S1 and S2 in Scotland and years 8 and 9 in Northern Ireland. The problems on the JMC are designed to make students think. Most are accessible, yet challenge those with more experience; they are also meant to be memorable and enjoyable.

Mathematics controls more aspects of the modern world than most people realise – from iPods, cash machines, telecommunications and airline booking systems to production processes in engineering, efficient distribution and stock-holding, investment strategies and 'whispering' jet engines. The scientific and industrial revolutions flowed from the realisation that mathematics was both the language of nature, and also a way of analysing – and hence controlling – our environment. In the last fifty years, old and new applications of mathematical ideas have transformed the way we live.

All of these developments depend on mathematical thinking – a mode of thought whose essential style is far more permanent than the wave of technological change which it has made possible. The problems on the JMC reflect this style, which pervades all mathematics, by encouraging students to think clearly about challenging problems.

The UK JMC has grown out of a national challenge first run in 1988. In recent years over 250,000 pupils have taken part from around 3,700 schools. Certificates are awarded to the highest scoring 40% of candidates (Gold : Silver : Bronze 1 : 2 : 3). From 2014, Certificates of Participation were awarded to all participants.

There is an Intermediate and Senior version for older pupils. All three events are organised by the United Kingdom Mathematics Trust and are administered from the School of Mathematics at the University of Leeds.

The UKMT is a registered charity. For more information about us please visit our website at www.ukmt.org.uk
Donations to support our work would be gratefully received and can be made at www.donate.ukmt.org.uk

The Junior Mathematical Olympiad

UK Junior Mathematical Olympiad 2014

Organised by The United Kingdom Mathematics Trust

Thursday 12th June 2014

RULES AND GUIDELINES : READ THESE INSTRUCTIONS CAREFULLY BEFORE STARTING

1. Time allowed: 2 hours.
2. **The use of calculators, measuring instruments and squared paper is forbidden.**
3. All candidates must be in *School Year 8 or below* (England and Wales), *S2 or below* (Scotland), *School Year 9 or below* (Northern Ireland).
4. For questions in Section A *only the answer is required.* Enter each answer neatly in the relevant box on the Front Sheet. Do not hand in rough work. Write in blue or black pen or pencil.

   For questions in Section B you must give *full written solutions*, including clear mathematical explanations as to why your method is correct.

   Solutions must be written neatly on A4 paper. Sheets must be STAPLED together in the top left corner with the Front Sheet on top.

   Do not hand in rough work.
5. Questions A1-A10 are relatively short questions. Try to complete Section A within the first 30 minutes so as to allow well over an hour for Section B.
6. Questions B1-B6 are longer questions requiring *full written solutions.*
   This means that each answer must be accompanied by clear explanations and proofs.
   Work in rough first, then set out your final solution with clear explanations of each step.
7. These problems are meant to be challenging! Do not hurry. Try the earlier questions in each section first (they tend to be easier). Try to finish whole questions even if you are not able to do many. A good candidate will have done most of Section A and given solutions to at least two questions in Section B.
8. Answers must be FULLY SIMPLIFIED, and EXACT using symbols like π, fractions, or square roots if appropriate, but NOT decimal approximations.

DO NOT OPEN THE PAPER UNTIL INSTRUCTED BY THE INVIGILATOR TO DO SO!

The United Kingdom Mathematics Trust is a Registered Charity.

Section A

A1. What is the largest digit that appears in the answer to the calculation $(3 \times 37)^2$?

A2. What is the sum of all fractions of the form $\frac{N}{7}$, where N is a positive integer less than 7?

A3. The six angles of two different triangles are listed in decreasing order. The list starts 115°, 85°, 75° and 35°. What is the last angle in the list?

A4. The figure shows two shapes that fit together exactly. Each shape is formed by four semicircles of radius 1. What is the total shaded area?

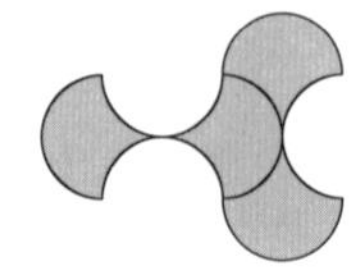

A5. The integer 113 is prime, and its 'reverse' 311 is also prime. How many two-digit primes are there between 10 and 99 which have the same property?

A6. A square of side length 1 is drawn. A larger square is drawn around it such that all parallel sides are a distance 1 apart. This process continues until the total perimeter of the squares drawn is 144.

What is the area of the largest square drawn?

A7. The time is 20:14. What is the smaller angle between the hour hand and the minute hand on an accurate analogue clock?

A8. Sam has four cubes all the same size: one blue, one red, one white and one yellow. She wants to glue the four cubes together to make the solid shape shown.

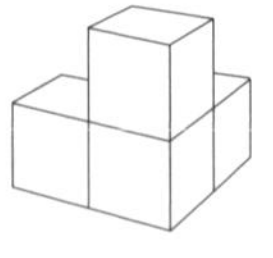

How many differently-coloured shapes can Sam make?

[Two shapes are considered to be the same if one can be picked up and turned around so that it looks identical to the other.]

A9. A rectangle is made by placing together three smaller rectangles P, Q and R, without gaps or overlaps. Rectangle P measures 3 cm × 8 cm and Q measures 2 cm × 5 cm.

How many possibilities are there for the measurements of R?

A10. My four pet monkeys and I harvested a large pile of peanuts. Monkey A woke in the night and ate half of them; then Monkey B woke and ate one third of what remained; then Monkey C woke and ate one quarter of the rest; finally Monkey D ate one fifth of the much diminished remaining pile. What fraction of the original harvest was left in the morning?

Section B

Your solutions to Section B will have a major effect on your JMO results. Concentrate on one or two questions first and then **write out full solutions** (not just brief 'answers').

B1. The figure shows an equilateral triangle ABC, a square $BCDE$, and a regular pentagon $BEFGH$.

What is the difference between the sizes of $\angle ADE$ and $\angle AHE$?

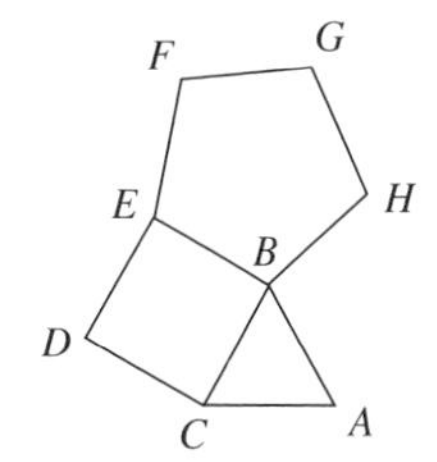

B2. I start at the square marked A and make a succession of moves to the square marked B. Each move may only be made downward or to the right. I take the sum of all the numbers in my path and add 5 for every black square I pass through.

How many paths give a sum of 51?

B3. A point lying somewhere inside a parallelogram is joined to the four vertices, thus creating four triangles T, U, V and W, as shown.

Prove that

$$\text{area } T + \text{area } V = \text{area } U + \text{area } W.$$

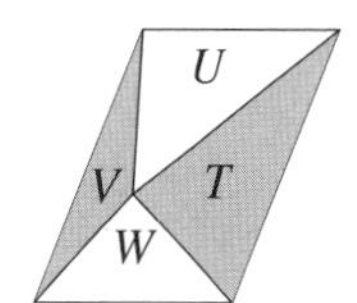

B4. There are 20 sweets on the table. Two players take turns to eat as many sweets as they choose, but they must eat at least one, and never more than half of what remains. The loser is the player who has no valid move.

Is it possible for one of the two players to force the other to lose? If so, how?

B5. Find a fraction $\frac{m}{n}$, with m not equal to n, such that all of the fractions

$$\frac{m}{n}, \frac{m+1}{n+1}, \frac{m+2}{n+2}, \frac{m+3}{n+3}, \frac{m+4}{n+4}, \frac{m+5}{n+5}$$

can be simplified by cancelling.

B6. The sum of four different prime numbers is a prime number. The sum of some pair of the numbers is a prime number, as is the sum of some triple of the numbers. What is the smallest possible sum of the four prime numbers?

UK Junior Mathematical Olympiad 2014 Solutions

A1 **3** Firstly, $3 \times 37 = 111$ and so $(3 \times 37)^2 = 111^2$. Now

$$\begin{aligned} 111^2 &= 1 \times 111 + 10 \times 111 + 100 \times 111 \\ &= 111 + 1110 + 11100 \\ &= 12\,321. \end{aligned}$$

Therefore the largest digit is 3.

A2 **3** The sum in question is

$$\frac{1}{7} + \frac{2}{7} + \frac{3}{7} + \frac{4}{7} + \frac{5}{7} + \frac{6}{7} = \frac{21}{7} = 3.$$

A3 **20°** First note that $115° + 85° > 180°$ and $115° + 75° > 180°$ so one triangle contains both the 75° and the 85° angles. Also note that $85° + 75° + 35° > 180°$ so that triangle does not contain the 35° angle. Hence one triangle must have internal angles including 85° and 75°, and the other triangle must have internal angles 115° and 35°. The two remaining angles are therefore $180° - (115° + 35°) = 30°$ and $180° - (85° + 75°) = 20°$. Therefore the last angle in the list is 20°.

A4 **8** The shapes can be cut and rearranged to make a 4×2 rectangle as shown.

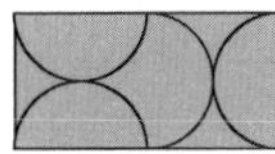

Therefore the shaded area is 8.

A5 **9** Any number ending in 2, 4, 6 or 8 is even. Similarly, any number ending in 5 is divisible by 5. Hence, for both a two-digit number and its reverse to be a prime, the original number can only start with 1, 3, 7 or 9. There are 10 two-digit primes starting with 1, 3, 7 or 9, namely 11, 13, 17, 19, 31, 37, 71, 73, 79 and 97 and, of these, only 19 does not have its reverse in the list. Hence there are 9 two-digit primes with the desired property.

A6 **121** The squares have side lengths 1, 3, 5, 7, 9, 11, . . . and so the sums of the perimeters are 4, 16, 36, 64, 100, 144, ... Thus the largest square has side-length 11 and area 121.

A7 **163°** The minute hand takes 60 minutes to make a complete turn, and so rotates through $360° \div 60 = 6°$ in one minute. Therefore, at 14 minutes past the hour, the minute hand has rotated by $14 \times 6° = 84°$. The hour hand takes 12 hours, or 720 minutes, to make a complete turn and so rotates through 0.5° in one minute. Therefore, at 20:14, the hour hand has rotated through $240° + 7° = 247°$. Thus the angle between the minute hand and the hour hand is $247° - 84° = 163°$.

A8 **8** The 'corner' cube may be chosen in four ways. Given a choice of the 'corner' cube, there are then three choices for the top cube and a further two choices for the left-hand cube. This gives $4 \times 3 \times 2 = 24$ different ways of arranging the cubes. However, the shape can be rotated so that each of the three faces of the 'corner' cube that are not joined to any other cube are at the bottom and the shape would then look the same. So the set of 24 arrangements contains groups of three that can be rotated into each other. Hence the number of differently-coloured shapes is $24 \div 3 = 8$.

A9 **4** The rectangles P and Q must be placed together edge-to-edge in one of the following ways.

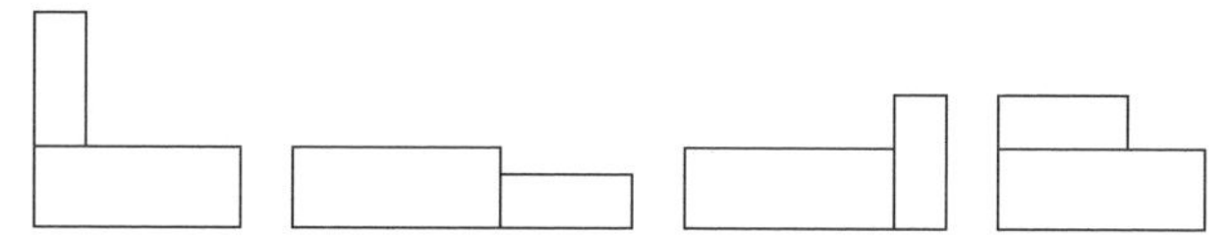

Therefore there are 4 possibilities for the measurements of R: 6×5, 1×5, 8×2 and 3×2.

A10 $\frac{1}{5}$ After Monkey A has eaten half of the pile, the fraction of the original pile that remains is $\frac{1}{2}$. Monkey B eats $\frac{1}{3}$ of the remaining pile and so leaves $\frac{2}{3} \times \frac{1}{2} = \frac{1}{3}$ of the original pile. Monkey C leaves $\frac{3}{4} \times \frac{1}{3} = \frac{1}{4}$; and Monkey D leaves $\frac{4}{5} \times \frac{1}{4} = \frac{1}{5}$ of the original pile.

B1 The figure shows an equilateral triangle ABC, a square $BCDE$, and a regular pentagon $BEFGH$.

What is the difference between the sizes of $\angle ADE$ and $\angle AHE$?

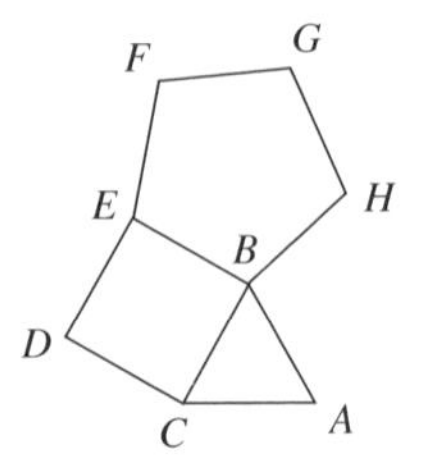

Solution

We calculate the sizes of $\angle ADE$ and $\angle AHE$ in turn. Since ABC is an equilateral triangle, $\angle ACB = 60°$. Since $BCDE$ is a square, $\angle BCD = 90°$. As edge BC is shared by the triangle and the square, $AC = CD$. Therefore the triangle ACD is isosceles. Now $\angle ACD = 60° + 90° = 150°$ and so $\angle ADC = 15°$. Therefore

$\angle ADE = \angle EDC - \angle ADC = 90° - 15° = 75°$.

Now, for $\angle AHE$, $\angle EBH = 108°$ as $BEFGH$ is a regular pentagon. By considering the angles around B, $\angle ABH = 360° - (108° + 90° + 60°) = 102°$. Since triangle ABH is isosceles, this means that $\angle AHB = 39°$. Also, triangle HBE is isosceles and so $\angle BHE = 36°$. Therefore $\angle AHE = \angle AHB + \angle BHE = 39° + 36° = 75°$.

So the difference between the sizes of the angles is zero.

B2 I start at the square marked A and make a succession of moves to the square marked B. Each move may only be made downward or to the right. I take the sum of all the numbers in my path and add 5 for every black square I pass through.

How many paths give a sum of 51?

Solution

Any path from A to B must pass through four black squares, contributing 20 to the sum. To have a path with sum 51, the numbers in the remaining three squares must sum to 31. Since all the numbers in the squares have two digits, the only possible way to make a sum of 31 is $10 + 10 + 11$. However any path must pass through the diagonal containing the numbers 13, 14 and 15. Thus there are no paths giving a sum of 51.

B3 A point lying somewhere inside a parallelogram is joined to the four vertices, thus creating four triangles T, U, V and W, as shown.

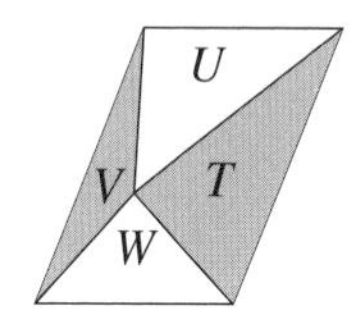

Prove that

$$\text{area } T + \text{area } V = \text{area } U + \text{area } W.$$

Solution

The parallelogram may also be split into four parallelograms, each having the point as a vertex.

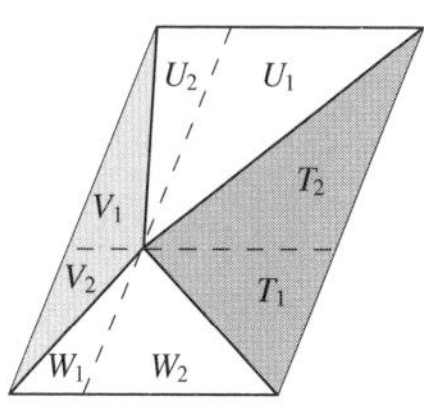

If we label the separate triangles formed as shown in the diagram then it can be seen that area V_1 = area U_2, area U_1 = area T_2, area T_1 = area W_2 and area W_1 = area V_2. Therefore

$$\begin{aligned}\text{area } T + \text{area } V &= \text{area } T_1 + \text{area } T_2 + \text{area } V_1 + \text{area } V_2 \\ &= \text{area } W_2 + \text{area } U_1 + \text{area } U_2 + \text{area } W_1 \\ &= \text{area } U_1 + \text{area } U_2 + \text{area } W_1 + \text{area } W_2 \\ &= \text{area } U + \text{area } W.\end{aligned}$$

B4 There are 20 sweets on the table. Two players take turns to eat as many sweets as they choose, but they must eat at least one, and never more than half of what remains. The loser is the player who has no valid move.

Is it possible for one of the two players to force the other to lose? If so, how?

Solution

The losing player is the one who is left with 1 sweet on the table, because taking that sweet would mean taking more than half of what remains. The first player can force the second to lose by leaving 15, 7, 3 and 1 sweets after successive turns. Call the first player A and the second player B. On her first turn, A should leave 15 sweets. Then B must leave between 8 and 14 sweets (inclusive). No matter how many sweets are left, A should leave 7 on her next turn. This will always be possible as 7 is at least half of the number of sweets remaining. Next, player B must leave between 4 and 6 sweets. Player A can then leave 3 sweets as 3 is at least half of the number of sweets remaining. Player B must now take 1 sweet, leaving 2 on the table. Finally, player A takes 1 sweet leaving player B with no valid move.

B5 Find a fraction $\frac{m}{n}$, with m not equal to n, such that all of the fractions

$$\frac{m}{n}, \frac{m+1}{n+1}, \frac{m+2}{n+2}, \frac{m+3}{n+3}, \frac{m+4}{n+4}, \frac{m+5}{n+5}$$

can be simplified by cancelling.

Solution

Suppose that $n > m$ and write $n = m + k$, where k is an integer. Then the six fractions are

$$\frac{m}{m+k}, \frac{m+1}{(m+1)+k}, \frac{m+2}{(m+2)+k}, \frac{m+3}{(m+3)+k}, \frac{m+4}{(m+4)+k}, \frac{m+5}{(m+5)+k}.$$

These fractions can all be cancelled provided that k is a multiple of each of the integers

$$m, m+1, m+2, m+3, m+4, m+5.$$

For example, take $m = 2$. Then k must be a common multiple of 2, 3, 4, 5, 6, 7; say $k = 420$. Then the six fractions are $\frac{2}{422}, \frac{3}{423}, \frac{4}{424}, \frac{5}{425}, \frac{6}{426}, \frac{7}{427}$; so $m = 2$ and $n = 422$ is a solution.

B6 The sum of four different prime numbers is a prime number. The sum of some pair of the numbers is a prime number, as is the sum of some triple of the numbers. What is the smallest possible sum of the four prime numbers?

Solution

One of the four primes must be 2. This is because the sum of four odd positive integers is even and bigger than 2, so cannot be prime. Similarly, 2 must be used in the pair. But 2 must not be used in the triple, otherwise its sum would be even and greater than 2.

The triple must sum to a prime that is also 2 smaller than a prime, so that the four chosen numbers sum to a prime. The sum of the three smallest odd primes is $3 + 5 + 7 = 15$, which is not prime, and so the sum of the triple must be greater than 15. The possible sums are therefore 17, 29, 41, ... In order to have sum 17, one of the numbers 3, 5 or 7 must be increased by 2. However, 3 and 5 cannot be increased by 2 as this would mean the primes in the triple are not all different, and 7 cannot be increased by 2 as 9 is not prime. Thus the triple cannot have sum 17. It is possible, however, to find three primes that sum to 29. For example, 5, 7 and 17.

Therefore the smallest possible sum of the four primes is $29 + 2 = 31$. (And an example of four primes with all of the desired properties is $\{2, 5, 7, 17\}$; the pair could then be $\{2, 5\}$and the triple $\{5, 7, 17\}$.)

The marking and results

The pupils' scripts began arriving very rapidly and the marking took place in Leeds on the weekend of 21st and 22nd June. The discussions as to how marks should be given and for what were ably led by Steven O'Hagan. A full list of markers appears in the Volunteers section.

As has been stated, the object of the JMO is for pupils to be *challenged*, possibly in ways they have not been before. Some participants may find all of Section B rather beyond them, but it is hoped that they achieve a degree of satisfaction from Section A. Satisfaction is an important aspect of this level of paper; nevertheless, those who do succeed in tackling Section B deserve credit for that and such credit is mainly dependent on getting solutions to questions in Section B which are 'perfect' or very nearly so. The awarding process is somewhat complicated, some might say bizarre. Firstly there are certificates which come in two versions, Participation and Distinction. The top 25% of scorers receive a Certificate of Distinction; candidates who score below this and who qualified automatically for the JMO via the JMC receive a Certificate of Participation. There were book prizes for the top fifty. The book prize for 2014 was *From 0 to infinity in 26 centuries: the extraordinary story of maths* by Chris Waring. Finally, there were medals of the traditional Gold, Silver, Bronze varieties of design introduced in 2004.

Average marks were down a little in comparsion to 2013, due in large part to a weaker performance in Section A.

The numbers of medals awarded were: 39 Gold, 92 Silver and 132 Bronze.

The list below includes all the medal winners in the 2014 JMO. Within each category, the names are in alphabetical order.

Special mention should be made of Alex Darby, Sam Ferguson, Thomas Hillman, Alex Song and Pasa Suksmith each of whom now have two JMO gold medals.

The results and all the extras (books, book plates, certificates and medals) were posted to schools by the middle of July. Where appropriate, some materials were e-mailed to schools.

GOLD MEDALS

Emilia Batory	English Martyrs Cath. Vol. Acad., Rutland
Naomi Bazlov	King Edward VI H. Sch. for Girls, Birmingham
Emily Beckford	Lancaster Girls' Grammar School
Oliver Beken	Horndean Technology College, Hampshire
Rose Blyth	Tonbridge Grammar School, Kent
Claire Carlotti	Sir Roger Manwood's School, Kent
Chihoon Choi	Regent International School Dubai
Alex Darby	Sutton Grammar School for Boys, Surrey
Sam Ferguson	King's College School, London
Max French	Millfield Preparatory School, Somerset
Freddie Hand	Cage Green Primary School, Kent
Thomas Hillman	Beechwood Park School, St Albans
Dion Huang	Westminster Under School
Takao Ito	Manchester Grammar School
Matthew Jolly	St Laurence School, Wiltshire
Brian Kim	British International School of Shanghai
Alex Lee	Taipei European School
Thomas Lunn	Belper School, Derbyshire
Robin Lyster	Matthew Arnold School, Oxford
Joe McGuire	Colet Court School, London
Navonil Neogi	Tiffin School, Kingston-upon-Thames
Tanish Patil	Institut International de Lancy, Switzerland
Frederick Phillips	Aylesbury Grammar School
Elijah Price	Reading School
David Rae	Mall School, Twickenham
Benedict Randall Shaw	Westminster Under School
Alexander Song	St Olave's Grammar School, Kent
Oliver Stubbs	Bristol Grammar School
Pasa Suksmith	Harrow International School, Bangkok
Mathilda Vere	Chenderit School, Northants
Tommy Walker Mackay	Stretford Grammar School, Manchester

Anyi Wang	King Edward's School, Birmingham
Chuan Chieh Wang	Beijing New Talent Academy
Patrick Winter	Thornden School, Hampshire
Harry Wright	Devonshire House Prep School, Hampstead
Yuqing Wu	Bangkok Patana School
James Xu	Chesterton Community College, Cambridge
Alex Yan	Bancroft's School, Essex
Tony Yang	North London Coll. Sch. Jeju, South Korea

SILVER MEDALS

Kaito Arai	American School in London
Tanvir Bakshi	Latymer School, London
Laura Bradby	St Francis Xavier School, North Yorkshire
Robin Bradfield	Cargilfield Preparatory, Edinburgh
Alex Buck	St Ninian's High School, Isle of Man
Jonathan Chen	King's College School, London
Xue Bang Chen	King Edward VI Camp Hill Boys' School
Pino Cholsaipant	Shrewsbury International School, Thailand
Joseph Cohen	King's College School, London
Thomas Connell	Ermysted's Grammar School, N. Yorks
Finn Corney	Penrice Community College, St Austell
Katie Cox	Gosforth East M. Sch., Newcastle-upon-Tyne
Catherine Cronin	West Exe Technology College, Exeter
Timothy De Goede	St James's C of E Secondary School, Bolton
Sam Dennison	Lawrence Sheriff School, Rugby
Angus Docherty	Grange Academy, Kilmarnock
Miu Endo	Overseas Family School, Singapore
Joel Fair	Bethany School, Sheffield
Sam Farmer	St Mary's RC High School, nr Preston
Rebekah Fearnhead	Lancaster Girls' Grammar School
Kit Foulkes	Wilson's School, Surrey
Owen Gilbert	Cheney School, Oxford
Jennifer Greenfield	The Grammar School at Leeds
Callum Gunning	The Chorister School, Durham

Arul Gupta	Eltham College, London
Ruiyang He	Glasgow Academy
Rachel Hewitt	St James Senior Girls' School, London
Jonny Heywood	Thomas's School Clapham
Robert Hillier	King Edward VI Camp Hill Boys' School
Matthew Hitchcock	Torquay Boys' Grammar School
Yang Hsu	Colet Court School, London
William Isotta	Colet Court School, London
Freddy Jiang	Renaissance College, Hong Kong
Stella Johnson	Sch. of St Helen and St Katharine, Abingdon
Isaac Kaufmann	City of London School
Hyeonji Kim	King Edward VII School, Sheffield
Yunjae Kim	City of London Freemen's School, Surrey
Bethany Kippin	Headington School, Oxford
Sebastian K. Wellsted	Dame Alice Owen's School, Herts
Jamie Lear	Hurstpierpoint College Junior Sch., W. Sussex
Yeasung Lee	North London Coll. Sch. Jeju, South Korea
Gordon Lee	Dame Alice Owen's School, Herts
Nathan Leon	Westminster Under School
Daniel Leung	Bancroft's School, Essex
Jonathan Liu	Liverpool Blue Coat School
Angus Macleod	Dollar Academy, Clackmannanshire
Danny Maddaford	Henry Beaufort School, Winchester
Stanley Mao	Beijing Dulwich International School
William Miles	Loughborough Grammar School
Rick Mukhopadhyay	Glasgow Academy
Aoi Nagahara	St Margaret's School, Bushey, Herts
Inkyung Nam	North London Coll. Sch. Jeju, South Korea
Jasper Newbold	St George's School, Windsor
Dillon Patel	King Edward VI Sch., Stratford-upon-Avon
Robert Peacock	Queen Mary's Grammar School, Walsall
Joshua Pursglove	Cranborne Middle School, Dorset
Geno Racklin-Asher	University College School, London

Alex Radcliffe	Stewart's Melville College, Edinburgh
Luke Remus Elliot	Westminster Under School
Max Rose	Hitchin Boys School, Hertfordshire
Peter Rose	Wymondham High School, Norfolk
David Rosof Williams	Altrincham Grammar Sch. for Boys, Cheshire
Nathan Ruegg	Reading School
Claire Rush	Latymer Upper School, Hammersmith
Julian Sadie	Reading School
Nick Scott	Dame Alice Owen's School, Herts
Oscar Selby	Stamford Green Primary School, Epsom
Andrea Sendula	Kenilworth School, Warks
Saksham Shah	King Edward VI Camp Hill Boys' School
Adithya Shenoy	Colchester Royal Grammar School
Zak Smith	Beaumont School, St Albans
Jude Smithers	Horris Hill School, Newbury
Oliver Sowden	Urmston Grammar School, Manchester
Kitty Sparrowhawk	Beaconsfield High School, Buckinghamshire
Sam Stansfield	King Edward VI Camp Hill Boys' School
James Stickland	Sancton Wood School, Cambridge
Matthew Strutton	Howard of Effingham School, Surrey
Louis Thomson	Lanesborough School, Guildford
Gemma Tipper	King William's College, Isle of Man
Owen Tyley	St Albans School
George Webber	John Mason School, Abingdon
Jamie Welsh	Dunblane High School, Perthshire
Sean White	City of London School
Peter Woo	Hampton Court House, Surrey
Joseph Wright	Altrincham Grammar Sch. for Boys, Cheshire
Yaning Wu	Harrow International School, Beijing
Ziqi Yan	The Tiffin Girls' Sch., Kingston-upon-Thames
Julian Yu	British School Manila, Phillipines
Joy Yu	Bilton Grange, Rugby
Will Zeng	Comberton Village College, Cambridgeshire

Lauren Zhang	King Edward VI H. Sch. for Girls, Birmingham
Christine Zhang	St Paul's Girls' School, Hammersmith

BRONZE MEDALS

Will Allfrey	Sandroyd School, Wiltshire
Taysir Barakat	Brighton College Abu Dhabi
Adam Barber	Parmiter's School, Watford
Victor Baycroft	Notre Dame High School, Sheffield
Charlie Betts	St Andrew's School, Berkshire
Jamie Biswas	Beaumont School, St Albans
Peter Brealey	Brambletye School, East Grinstead, Sussex
Emma Brightman	Wakefield Girls' High School
David Bunn	Abingdon School
Joseph Butterfield	Rednock School, Gloucestershire
Ariff Castronovo	Colet Court School, London
Elena Cates	Perse School, Cambridge
Dimitri Chamay	Beechwood Park School, St Albans
Richard Chappell	Aylesbury Grammar School
Soren Choi	Westminster Under School
Pavani Chotai	Watford Grammar School for Girls
Usman Choudahary	Twyford CofE High School, Acton
Matt Cocker	Warwick School
Amy Collis	Guildford High School
Jonathan Coombe	Wilson's School, Surrey
James Copeland	Toot Hill School, Notts
Stephen Darby	Sutton Grammar School for Boys, Surrey
Callum Davies	Teesside High School, nr Stockton-on-Tees
Nicholas Dibb-Fuller	Hampton School, Middlesex
Max Dormon	Solihull School
Siwei Dou	Leys School, Cambridge
Silas Doye	The Cherwell School, Oxford
Andrew Dubois	Wellsway School, Bristol
Jamie Dunsmore	St Olave's School, York
Thomas Durrant	Simon Langton Boys' Gram. Sch., Canterbury
Eamon Dutta Gupta	King Edward VI Grammar Sch., Chelmsford

Camille Fontaine	Colet Court School, London
Cameron Fraser	Merchant Taylors' School, Middlesex
Daniel Gallagher	King Edward VI Grammar Sch., Chelmsford
Levi Grange	Bydales Sp. T. Coll., Redcar and Cleveland
Timothy Groves	Robert Gordon's College, Aberdeen
Akash Gupta	Wilson's School, Surrey
Faiz Haris	British School of Brussels
Joel Harris	University College School, London
Isaac Harris Holt	Adams Grammar School, Shropshire
Katie Harrison	The King's School, Peterborough
Joseph Harrison	London Oratory School
Simeon Hellsten	Bournemouth School
Liam Hill	Gosforth East M. Sch., Newcastle-upon-Tyne
Jamie Hood	Skinners' School, Tunbridge Wells
Alastair Horn	Ermysted's Grammar School, N. Yorks
Charlie Howlett	Colchester Royal Grammar School
Jennifer Hu	Loughborough High School
Nefeli Hutton	Dame Alice Owen's School, Herts
Pip Jackson	Perse School, Cambridge
Samuel Ketchell	Weaverham High School, Cheshire
Mihnki Kim	Clifton College Prep School, Bristol
Hajun Kim	Gosford Hill School, Oxon
Fredric Kong	Beijing Dulwich International School
Soumya Krishna Kumar	Bancroft's School, Essex
Norbert Kulesza	Colston's School, Bristol
Avish Kumar	Westminster Under School
Alex Lee	North London Coll. Sch. Jeju, South Korea
Anthony Lee	Garden International School, Malaysia
Sein Lee	North London Coll. Sch. Jeju, South Korea
Kyung Jae Lee	Garden International School, Malaysia
Rhys Lewis	Tasker Milward VC, Haverfordwest
Jerry Lin	Discovery College, Hong Kong
Alex Linfield	Durrington High School, Worthing
Jonathan Liu	Beijing Dulwich International School

Emma Main	Churchill Academy, North Somerset
Saul Manasse	Lancaster Royal Grammar School
Fraser Mason	St Mary's Music School, Edinburgh
Peter Massey	Pocklington School, nr York
Matthew Masterman	Richmond School, N. Yorks
Samuel McConnell	Westminster Under School
Chris Mckie	Sullivan Upper Sch., Holywood, Co. Down
Samuel Mellis	St Olave's Grammar School, Kent
Jay Milligan	University College School, London
Edmund Milwain	Bradford Grammar School
Samuel Minc	British School Manila, Phillipines
Ryusei Miyamoto	Overseas Family School, Singapore
Isaac Moselle	City of London School
Angela Ng	Harrow International School, Hong Kong
Kilesh Nundlall	Upton Court Grammar School, Slough
Oscar Obrien	Colet Court School, London
Damola Odeyemi	Horris Hill School, Newbury
Mofe Owolabi	City of London School
James Panayis	St Albans School
Yunsoo Park	North London Coll. Sch. Jeju, South Korea
Charlotte Parry	Wycombe Abbey School, High Wycombe
Ben Patterson	Howard of Effingham School, Surrey
Mingke Peng	King Edward's School, Birmingham
Jonathan Peters	Bishop Challoner RC School, Basingstoke
Brnthan Pratheepan	Latymer School, London
Toby Proudfoot	Perse School, Cambridge
Gunn Pungpapong	Bangkok Patana School
Nico Puthu	Queen Elizabeth's School, Barnet
Ben Pymer	Monkton Combe School, Bath
Gordon Qiu	Douglas Academy, East Dunbartonshire
Yousuf Qureshi	Teesside High School, nr Stockton-on-Tees
Ria Ramkumar	Henrietta Barnett School, London
Benjamin Rienecker	Colet Court School, London
Molly Roberts	Wycombe High School, Buckinghamshire

Oliver Ross	Yateley School, Hampshire
Purushot Sadagopan	Haberdashers' Aske's School for Boys, Herts
Neel Sen	UWCSEA Dover Campus, Singapore
Max Shen	Queen Elizabeth's School, Barnet
Jaeheon Shim	Perse School, Cambridge
Jinho Shin	Yokohama International School
Charley Smith	Watford Grammar School for Boys
Daniel Smith	St John's Marlborough, Wiltshire
Harry Snell	Dunhurst School, Hampshire
Mikhail Sorokin	Bournemouth School
Vikram Suresh	Manor High School, Leicester
Kobe Thielemans	King's College School, London
Daniel Thompson	Cheadle Hulme High School, Cheshire
Adam Thompson	Colet Court School, London
Matthew Thomson	Wildern School, Southampton
Naren Tirumularaju	King Edward's School, Birmingham
Vincent Trieu	Tiffin School, Kingston-upon-Thames
Thien Udomsrirungruang	Shrewsbury International School, Thailand
Joshua Van der Merwe	Magdalen College School, Oxford
Jianshi Wang	Beijing New Talent Academy
Peter Westbrooke	Sevenoaks School, Kent
Edwin Wilkinson	Horringer Court M. Sch., Bury St Edmunds
Sophie Wilson	St Paul's Girls' School, Hammersmith
Isolel Wolf	St Swithun's School, Winchester
William Wright	Christopher Whitehead Lang. Coll., Worcester
Adam Xu	Alleyn's School, Dulwich
Colbert Xuan	King Edward's School, Birmingham
Takato Yamada	Lyndhurst House Prep. School, Hampstead
Woosuk Yang	Hampton School, Middlesex
Zhang Yazhou	Packwood Haugh, Shropshire
Keerthika Yoganathan	The Tiffin Girls' Sch., Kingston-upon-Thames
Will Yun Farmbrough	Rokeby School, Kingston-upon-Thames
Annie Zhao	Oxford High School

The Intermediate Mathematical Challenge and its follow-up events

The Intermediate Mathematical Challenge was held on Thursday 6th February 2014. Entries numbered 254,130 and 205,550 pupils took part. There were several different IMOK follow-up competitions and pupils were invited to the one appropriate to their school year and mark in the IMC. Around 500 candidates in each of Years 9, 10 and 11 sat the Olympiad papers (Cayley, Hamilton and Maclaurin respectively) and approximately 2500 more in each year group took a Kangaroo paper. We start with the IMC paper.

UK INTERMEDIATE MATHEMATICAL CHALLENGE

THURSDAY 6TH FEBRUARY 2014

Organised by the **United Kingdom Mathematics Trust**
and supported by

RULES AND GUIDELINES (to be read before starting)

1. Do not open the paper until the Invigilator tells you to do so.
2. Time allowed: **1 hour**.
   No answers, or personal details, may be entered after the allowed hour is over.
3. The use of rough paper is allowed; **calculators** and measuring instruments are **forbidden**.
4. Candidates in England and Wales must be in School Year 11 or below.
   Candidates in Scotland must be in S4 or below.
   Candidates in Northern Ireland must be in School Year 12 or below.
5. **Use B or HB pencil only**. Mark *at most one* of the options A, B, C, D, E on the Answer Sheet for each question. Do not mark more than one option.
6. *Do not expect to finish the whole paper in 1 hour.* Concentrate first on Questions 1-15. When you have checked your answers to these, have a go at some of the later questions.
7. Five marks are awarded for each correct answer to Questions 1-15.
   Six marks are awarded for each correct answer to Questions 16-25.
   Each incorrect answer to Questions 16-20 loses 1 mark.
   Each incorrect answer to Questions 21-25 loses 2 marks.
8. Your Answer Sheet will be read only by a *dumb machine*. **Do not write or doodle on the sheet except to mark your chosen options**. The machine 'sees' all black pencil markings even if they are in the wrong places. If you mark the sheet in the wrong place, or leave bits of rubber stuck to the page, the machine will 'see' a mark and interpret this mark in its own way.
9. The questions on this paper challenge you to **think**, not to guess. You get more marks, and more satisfaction, by doing one question carefully than by guessing lots of answers. The UK IMC is about solving interesting problems, not about lucky guessing.

The UKMT is a registered charity

http://www.ukmt.org.uk

1. What is 25 % of $\frac{3}{4}$?

   A $\dfrac{3}{16}$ B $\dfrac{1}{4}$ C $\dfrac{1}{3}$ D 1 E 3

2. Which is the smallest positive integer for which all these are true?

   (i) It is odd.

   (ii) It is not prime.

   (iii) The next largest odd integer is not prime.

   A 9 B 15 C 21 D 25 E 33

3. An equilateral triangle is placed inside a larger equilateral triangle so that the diagram has three lines of symmetry. What is the value of x?

   A 100 B 110 C 120 D 130 E 150

4. You are given that m is an even integer and n is an odd integer. Which of these is an odd integer ?

   A $3m + 4n$ B $5mn$ C $(m + 3n)^2$ D m^3n^3 E $5m + 6n$

5. A ship's bell is struck every half hour, starting with one bell at 0030, two bells (meaning the bell is struck twice) at 0100, three bells at 0130 until the cycle is complete with eight bells at 0400. The cycle then starts again with one bell at 0430, two bells at 0500 and so on. What is the total number of times the bell is struck between 0015 on one day and 0015 on the following day?

   A 24 B 48 C 108 D 144 E 216

6. The shape shown on the right was assembled from three identical copies of one of the smaller shapes below, without gaps or overlaps. Which smaller shape was used?

   A B C D E

7. Just one positive integer has exactly 8 factors including 6 and 15. What is the integer?

   A 21 B 30 C 45 D 60 E 90

8. A large cube is made by stacking eight dice. The diagram shows the result, except that one of the dice is missing. Each die has faces with 1, 2, 3, 4, 5 and 6 pips and the total number of pips on each pair of opposite faces is 7. When two dice are placed face to face, the matching faces must have the same number of pips. What could the missing die look like?

   A 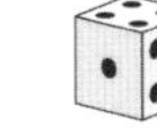  B  C  D  E 

9. At the age of twenty-six, Gill has passed her driving test and bought a car. Her car uses p litres of petrol per 100 km travelled. How many litres of petrol would be required for a journey of d km?

A $\frac{pd}{100}$ B $\frac{100p}{d}$ C $\frac{100d}{p}$ D $\frac{100}{pd}$ E $\frac{p}{100d}$

10. The diagram shows five touching semicircles, each with radius 2.

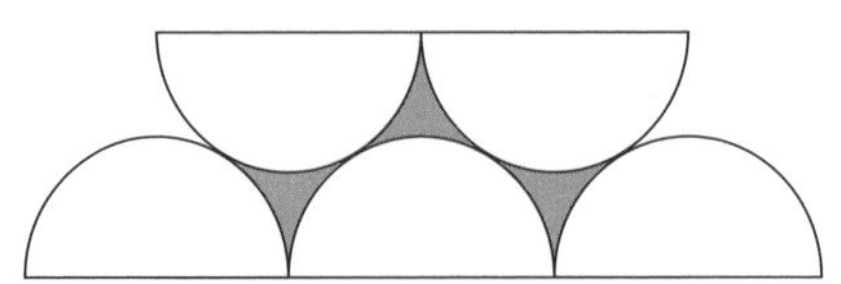

What is the length of the perimeter of the shaded shape?

A 5π B 6π C 7π D 8π E 9π

11. Not all characters in the Woodentops series tell the truth. When Mr Plod asked them, "How many people are there in the Woodentops family?", four of them replied as follows:

Jenny: "An even number." Willie: "An odd number." Sam: "A prime number."

Mrs Scrubitt: "A number which is the product of two integers greater than one."

How many of these four were telling the truth?

A 0 B 1 C 2 D 3 E 4

12. The diagram shows an isosceles right-angled triangle divided into strips of equal width. Four of the strips are shaded.
What fraction of the area of the triangle is shaded?

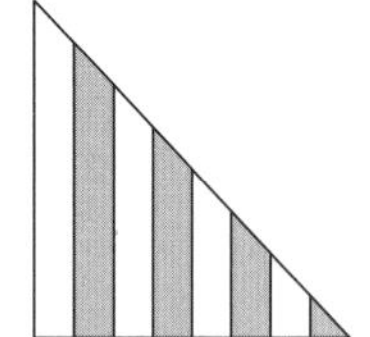

A $\frac{11}{32}$ B $\frac{3}{8}$ C $\frac{13}{32}$ D $\frac{7}{16}$ E $\frac{15}{32}$

13. How many numbers can be written as a sum of two different positive integers each at most 100?

A 100 B 197 C 198 D 199 E 200

14. This year the *Tour de France* starts in Leeds on 5 July. Last year, the total length of the *Tour* was 3404 km and the winner, Chris Froome, took a total time of 83 hours 56 minutes 40 seconds to cover this distance. Which of these is closest to his average speed over the whole event?

A 32 km/h B 40 km/h C 48 km/h D 56 km/h E 64 km/h

15. Zac halves a certain number and then adds 8 to the result. He finds that he obtains the same answer if he doubles his original number and then subtracts 8 from the result.
What is Zac's original number?

A $8\frac{2}{3}$ B $9\frac{1}{3}$ C $9\frac{2}{3}$ D $10\frac{1}{3}$ E $10\frac{2}{3}$

16. The base of a triangle is increased by 25% but the area of the triangle is unchanged. By what percentage is the corresponding perpendicular height decreased?

A $12\frac{1}{2}\%$ B 16% C 20% D 25% E 50%

17. How many weeks are there in $8 \times 7 \times 6 \times 5 \times 4 \times 3 \times 2 \times 1$ minutes?

A 1 B 2 C 3 D 4 E 5

18. Consider looking from the origin (0, 0) towards all the points (m, n), where each of m and n is an integer. Some points are *hidden*, because they are directly in line with another nearer point. For example, (2, 2) is hidden by (1, 1).

How many of the points (6, 2), (6, 3), (6, 4), (6, 5) are *not* hidden points?

A 0 B 1 C 2 D 3 E 4

19. Suppose that $8^m = 27$. What is the value of 4^m?

A 3 B 4 C 9 D 13.5 E there is no such m

20. The diagram shows a regular pentagon and five circular arcs. The sides of the pentagon have length 4. The centre of each arc is a vertex of the pentagon, and the ends of the arc are the midpoints of the two adjacent edges.

What is the total shaded area?

A 8π B 10π C 12π D 14π E 16π

---

21. In King Arthur's jousting tournament, each of the several competing knights receives 17 points for every bout he enters. The winner of each bout receives an extra 3 points. At the end of the tournament, the Black Knight has exactly one more point than the Red Knight.

What is the smallest number of bouts that the Black Knight could have entered?

A 3 B 4 C 5 D 6 E 7

22. The positive integers a, b and c are all different. None of them is a square but all the products ab, ac and bc are squares. What is the least value that $a + b + c$ can take?

A 14 B 28 C 42 D 56 E 70

23. A sector of a disc is removed by making two straight cuts from the circumference to the centre. The perimeter of the sector has the same length as the circumference of the original disc. What fraction of the area of the disc is removed?

A $\frac{\pi - 1}{\pi}$ B $\frac{1}{\pi}$ C $\frac{\pi}{360}$ D $\frac{1}{3}$ E $\frac{1}{2}$

24. How many 4-digit integers (from 1000 to 9999) have at least one digit repeated?

A 62×72 B 52×72 C 52×82 D 42×82 E 42×92

25. The diagram shows two concentric circles with radii 1 and 2 units, together with a shaded octagon, all of whose sides are equal.

What is the length of the perimeter of the octagon?

A $8\sqrt{2}$ B $8\sqrt{3}$ C $8\sqrt{3}\pi$ D $2\sqrt{5 + 2\sqrt{2}}$ E $8\sqrt{5 - 2\sqrt{2}}$

The IMC solutions

As with the Junior Challenge, a solutions leaflet was sent out.

UK INTERMEDIATE MATHEMATICAL CHALLENGE

THURSDAY 6TH FEBRUARY 2014

Organised by the **United Kingdom Mathematics Trust from the School of Mathematics, University of Leeds**

http://www.ukmt.org.uk

SOLUTIONS LEAFLET

This solutions leaflet for the IMC is sent in the hope that it might provide all concerned with some alternative solutions to the ones they have obtained. It is not intended to be definitive. The organisers would be very pleased to receive alternatives created by candidates. More comprehensive solutions are on the website at: http://www.ukmt.org.uk/

The UKMT is a registered charity

1. A 25% of $\frac{3}{4} = \frac{1}{4} \times \frac{3}{4} = \frac{3}{16}$.

2. D The first four options are the smallest positive integers which are both odd and not prime. However, the next largest odd numbers after 9, 15, 21 are 11, 17, 23 respectively and these are all prime. The next largest odd number after 25 is 27, which is not prime. So 25 is the smallest positive integer which satisfies all three conditions.

3. E Clearly AD lies along one of the lines of symmetry of the figure. So $\angle FDA = \angle EDA = x°$. Triangle DEF is equilateral so $\angle EDF = 60°$.
The angles which meet at a point sum to 360°, so $x + x + 60 = 360$.
Therefore $x = 150$.

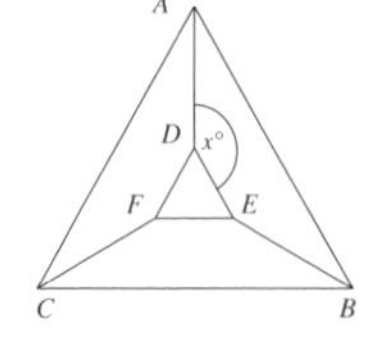

4. C Since m is even, $m = 2k$ for some integer k. So $3m + 4n = 2(3k + 2n)$; $5mn = 2(5kn)$; $m^3n^3 = 8k^3n^3$ and $5m + 6n = 2(5k + 3n)$, which are all even. As n is odd, $3n$ is also odd. So $m + 3n$ is an even integer plus an odd integer and is therefore odd. The square of an odd integer is odd so $(m + 3n)^2$ is odd.

5. **E** In one complete cycle of 4 hours, the clock is struck $1 + 2 + 3 + 4 + 5 + 6 + 7 + 8 = 36$ times. So in 24 hours the clock is struck $6 \times 36 = 216$ times.

6. **E** The large shape consists of 21 small squares, so the required shape is made up of 7 small squares. So A and C may be eliminated. The diagram on the right shows that shape E is as required. It is left to the reader to check that neither B nor D was the shape used.

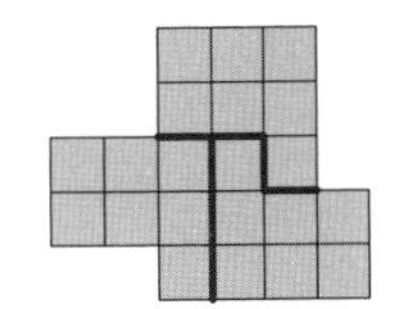

7. **B** Since 6 and 15 are factors of the integer, its prime factors will include 2, 3 and 5. So 10 and 30 will also be factors of the required integer. Seven of its factors are now known and as 1 must also be a factor, the required integer is 30, the factors of which are 1, 2, 3, 5, 6, 10, 15, 30.
(Positive integers with exactly 8 factors are of the form pqr or pq^3 or p^7 where p, q, r are distinct primes.)

8. **C** The missing die, if correctly placed in the figure, would show faces 1, 3, 5 placed in a clockwise direction around the nearest corner. An examination of each of the five proposed dice shows that only C has this property.

9. **A** Gill's car uses $p / 100$ litres of petrol for every one kilometre travelled. So for a journey of length d km, $pd / 100$ litres of petrol are required.

10. **B** A, B, C, D, E are the centres of the five semicircles. Note that AC joins the centres of two touching semicircles and therefore passes through the point of contact of the semicircles. So AC has length $2 + 2 = 4$. This also applies to all of the other sides of triangles ACD and BED. Hence both triangles are equilateral. So each of the nine arcs which make up the perimeter of the shaded shape subtends an angle of 60° at the centre of a semicircle.

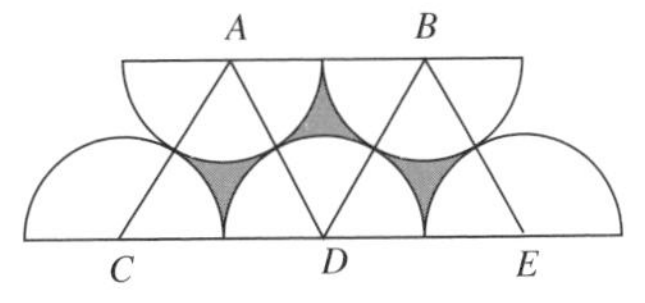

So the length of the perimeter of the shaded figure is $9 \times \frac{1}{6} \times 2 \times \pi \times 2 = 6\pi$.

11. **C** Precisely one of Jenny and Willie is telling the truth since the number of people is either even or odd. Similarly, precisely one of Sam and Mrs Scrubitt is telling the truth since the number of people is either a prime number or a number which is the product of two integers greater than one. So although it is not possible to deduce who is telling the truth, it is possible to deduce that exactly two of them are doing so.

12. **D** Let the width of each strip be 1 unit. Then the triangle has base 8 and perpendicular height 8. So its area is equal to $\frac{1}{2} \times 8 \times 8 = 32$. Looking from the right, the area of the first shaded strip is 1 unit of area less than the first unshaded strip. This difference of 1 unit also applies to the other three pairs of strips in the triangle, which means that the shaded area is 4 less than the unshaded area. So the total shaded area is $\frac{1}{2}(32 - 4) = 14$. Therefore the required fraction is $\frac{14}{32} = \frac{7}{16}$.

13. B The smallest such number is $1 + 2 = 3$, whilst the largest is $99 + 100 = 199$. Every number between 3 and 199 may be written as $1 + n$ with $n = 2, 3, \ldots, 99$ or as $100 + n$ with $n = 1, \ldots, 99$. So in total there are $(199 - 3) + 1 = 197$ such numbers.

14. B Chris Froome's average speed $\approx \frac{3400}{84}$ km/h $\approx \frac{3400}{85}$ km/h $= \frac{200}{5}$ km/h $= 40$ km/h.

15. E Let Zac's number be x. Then $\frac{1}{2}x + 8 = 2x - 8$. So $x + 16 = 4x - 16$. Therefore $32 = 3x$, that is $x = 10\frac{2}{3}$.

16. C If the areas of the original and new triangles are the same then the product of the base and the perpendicular height must be the same for the two triangles. When the base of the original triangle is increased by 25%, its value is multiplied by $\frac{5}{4}$. So if the area is to remain unchanged then the perpendicular height must be multiplied by $\frac{4}{5}$, which means that its new value is 80% of its previous value. So it is decreased by 20%.

17. D The number of minutes in one week is $7 \times 24 \times 60$, which may be written as $7 \times (6 \times 4) \times (5 \times 3 \times 2 \times 2) = (7 \times 6 \times 5 \times 4 \times 3 \times 2) \times 2$. So the number of weeks in $8 \times 7 \times 6 \times 5 \times 4 \times 3 \times 2 \times 1$ minutes is $8 \div 2 = 4$.

18. B The point (m, n) is hidden if and only if m and n share a common factor greater than 1. So (6, 2) is hidden by (3, 1) since 6 and 2 have common factor 2. Also (6, 3) is hidden by (2, 1) whilst (6, 4) is hidden by (3,2). However, 6 and 5 have no common factor other than 1 and therefore (6, 5) is not a hidden point.

19. C Note that $8^m = (2^3)^m = 2^{3m} = (2^m)^3$ and $27 = 3^3$; so $2^m = 3$. Therefore $4^m = 2^m \times 2^m = 9$.

20. D Each exterior angle of a regular pentagon is $\frac{1}{5} \times 360° = 72°$. So each of the five circular arcs has radius 2 and so subtends an angle of $(180 + 72)°$ at a vertex of the pentagon. Therefore the area of each of the five shaded major sectors is $\frac{252}{360} \times \pi \times 2^2 = \frac{7}{10} \times \pi \times 4 = \frac{14\pi}{5}$. So the total shaded area is 14π.

21. D Firstly suppose that any two knights X and Y win x and y bouts respectively and that x is at least as large as y. The difference between their total scores would be the same as if X had won $x - y$ bouts and Y had won none, since each of the separate totals would have been reduced by the same amount, namely $20y$. A similar procedure applies to losses. For example, if X won 3 and lost 6, while Y won 8 and lost 2, the difference between their total scores is the same as if X won 0 and lost 4, while Y won 5 and lost 0. In each case the difference is 32. This argument shows that, in the case of the Black Knight, B, and the Red Knight, R, the smallest number of bouts will be achieved when one of B, R wins all his bouts and the other loses all his bouts. Also B has to score one more point than R. The possible scores for the knight who wins all his bouts are 20, 40, 60, 80, 100, 120, … . while the possible scores for the knight who loses all his bouts are 17, 34, 51, 68, 85, 102, 119, 136, … .

The first two numbers to differ by 1 are 119 and 120. Thus the Black Knight has a total of 120 corresponding to winning all of his 6 bouts and the Red Knight has a total of 119 corresponding to losing all of his 7 bouts.

22. B Let $a = a_1a_2$ where a_2 is the largest square dividing a. Note that a_1 is then a product of distinct primes. Similarly write $b = b_1b_2$ and $c = c_1c_2$. Since ab is a square, a_1b_1 must be a square; so $a_1 = b_1 = k$ say. Similarly $c_1 = k$. The smallest possible value of k is 2 (since a is not a square); and the smallest possible values for a_2, b_2, c_2 are 1, 4 and 9 in some order. This makes $a + b + c = 2 + 8 + 18 = 28$.

23. A Let the radius of the circle be r and let the angle of the sector be $a°$.

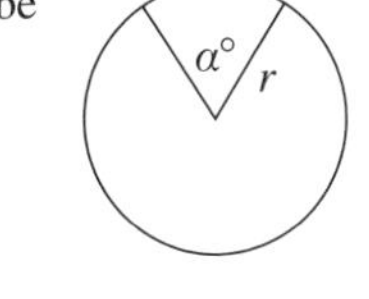

Then the perimeter of the sector is $2r + \frac{a}{360} \times 2\pi r$.
This equals $2\pi r$, the circumference of the original circle.
So $2r + \frac{a}{360} \times 2\pi r = 2\pi r$.
Therefore the fraction of the area of the disc removed is
$\frac{a}{360} = \frac{2\pi r - 2r}{2\pi r} = \frac{\pi - 1}{\pi}$.

24. A There are 9000 four-digit integers. To calculate the number of these which have four different digits, we note that we have a choice of 9 for the thousands digit. We now have a choice of 9 for the hundreds digit (since we can choose 0 as a possible digit). After these two digits have been chosen, we have a choice of 8 for the tens digit and then 7 for the units digit. So the number of four-digit numbers in which all digits are different is $9 \times 9 \times 8 \times 7$.
Therefore the number of four-digit numbers which have at least one digit repeated is $9000 - 9 \times 9 \times 8 \times 7 = 9(1000 - 9 \times 8 \times 7) =$
$9 \times 8 \times (125 - 9 \times 7) = 72 \times (125 - 63) = 72 \times 62$.

25. E Let each side of the octagon have length x. The octagon may be divided into eight triangles by joining the centre of the circle to the vertices of the octagon. One such triangle is shown. Each of these triangles has one side of length 1 (the radius of the smaller circle), one side of length 2 (the radius of the larger circle) and one side of length x. So all eight triangles are congruent. Therefore $\angle AOB = 360° \div 8 = 45°$.

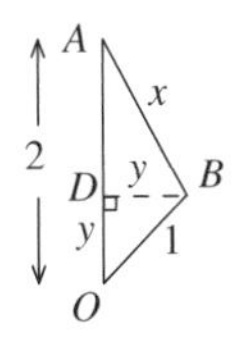

Let D be the foot of the perpendicular from B to AO. Then triangle BDO is an isosceles right-angled triangle.
Let $OD = DB = y$. Applying Pythagoras' Theorem to triangle BDO:
$y^2 + y^2 = 1$. So $y = \frac{1}{\sqrt{2}}$.
Applying Pythagoras' Theorem to triangle ADB:
$x^2 = (2 - y)^2 + y^2 = \left(2 - \frac{1}{\sqrt{2}}\right)^2 + \left(\frac{1}{\sqrt{2}}\right)^2 = 4 - 2 \times 2 \times \frac{1}{\sqrt{2}} + \frac{1}{2} + \frac{1}{2} = 5 - \frac{4}{\sqrt{2}} = 5 - 2\sqrt{2}$.
So the length of the perimeter is $8x = 8\sqrt{5 - 2\sqrt{2}}$.
(Note that the length of AB may also be found by applying the Cosine Rule to triangle OAB.)

The answers

The table below shows the proportion of pupils' choices. The correct answer is shown in bold. [The percentages are rounded to the nearest whole number.]

Qn	A	B	C	D	E	Blank
1	**72**	11	9	2	4	2
2	12	9	8	**49**	19	2
3	1	3	15	5	**74**	2
4	7	12	**58**	16	4	3
5	4	20	17	12	**42**	3
6	4	4	4	11	**73**	2
7	1	**58**	3	20	15	2
8	39	9	**28**	15	6	3
9	**33**	24	17	8	14	4
10	20	**39**	9	13	12	7
11	3	10	**56**	26	2	4
12	9	24	12	**29**	17	7
13	17	**14**	22	18	18	9
14	13	**56**	16	7	3	4
15	15	9	12	14	**41**	8
16	13	4	**16**	14	4	48
17	7	8	11	**32**	7	34
18	7	**9**	10	4	9	60
19	2	1	**5**	17	22	53
20	4	8	6	**10**	7	65
21	4	6	6	**11**	4	69
22	4	**9**	6	3	1	77
23	**4**	3	5	4	3	81
24	**4**	4	3	4	3	82
25	3	3	5	3	**3**	84

IMC 2014: Some comments on the pupils' choice of answers as sent to schools in the letter with the results

The mean score this year of 40.9 is a little lower than last year. No question was answered correctly by more than 80% of the pupils, and several of the first ten questions turned out to be rather harder than the Problems Group expected. In many cases we are left with the impression that many pupils guessed a plausible answer instead of thinking their way through to the correct answer.

We hope that you will look at the table comparing the answers given by your pupils with the national distribution, and that you will find this informative. For example, in Question 1 only 73% of the pupils were able to give the correct value for 25% of. If your pupils did not do any better than this, is this because of a lack of understanding of percentages and fractions, or just carelessness?

Question 2 is not difficult, but it contains a lot of words and needs to be read carefully. No doubt this explains why only half the pupils gave the correct answer.

It is good to see that 75% of the pupils found the correct value for the angle in Question 3. Did the 15% who chose 120 as their answer think about the question or just make a guess based on the diagram?

Question 8 does not involve any mathematical techniques but just the ability to imagine cubes in three dimensions. So it is a little disappointing that only 29% of the pupils gave the correct answer. They were not much more successful with Question 9. This uses algebra, but, as indicated in the Solutions and Investigations, it should not have been difficult to work out that only option A could possibly be correct. They had more success with Question 15 which also involves algebra, but, perhaps, is of a more familiar type. The outcomes on Question 11 which uses logic applied to number facts, and Question 14 about estimating an average speed, were also encouraging.

The later questions are intended to be harder, and are used to help us select the pupils who are invited to take the Cayley, Hamilton and Maclaurin and Kangaroo papers. Many of these questions are very challenging and most students did not attempt them. Pupils who did well enough on these later, harder questions to qualify for one of the follow-on events should be congratulated on their excellent achievement.

The profile of marks obtained is shown below.

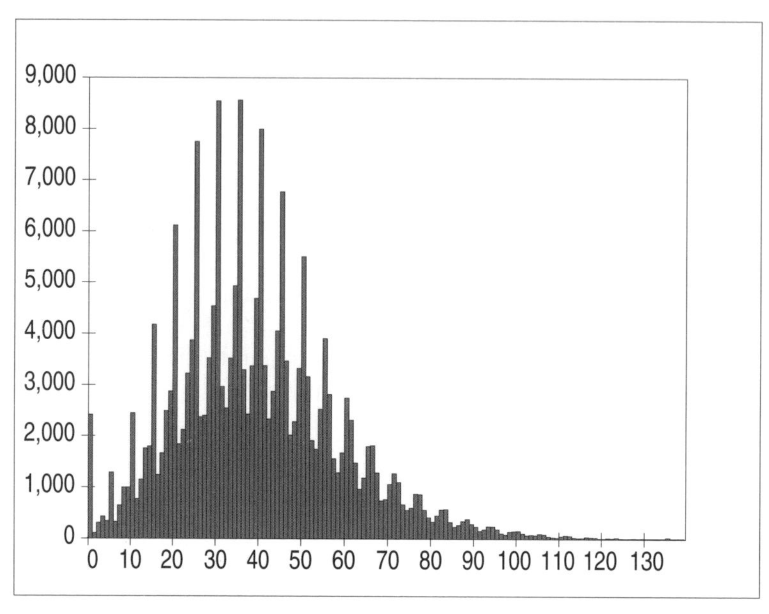

Bar chart showing the actual frequencies in the 2014 IMC

On the basis of the standard proportions used by the UKMT, the cut-off marks were set at

GOLD – 72 or over SILVER – 55 to 71 BRONZE – 42 to 54

The certificates were virtually identical in design to those used for the JMC.

The cut-off scores for the follow-up competitions were

Year (E&W)		Minimum mark	Event		Minimum mark	Event
11		103	Maclaurin		78	Kangaroo Pink
10		96	Hamilton		78	Kangaroo Pink
9		90	Cayley		67	Kangaroo Grey

The Intermediate Mathematical Olympiad and Kangaroo

(a) *Kangaroo*

The 2014 European Kangaroo (a multiple choice paper with 25 questions) took place on Thursday 20th March. It was also held in many other countries across Europe and beyond with over five million candidates. As in previous years, the UKMT constructed two Kangaroo papers.

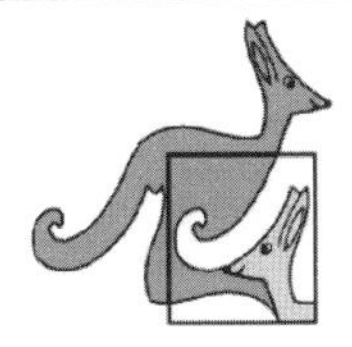

EUROPEAN 'KANGAROO' MATHEMATICAL CHALLENGE
'GREY'
Thursday 20th March 2014

Organised by the United Kingdom Mathematics Trust and the Association Kangourou Sans Frontières

This competition is being taken by 5 million students in over 40 countries worldwide.

RULES AND GUIDELINES (to be read before starting):

1. Do not open the paper until the Invigilator tells you to do so.
2. Time allowed: **1 hour**.
   No answers, or personal details, may be entered after the allowed hour is over.
3. The use of rough paper is allowed; **calculators** and measuring instruments are **forbidden**.
4. Candidates in England and Wales must be in School Year 9 or below.
   Candidates in Scotland must be in S2 or below.
   Candidates in Northern Ireland must be in School Year 10 or below.
5. **Use B or HB pencil only**. For each question mark *at most one* of the options A, B, C, D, E on the Answer Sheet. Do not mark more than one option.
6. Five marks will be awarded for each correct answer to Questions 1 - 15.
   Six marks will be awarded for each correct answer to Questions 16 - 25.
7. *Do not expect to finish the whole paper in 1 hour*. Concentrate first on Questions 1-15. When you have checked your answers to these, have a go at some of the later questions.
8. The questions on this paper challenge you **to think**, not to guess. Though you will not lose marks for getting answers wrong, you will undoubtedly get more marks, and more satisfaction, by doing a few questions carefully than by guessing lots of answers.

Enquiries about the European Kangaroo should be sent to:
Maths Challenges Office,
School of Maths Satellite, University of Leeds, Leeds, LS2 9JT.
(Tel. 0113 343 2339)
http://www.ukmt.org.uk

2014 European Grey Kangaroo

1. Each year, the Kangaroo competition is held on the the third Thursday of March. What is the latest possible date of the competition in any year?

   A 14th March B 15th March C 20th March D 21st March E 22nd March

2. The area of rectangle $PQRS$ is 10 cm^2. Points M and N are the midpoints of the sides PQ and SR.
   What is the area in cm^2 of quadrilateral $MRNP$?

   A 4 B 4.5 C 5 D 6 E 10

3. Rachel has several square pieces of paper of area 4 cm^2. She cuts each of them into smaller squares and right-angled triangles in the manner shown in the first diagram. She takes some of the pieces and makes the shape shown in the second diagram.
   What is the area in cm^2 of the shape?

   A 3 B 4 C 9/2 D 5 E 6

4. A bucket was half full. A cleaner added two litres of water to the bucket. The bucket was then three-quarters full. How many litres can the bucket hold?

   A 10 B 8 C 6 D 4 E 2

5. Carl built the shape shown using seven unit cubes. How many such cubes does he have to add to make a cube with edges of length 3?

   A 12 B 14 C 16 D 18 E 20

6. Which of the following calculations gives the largest result?

   A 44×777 B 55×666 C 77×444 D 88×333 E 99×222

7. Jack has a piano lesson twice a week and Jill has a piano lesson every other week. Since they started playing, Jack has had 15 more lessons than Jill.
   How many weeks have they been playing?

   A 30 B 25 C 20 D 15 E 10

8. In the diagram, the area of each circle is 1 cm^2. The area common to any two overlapping circles is $\frac{1}{8}$ cm^2. What is the area of the region covered by the five circles?

   A 4 cm^2 B $\frac{9}{2}$ cm^2 C $\frac{35}{8}$ cm^2 D $\frac{39}{8}$ cm^2 E $\frac{19}{4}$ cm^2

9. This year a grandmother, her daughter and her granddaughter noticed that the sum of their ages is 100 years. Each of their ages is a power of 2. How old is the granddaughter?

   A 1 B 2 C 4 D 8 E 16

10. The heart and the arrow are in the positions shown in the figure. At the same time the heart and the arrow start moving. The arrow moves three places clockwise and then stops and the heart moves four places anticlockwise and then stops. They repeat the same routine over and over again.
    After how many routines will the heart and the arrow land in the same place as each other for the first time?

    A 7 B 8 C 9 D 10 E It will never happen

11. Five equal rectangles are placed inside a square with side 24 cm, as shown in the diagram. What is the area in cm^2 of one rectangle?

A 12 B 16 C 18 D 24 E 32

12. The diagram shows the triangle PQR in which RH is a perpendicular height and PS is the angle bisector at P. The obtuse angle between RH and PS is four times angle SPQ. What is angle RPQ?

A 30° B 45° C 60° D 75° E 90°

13. Six boys share a flat with two bathrooms which they use every morning beginning at 7:00 o'clock. In each bathroom there is never more than one person at any one time. The times they spend in the bathroom are 8, 10, 12, 17, 21 and 22 minutes.
What is the earliest time that they can finish using the bathrooms?

A 7:45 B 7:46 C 7:47 D 7:48 E 7:50

14. A rectangle has sides of length 6 cm and 11cm. The bisectors of the angles at either end of one 11 cm side are drawn. These bisectors divide the other 11 cm side into three parts. What are the lengths of these parts?

A 1 cm, 9 cm, 1 cm B 6 cm, 1 cm, 6 cm C 3 cm, 5 cm, 3 cm
D 4 cm, 3 cm, 4 cm E 5 cm, 1 cm, 5 cm

15. Captain Sparrow and his pirate crew dug up several gold coins. They divided the coins amongst themselves so that each person received the same number of coins.
If there had been four fewer pirates, then each person would have received 10 more coins.
However, if there had been 50 fewer coins, then each person would have received 5 fewer coins. How many coins did they dig up?

A 80 B 100 C 120 D 150 E 250

16. The mean of two positive numbers is 30% less than one of the numbers.
By what percentage is the mean greater than the other number?

A 75% B 70% C 30% D 25% E 20%

17. Janet enters all the digits from 1 to 9 in the cells of a 3×3 table, so that each cell contains one digit. She has already entered 1, 2, 3 and 4, as shown. Two numbers are considered to be 'neighbours' if their cells share an edge. After entering all the numbers, she notices that the sum of the neighbours of 9 is 15.
What is the sum of the neighbours of 8?

1		3
2		4

A 12 B 18 C 20 D 26 E 27

18. The numbers a, b and c satisfy the equations $a + b + c = 500$ and $3a + 2b + c = 1000$.
What is $3a + 4b + 5c$?

A 2000 B 1900 C 1700 D 1600 E 1500

19. Liz and Mary compete in solving problems. Each of them is given the same list of 100 problems. For any problem, the first of them to solve it gets 4 points, while the second to solve it gets 1 point. Liz solved 60 problems, and Mary also solved 60 problems. Together, they got 312 points.

How many problems were solved by both of them?

A 53 B 54 C 55 D 56 E 57

20. Peter set off on his bike to go to Oxford from his cottage. He aimed to arrive at 15:00. When he had used up $\frac{2}{3}$ of the time available, he realised that he had covered $\frac{3}{4}$ of the distance. He then changed his speed so he arrived exactly on time.

What is the ratio of the speed for the first part of the journey to the speed for the second part?

A 5:4 B 4:3 C 3:2 D 2:1 E 3:1

21. An antique set of scales is not working properly. If something is lighter than 1000g, the scales show the correct weight, otherwise the scales can show any value greater then 1000g.

Jenny grows giant fruit and vegetables. She has a pumpkin, a quince, a radish, a swede and a turnip whose weights are all less than 1000g and, in grams, are P, Q, R, S and T.

When she weighs them in pairs, the scale shows the following:

quince and swede: 1200g radish and turnip: 2100g quince and turnip: 800g

quince and radish: 900g pumpkin and turnip: 700g

Which of the following lists gives the masses in descending order?

A *SRTQP* B *STRQP* C *SRTPQ* D *STRPQ* E *SRQTP*

22. A group of 25 people consists of knights, serfs and damsels. Each knight always tells the truth, each serf always lies, and each damsel alternates between telling the truth and lying. When each of them was asked: "Are you a knight?", 17 of them said "Yes". When each of them was then asked: "Are you a damsel?", 12 of them said "Yes". When each of them was then asked: "Are you a serf?", 8 of them said "Yes".

How many knights are in the group?

A 4 B 5 C 9 D 13 E 17

23. Dean's teacher asks him to write several different positive integers on the board. Exactly two of them are to be divisible by 2 and exactly 13 of them are to be divisible by 13. M is the greatest of these numbers.

What is the least possible value of M?

A 169 B 260 C 273 D 299 E 325

24. A 5×5 square is made from 1×1 tiles, all with the same pattern, as shown. Any two adjacent tiles have the same colour along the shared edge. The perimeter of the 5×5 square consists of black and white segments of length 1.

What is the smallest possible number of black segments on the perimeter of the 5×5 square?

A 4 B 5 C 6 D 7 E 8

25. Quadrilateral *PQRS* has right angles at vertices P and Q only. The numbers show the areas in cm^2 of two of the triangles.

What is the area in cm^2 of *PQRS*?

A 60 B 45 C 40 D 35 E 30

Solutions to the 2014 European Grey Kangaroo

1. D Thursdays occur every seven days. The latest date for the first Thursday in March would be 7th March and hence the latest date for the third Thursday in March would be 21st March.

2. C Draw the line MN. The rectangle is now divided into four identical triangles. Quadrilateral $MRNP$ consists of two of these triangles, so its area is half of the area of rectangle $PQRS$, that is, 5 cm^2.

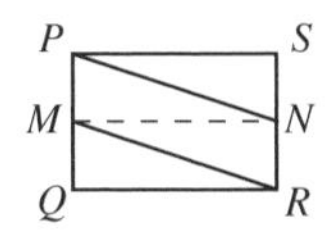

3. E The shape is made up of four pieces from one large square plus three further pieces making up half of a large square. Hence the area in cm^2 is $4 + \frac{1}{2} \times 4 = 6$.

4. B Two litres represents $\frac{3}{4} - \frac{1}{2} = \frac{1}{4}$ of the capacity of the bucket. Hence the capacity of the bucket in litres is $4 \times 2 = 8$.

5. E A cube with edges of length 3 is made up of $3^3 = 27$ unit cubes. Carl has already used seven cubes to build the initial shape so the number of cubes he needs to add is $27 - 7 = 20$.

6. B Each product is of the form $aa \times bbb = a \times b \times 11 \times 111$. The largest result will come when the value of $a \times b$ is largest. These values are 28, 30, 28, 24 and 18 respectively. Hence, the largest result comes when $a \times b = 30$ in calculation B.

7. E In each two week period, Jack has four piano lessons while Jill has one lesson. Therefore Jack has three extra lessons in each two week period. Hence it has taken $15 \div 3 = 5$ two week periods for Jack to have the extra 15 lessons. So they have been playing for $5 \times 2 = 10$ weeks.

8. B There are four regions where two circles overlap. Therefore the area covered by the five circles in cm^2 is $5 \times 1 - 4 \times \frac{1}{8} = \frac{9}{2}$.

9. C The powers of 2 under 100 are 1, 2, 4, 8, 16, 32 and 64. The sum of the first six of these is 63 so, to have a sum of three such ages adding to 100, one of them must be 64 (the grandmother). This leaves 36 as the sum of the ages of the daughter and the granddaughter. The sum of the first five powers of 2 is 31 so, to have a sum of two such ages adding to 36, one of them must be 32 (the daughter). This leaves 4 as the age of the granddaughter.

10. E The figure contains seven regions. An anticlockwise rotation of four regions on such a figure is equivalent to a clockwise rotation of three regions. Hence, each routine involves the two symbols moving three regions clockwise and so they will never land in the same region.

11. E Let the length and height of the small rectangle be x cm and y cm respectively. From the arrangement of the small rectangles within the square it can be seen that $x - y + x + y + x = 24$ (horizontally) and $y + x + x + y = 24$ (vertically). These simplify to $3x = 24$ and $2y + 2x = 24$ respectively. Hence the value of x is 8 and the value of y is 4. The area of each small rectangle in cm^2 is then $8 \times 4 = 32$.

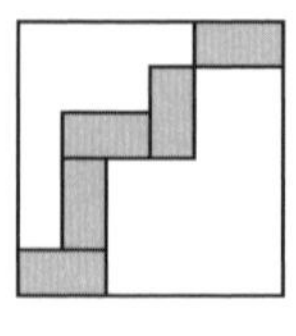

12. C Let X be the point where RH meets PS. In ΔHXP, $\alpha + 90° + \angle HXP = 180°$. This gives $\angle HXP = 90° - \alpha$. Angles on a straight line add to $180°$ so $4\alpha + 90° - \alpha = 180°$ with solution $\alpha = 30°$. Hence the size of $\angle RPQ$ is $2 \times 30° = 60°$.

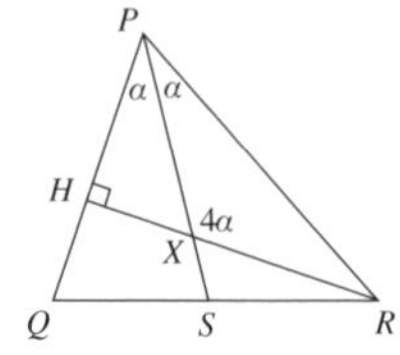

Alternative solution: For any triangle, the exterior angle at one vertex is equal to the sum of the interior angles at the other two vertices. If we apply this to triangle XPH we get $4\alpha = 90° + \alpha$, so $\alpha = 30°$. Therefore $\angle RPQ = 2 \times \alpha = 60°$.

13. B The total length of time in minutes spent in the two bathrooms is $8 + 10 + 12 + 17 + 21 + 22 = 90$. So, if it can be arranged that one bathroom is being used for exactly 45 minutes at the same time as the other bathroom is also being used for 45 minutes then the boys would be finished at 7:45. Consider the bathroom used by the boy taking 22 minutes. For an optimal solution, the other boys using the same bathroom would need to take 23 minutes in total and it can easily be seen that no such combination of two or more times can give this time. The closest is 22 minutes from the boy who takes 10 minutes and the boy who takes 12 minutes. This would mean one bathroom was in use for 44 minutes and the other for 46 minutes. Hence the earliest time they can finish using the bathrooms is 7:46.

14. E Label the rectangle as shown in the diagram. The bisectors of angles SPQ and RSP form the hypotenuses of two isosceles right-angled triangles PQV and URS. Let the length of UV be x cm. The lengths of QV and RU are both 6 cm. QR has length 11cm so $QV + RU > QR$ and hence U and V are placed as shown. Hence, the length of QU and of

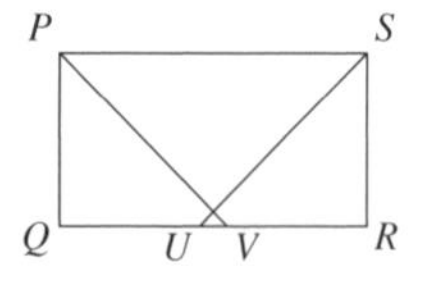

VR is $(6 - x)$ cm. The length of QR is 11 cm so $6 - x + x + 6 - x = 11$. This has solution $x = 1$ so the lengths of the three parts of QR formed by the angle bisectors are 5 cm, 1 cm and 5 cm respectively.

15. D Let the number of coins and the number of pirates be N and x respectively. From the information in the question, we have the equations $\dfrac{N}{x-4} = \dfrac{N}{x} + 10$ and $\dfrac{N-50}{x} = \dfrac{N}{x} - 5$. Multiply the second equation through by x to obtain $N - 50 = N - 5x$ which has solution $x = 10$. Now substitute this value into the first equation to obtain $\frac{1}{6}N = \frac{1}{10}N + 10$. This reduces to $\frac{1}{15}N = 10$ with solution $N = 150$. Hence the pirates dug up 150 coins.

16. A Let the two numbers be x and y with $x > y$. The mean of the two numbers is 30% less than one of the numbers, which must be the larger number. So the mean, $\frac{1}{2}(x+y)$, is 30% less than x. Therefore, $\frac{1}{2}(x + y) = \frac{70}{100}x$, that is $\frac{1}{2}(x + y) = \frac{7}{10}x$. If we multiply both sides of the equation by 10, we obtain $5(x + y) = 7x$. So $5y = 2x$ and hence $x = \frac{5}{2}y$. Therefore $\frac{1}{2}(x+y) = \frac{7}{10} \times \frac{5}{2}y = \frac{35}{20}y = \frac{7}{4}y = 1\frac{3}{4}y = 1.75y$. Therefore, the mean is 75% greater than the smaller number.

17. E The sum of the neighbours of 9 is 15. If 9 were to be placed in the central cell, its neighbours would be 5, 6, 7 and 8 with sum 26 so 9 must be placed in one of the cells on the perimeter of the table. So the neighbours of 9 will be the numbers in the middle cell and the two corner cells which are in either the same row or the same column of the table. The largest sum of two such corner cells is $3 + 4 = 7$ so, for the sum of the neighbours of 9 to be 15, the number in the middle cell cannot be smaller than 8. However, the middle square cannot be larger than 8 since we already know 9 is in a perimeter cell. Therefore the number in the middle cell is 8 and its neighbours are 5, 6, 7 and 9 with sum 27.

18. A Note that $(3a + 4b + 5c) + (3a + 2b + c) = 6(a + b + c)$. Hence the value of $3a + 4b + 5c$ is $6 \times 500 - 1000 = 2000$.

19. D The total number of points scored for any question answered by both Liz and Mary is 5 whereas the total number of points scored for any question answered by only one of them is 4. Let x be the number of questions answered by both. Therefore, as the number of questions answered only by Liz and the number answered only by Mary were both $60 - x$, we have $5x + 2 \times 4(60 - x) = 312$. This reduces to $480 - 3x = 312$ with solution $x = 56$. Hence the number of problems solved by both is 56.

20. C Let the distance Peter planned to cycle and the time he planned to take be x and t respectively. On the first part of his journey, he travelled a distance $\frac{3}{4}x$ in time $\frac{2}{3}t$ at an average speed of $\frac{3}{4}x \div \frac{2}{3}t = \frac{9x}{8t}$. On the second part of his journey, he travelled a distance $\frac{1}{4}x$ in time $\frac{1}{3}t$ at an average speed of $\frac{1}{4}x \div \frac{1}{3}t = \frac{3x}{4t}$. Hence the ratio of his average speeds for the two parts of the journey is $\frac{9x}{8t} : \frac{3x}{4t} = \frac{9}{8} : \frac{3}{4} = 36 : 24 = 3 : 2$.

21. A Consider the results of the weighings in pairs. The pair $Q + S = 1200$ and $Q + R = 900$ tell us that $S > R$. Similarly the pair $Q + R = 900$ and $Q + T = 800$ tell us that $R > T$, the pair $R + T = 2100$ and $Q + R = 900$ tell us that $T > Q$ and finally the pair $Q + T = 800$ and $P + T = 700$ tell us that $Q > P$. If we combine these inequalities, we obtain $S > R > T > Q > P$. Hence, the list in decreasing order of mass is $SRTQP$.

22. B Let there be k knights and s serfs altogether, and let there be d damsels who lied to the first question. In answer to the first question, the people who answered yes were the knights (truthfully), the serfs (untruthfully) and the damsels who lied to the first question they were asked. This gives the equation $k + s + d = 17$. In answer to the second question, the people who answered yes were the serfs (untruthfully) and the damsels who lied to the first question they were asked but who then answered truthfully. This gives the equation $s + d = 12$. Subtract the second equation from the first to give $k = 5$. Hence, the number of knights in the group is 5.

23. C The list of integers must contain 13 numbers divisible by 13, no more than two of which can be even. Therefore the list must contain at least 11 distinct odd multiples of 13. The minimum value for the largest of these occurs when there are exactly 11 odd multiples of 13 and they are the first 11 odd multiples of 13. The 11th odd integer is 21 so the 11th odd multiple of 13 is $21 \times 13 = 273$. A list of integers containing two small even multiples of 13 such as 26 and 52 and the first 11 odd multiples of 13 satisfies the conditions in the question and so the least possible value of M is 273.

24. B All the tiles on the perimeter of the 5×5 square contribute either one or two segments of length 1 to the perimeter with those contributing two segments being the four tiles at the corners. Each tile has only one white edge so there must be a minimum of four black segments on the perimeter. Now consider the central 3×3 square of the larger square. Adjacent tiles must be the same colour along a common edge so only eight of the nine tiles in the central square can have their white edge joined to another tile in the central square leaving at least one tile with its white edge not joined to any other tile in the central square. Hence, at least one tile on the perimeter must join its white edge to that of a tile from the central 3×3 square. The diagram above shows that an arrangement with only one tile on the perimeter joining its white edge to that of a central tile is possible. Hence, the smallest possible number of black segments on the perimeter of the 5×5 square is 5.

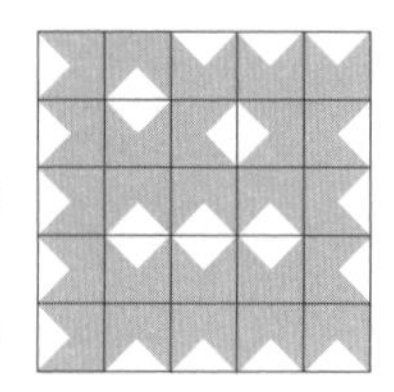

25. B Let T be the intersection of PR and QS. Let x and y be the areas in cm^2 of triangles STR and QRT respectively as shown in the diagram. Angles SPQ and PQR are 90° so PS and QR are parallel. Triangles SPQ and SPR have the same base and the same height so must have the same area. Hence $x = 10$. Triangle SPT has the same base as triangle SPQ but only a third of the area. Therefore the height of triangle SPT is a third of the height of triangle SPQ and so the height of triangle QRT is $\frac{2}{3}$ the height of triangle QRP. Triangles QRT and QRP have the same base so their areas are in the ratio of their heights. Therefore $y = \frac{2}{3}(y + 10)$ which has solution $y = 20$. Hence the total area in cm^2 of quadrilateral $PQRS$ is $5 + 10 + x + y = 45$.

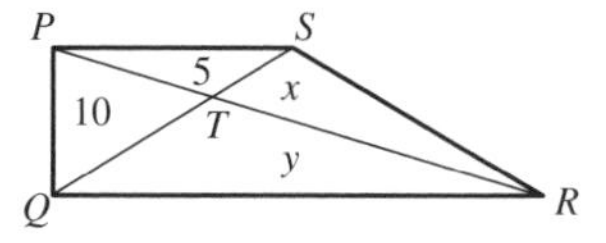

2014 European Pink Kangaroo

1. The MSC Fabiola holds the record for being the largest container ship to enter San Francisco Bay. It carries 12 500 containers which, if placed end to end, would stretch about 75 km.

   Roughly, what is the length of one container?

   A 0.6 m B 1.6 m C 6 m D 16 m E 60 m

2. If r, s, and t denote the lengths of the 'lines' in the picture, then which of the following inequalities is correct?

   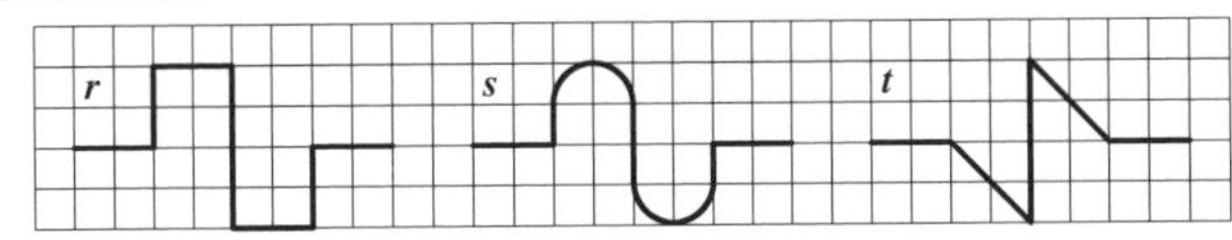

   A $r < s < t$ B $r < t < s$ C $s < r < t$ D $s < t < r$ E $t < s < r$

3. Which of the following is halfway between $\frac{2}{3}$ and $\frac{4}{5}$?

   A $\frac{11}{15}$ B $\frac{7}{8}$ C $\frac{3}{4}$ D $\frac{6}{15}$ E $\frac{5}{8}$

4. In the number 2014 the last digit is larger than the sum of the other three digits. How many years ago was this last true for the calendar year?

   A 1 B 3 C 5 D 7 E 11

5. In a certain village, the ratio between adult men and adult women is 2 : 3 and the ratio between adult women and children is 8 : 1. What is the ratio between adults (men and women) and children?

   A 5 : 1 B 10 : 3 C 13 : 1 D 12 : 1 E 40 : 3

6. The big wheel of this penny-farthing bicycle has perimeter 4.2 metres. The small wheel has perimeter 0.9 metres. At a certain moment, the valves of both wheels are at their lowest points. The bicycle begins to roll.

   How many metres will the bicycle have rolled forward when both valves are next at their lowest points at the same time?

   A 4.2 B 6.3 C 12.6 D 25.2 E 37.8

7. Doris, her daughter and granddaughter were all born in the month of January. Today their ages are all powers of 2. Moreover, the sum of their ages is 100. In which year was the granddaughter born?

   A 1998 B 2006 C 2010 D 2012 E 2013

8. Six girls share a flat which has two bathrooms. Every morning, beginning at 7:00, they use the bathrooms (one girl at a time per bathroom!). As soon as the last girl has finished, they sit down to eat breakfast together. The times they spend in the bathroom are 9, 11, 13, 18, 22, and 23 minutes. If they organise themselves well, what is the earliest they can have breakfast together?

   A 7:48 B 7:49 C 7:50 D 7:51 E 8:03

9. The diagram shows a regular octagon, with a line drawn between two of its vertices. The shaded area measures 3 cm^2.

   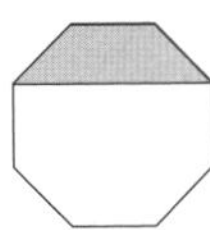

   What is the area of the octagon in square centimetres?

   A 9 B 10 C $8\sqrt{2}$ D 12 E $8 + 4\sqrt{2}$

10. The length of my crocodile's tail is a third of its entire length. Its head is 93 cm long and this is a quarter of the crocodile's length (not counting the tail).
How long is my crocodile in centimetres?

A 558 B 496 C 490 D 372 E 186

11. The diagram shows a special die. Each pair of numbers on opposite faces has the same sum. The numbers on the hidden faces are all prime numbers. Which number is opposite to the 14 shown?

A 11 B 13 C 17 D 19 E 23

12. After walking 8 km at a speed of 4 km/h, Ann starts to run at a speed of 8 km/h.
For how many minutes will she have to run in order to have an average speed of 5 km/h over her complete journey?

A 15 B 20 C 30 D 35 E 40

13. Cleo played 40 games of chess and scored 25 points. (A win counts as one point, a draw counts as half a point, and a loss counts as zero points.)
How many more games did she win than lose?

A 5 B 7 C 10 D 12 E 15

14. Triplets Jane, Danielle and Hannah wanted to buy identical hats. However, Jane lacked a third of their price, Danielle a quarter and Hannah a fifth. When the price of each hat was reduced by €9.40, the sisters combined their savings and bought a hat each. Not a cent was left over!
What was the price of a hat before the price reduction?

A €12 B €16 C €28 D €36 E €112

15. Let p, q, r be positive integers such that

$$p + \frac{1}{q + \frac{1}{r}} = \frac{25}{19}.$$

Which of the following is equal to pqr ?

A 6 B 10 C 18 D 36 E 42

16. In the equation $N \times U \times (M + B + E + R) = 33$, each letter stands for a different digit (0, 1, 2, . . . , 9).
How many different ways are there to choose the values of the letters?

A 12 B 24 C 30 D 48 E 60

17. The picture shows seven points and the connections between them. What is the least number of connecting lines that could be added to the picture so that each of the seven points has the same number of connections with other points? (Connecting lines are allowed to cross each other.)

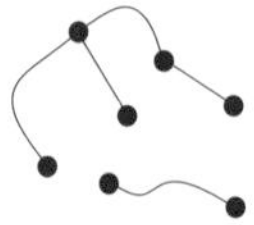

A 4 B 5 C 6 D 9 E 10

18. The picture shows the same cube from two different views. It is built from 27 smaller cubes, some of which are grey and some white.
What is the largest number of grey cubes there could be?

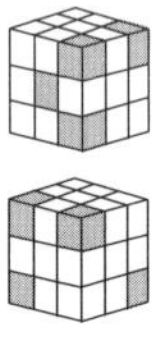

A 5 B 7 C 8 D 9 E 10

19. In a certain forest, frogs are either green or blue. Since last year, the number of blue frogs has increased by 60%, while the number of green frogs has decreased by 60%. It turns out that the new ratio of blue frogs to green frogs is the same as the previous ratio in the opposite order (i.e. the same as the previous ratio of green frogs to blue frogs).
By what percentage did the overall number of frogs change?

A 0 B 20 C 30 D 40 E 50

20. Tomas wrote down several distinct positive integers, none of which exceeded 100. Their product was not divisible by 18.
At most how many numbers could he have written?

A 5 B 17 C 68 D 69 E 90

21. Any three vertices of a given cube form the vertices of a triangle.
What is the number of triangles formed in this way whose three vertices are not all in the same face of the cube?

A 16 B 24 C 32 D 40 E 48

22. In the picture, PT is a tangent to the circle with centre O and PS is the angle bisector of angle RPT.
What is the size of angle TSP?

A $30°$ B $45°$ C $50°$ D $60°$
E It depends on the position of point P.

23. Tatiana wrote down in ascending order the list of all 7-digit numbers that contain each of the digits 1, 2, 3, . . . , 7. She then split the list exactly at the middle into two parts of the same size.
What is the largest number in the first half?

A 1 234 567 B 3 765 421 C 4 123 567 D 4 352 617 E 4 376 521

24. The diagram shows a triangle FHG with $FH = 6$, $GH = 8$ and $FG = 10$. The point I is the midpoint of FG, and $HIJK$ is a square. The line segment IJ intersects GH at L.
What is the area of the shaded quadrilateral $HLJK$?

A $\frac{124}{8}$ B $\frac{125}{8}$ C $\frac{126}{8}$ D $\frac{127}{8}$ E $\frac{128}{8}$

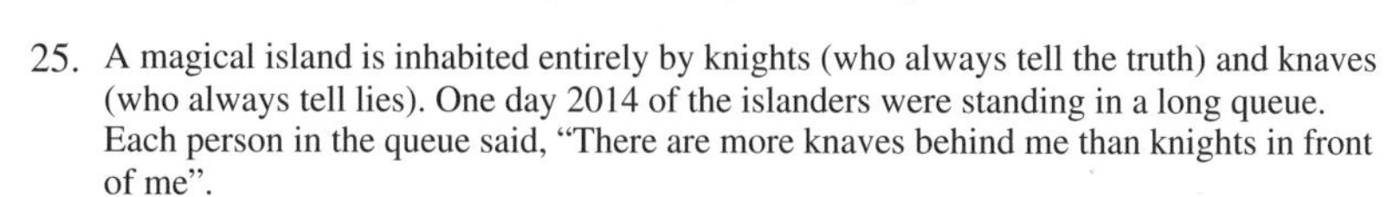

25. A magical island is inhabited entirely by knights (who always tell the truth) and knaves (who always tell lies). One day 2014 of the islanders were standing in a long queue. Each person in the queue said, "There are more knaves behind me than knights in front of me".
How many knights were in the queue?

A 1 B 504 C 1007 D 1008 E 2014

Solutions to the 2014 European Pink Kangaroo

1. **C** Dividing 75 km (75 000 m) by 12 500 gives the length of a container as 6 m.

2. **E** If each square has side-length one unit, then the length r is 16 units. The length s consists of 8 straight unit lengths and two semicircles with radius 1 unit, so $s = 8 + 2\pi$. The length t consists of 8 straight unit lengths and two diagonals (that together make the hypotenuse of a right-angled triangle with short sides both of length 4 units), so $t = 8 + 2\sqrt{8}$. Since $\sqrt{8} < 3 < \pi < 4$, we have $t < s < r$.

3. **A** Since $\frac{2}{3} = \frac{10}{15}$ and $\frac{4}{5} = \frac{12}{15}$, the number halfway between $\frac{2}{3}$ and $\frac{4}{5}$ is $\frac{11}{15}$.

4. **C** Working backwards one year at a time, we see that the last digits of 2013, 2012, 2011, 2010 are not larger than the sum of the other digits, but for 2009 the last digit is larger than $2 + 0 + 0$. This was 5 years ago.

5. **E** The ratio of men to women (2 : 3) is equivalent to 16 : 24; the ratio of women to children (8 : 1) is equivalent to 24 : 3. Hence the ratio of men to women to children is 16 : 24 : 3. Combining men and women gives the ratio of adults to children as 40 : 3.

6. **C** Note that $4.2 = 14 \times 0.3$ and that $0.9 = 3 \times 0.3$. So to determine when the valves are next at their lowest point at the same time we need the lowest common multiple (LCM) of 14 and 3. As these two numbers are coprime, their LCM is their product, that is 42. So the required distance is 42×0.3 m $= 12.6$ m.

7. **C** The three ages are powers of two and also under 100, so must be three of 1, 2, 4, 8, 16, 32, 64. The sum of the first five is only 63, so to make 100, one of them (the grandmother) must be aged 64. This leaves 36 years as the total of the other two ages. The only two that add to 36 are 32 and 4. Hence the granddaughter is four years old, so she was born in 2010.

8. **B** The total time spent in a bathroom is $9 + 11 + 13 + 18 + 22 + 23 = 96$ minutes. Hence they must use at least $\frac{1}{2} \times 96 = 48$ minutes in one of the bathrooms. However, we can show that no combination of these times gives 48 minutes. For one bathroom must take the 23 minute girl and we would need to find other girls' times adding to 25 minutes. This is impossible for any two girls and yet any three girls have a total time greater than 25 minutes. Notice, though, that $11 + 13 = 24$; so we get $11+13 + 23 = 47$ and $9 + 18 + 22 = 49$. Hence they can have breakfast at 7:49am.

9. **D** The original shaded piece can be split into two isosceles right-angled triangles and a rectangle. The remainder of the octagon can be filled with three shapes of area equal to that of the original shaded shape, as shown. The area is then four times the shaded area, namely 12 cm^2.

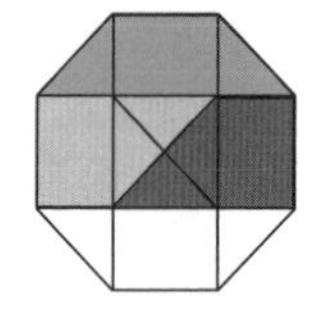

10. A Since the head of my crocodile is a quarter of the length of it (not counting the tail), this length is 4×93 cm $= 372$ cm. This is also two-thirds of the total length (with the tail as the other third). Hence one-third of the total length is $\frac{1}{2} \times 372$ cm $= 186$ cm, and the total length is 3×186 cm $= 558$ cm.

11. E The only even prime number is 2. The numbers opposite the 18 and 14 are different primes, so at least one of them must be odd. Thus the sum of the opposite pairs must be odd. But then the number opposite 35 must be even and a prime, so it is 2. The sum of opposite pairs is then $35 + 2 = 37$. Hence the number opposite to 14 must be $37 - 14 = 23$.

12. E Let the time for which Ann needs to run be T hours. So the total time for her journey will be $(T + 2)$ hours. In order to have an average speed of 5 km/h over this time she will need to travel $5(T + 2)$ km. After walking 8 km in 2 hours, she will run a distance of $8T$ km if she runs for T hours at 8 km/h. So her total distance travelled will be $(8 + 8T)$ km. Therefore $(8 + 8T) = 5(T + 2)$, that is $8 + 8T = 5T + 10$. So $T = \frac{2}{3}$ and two-thirds of an hour is 40 minutes.

13. C Let W be the number of wins, and L the number of losses. Each win is one point, giving W points for the wins. The number of draws is $40 - W - L$, giving a score of $(40 - W - L)/2$ for the draws. In total the score is 25 points, so we have $W + (40 - W - L)/2 = 25$, leading to $\frac{1}{2}W - \frac{1}{2}L + 20 = 25$, so $\frac{1}{2}W - \frac{1}{2}L = 5$ and $W - L = 10$. Hence the difference between the number of wins and losses is 10.

14. D The total reduction in the price of the three hats is $3 \times 9.40 = €28.20$. Between them they lack $\frac{1}{3} + \frac{1}{4} + \frac{1}{5} = \frac{20 + 15 + 12}{60} = \frac{47}{60}$ of the price of a hat. Thus we know that $\frac{47}{60}$ of the price of one hat is €28.20. Thus the price of a hat is $28.20 \times 60 \div 47 = €36$.

15. C We have $p + \frac{1}{q + \frac{1}{r}} = \frac{25}{19} = 1 + \frac{6}{19}$. Since p, q and r are positive integers, $\frac{1}{q + \frac{1}{r}} < 1$. It follows that $p = 1$ and $\frac{1}{q + \frac{1}{r}} = \frac{6}{19}$. Therefore $q + \frac{1}{r} = \frac{19}{6} = 3 + \frac{1}{6}$. Hence, by a similar argument, $q = 3$ and $r = 6$. Hence $pqr = 1 \times 3 \times 6 = 18$.

16. D The prime factorisation of 33 is 3×11, so apart from a change of order the only way to write 33 as a product of three integers is $1 \times 3 \times 11$. Now $M + B + E + R \geqslant 0 + 1 + 2 + 3 = 6$ so we must have $M + B + E + R = 11$ and N and U are 1 and 3 in either order. The four smallest integers that remain are 0, 2, 4, 5 which sum to 11, so the values of M, B, E, R must in fact be 0, 2, 4, 5 in some order. There are 4 choices for the value of M, leaving three for B, two for E and one for R, giving 24 choices. The total for all the choices is two (for N, U) times 24 (for M, B, E, R), giving 48 choices altogether.

17. D Let n be the smallest number of connections that each point could have; then the total number of connections from all the points together would be $7n$. Every connecting line has two ends, so contributes two to the number of connections coming from the points. Hence $7n$ must be even, so n must be even. One of the points has 3 connections already, so the smallest possible would be 4 connections from each point. The total number of connections would then be $7 \times 4 = 28$, requiring 14 connecting lines. Subtracting the 5 already there, we would need to add 9 more. This can be achieved as shown in the diagram.

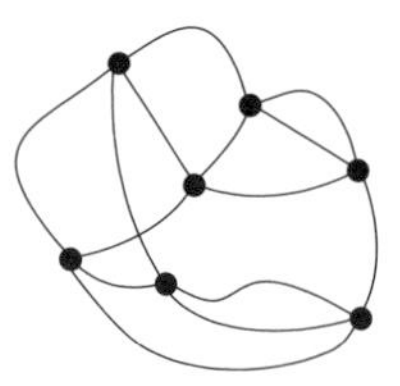

18. D In the two diagrams we can see that the large cube has four white vertices and four grey vertices. Three of the grey vertices lie in the same face; they are in the right hand face of the top diagram, and in the left hand face of the bottom diagram. Hence the lower cube is the upper cube rotated 90° clockwise, as viewed from above. Out of the six cubes in the centres of the faces, we can see that three of them are white, so at most three of them could be grey. Out of the 12 cubes in the middle of the edges, we can see that the top face has no grey ones, the middle layer has no grey ones, and the bottom layer may have one grey cube.

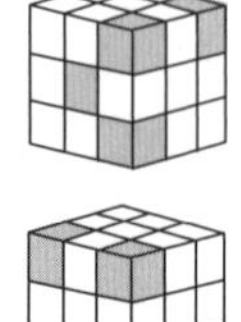

The largest number of grey cubes would therefore arise from four grey cubes at vertices, three in the centres of faces, one in the middle of an edge and the cube in the very centre of the large cube, making a total of nine in all.

19. B Let b be the original number of blue frogs, and g the number of green frogs. The new number of blue frogs is $1.6b$, and the number of green frogs is $0.4g$. The new ratio of blue frogs to green frogs is $1.6b : 0.4g$ and is the same as the previous ratio in the opposite order $g : b$. Hence $\frac{1.6b}{0.4g} = \frac{g}{b}$. This gives $1.6b^2 = 0.4g^2$. which simplifies to $g^2 = 4b^2$ so $g = 2b$. Then the original population of frogs is $b + g = b + 2b = 3b$; and the new population is $1.6b + 0.4g = 1.6b + 0.8b = 2.4b$. This is a reduction of $0.6b$ from the original $3b$, which is a fifth (or 20%).

20. C Since the prime factorisation of 18 is 2×3^2, Tomas must ensure that he does not have any multiple of 2 together with two or more multiples of 3 in the numbers he writes down. If he excludes all multiples of 2, then he writes down 50 numbers. However, if he excludes all but one multiple of 3 (of which there are 33, though the one he includes mustn't be a multiple of 9), then he writes down $100 - 32 = 68$ numbers.

21. C There are eight vertices on a cube. To pick three of these to form a triangle, there are 8 choices for the first vertex, 7 choices for the second vertex, and 6 choices for the third, making $8 \times 7 \times 6 = 336$ choices. However, some of these choices form the same triangles, so we must only count each set of three vertices once. Since each set of three vertices can be arranged in six different ways, we must divide the 336 by 6 to get 56 possible triangles. Now for a particular face, there are 4 possible triangles that can be formed in that face. As there are 6 faces, there are $6 \times 4 = 24$ triangles whose vertices all lie in the same face, and hence $56 - 24 = 32$ triangles whose vertices do not all lie in the same face.

22. B

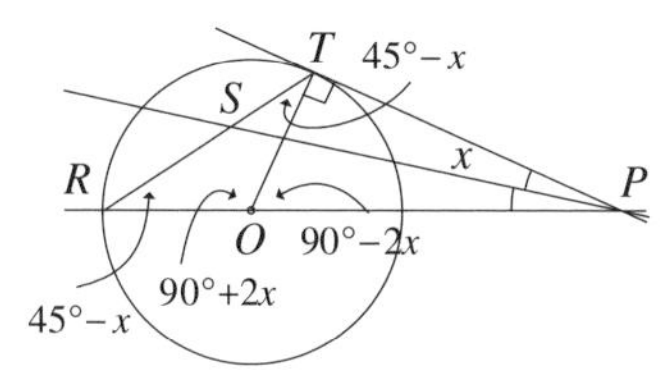

Denote $\angle SPT$ by x. Since TP is a tangent and OT is a radius, $\angle OTP = 90°$. So $\angle TOP = 180° - \angle OTP - \angle OPT = 180° - 90° - 2x = 90° - 2x$. Then $\angle TOR = 90° + 2x$ (angles on a straight line). But triangle TOR is isosceles (OT and OR are both radii), so $\angle ORT = \angle OTR$. Therefore by considering the angles in the triangle TOR, we have $\angle ORT = \frac{1}{2}(\angle ORT + \angle OTR) = \frac{1}{2}(180° - (90° + 2x)) = 45° - x$. By considering the angles in the triangle TSP, we see $\angle TSP = 180° - \angle SPT - \angle STP = 180° - x - (90° + 45° - x) = 45°$.

23. E The number of integers on Tatiana's list that start with 1, 2 or 3 will be the same as the number of integers that start with 5, 6 or 7. Hence the integers around the middle will all start with the digit 4. Just considering the integers that start with a 4, the number of these whose second digit is 1,2 or 3 will be the same as the number whose second digit is 5, 6 or 7; hence the largest one of the first half of the list will be the largest integer that starts with '43', namely 4 376 521.

24. B Triangle FGH is right-angled with the right angle at H because its sides 6, 8, 10 form a Pythagorean triple. Using the converse of 'angles in a semicircle are right angles', we deduce that FG is the diameter of a circle with centre at I (midpoint of FG) and radius 5 (half of the length FG). Thus IH has length 5 units, and the square $HIJK$ has area $5 \times 5 = 25$. By subtracting the area of triangle HIL we will be able to find the area of quadrilateral $HLJK$ as required. We can find the area of triangle HIL by showing it is similar to triangle FGH: let the angle HFG be x; then the angles in triangle FGH are $90°$, x and $90° - x$. Since HI and FI are both 5 units long, triangle HFI is isosceles so we have $\angle IHF = \angle HFG = x$. But then $\angle IHL = 90° - x$, so the angles of triangle HIL are $90°$, x and $90° - x$, the same as triangle FGH. Using this similarity $\frac{IL}{IH} = \frac{FH}{HG}$ so $\frac{IL}{5} = \frac{6}{8}$. Hence $IL = \frac{30}{8}$ and area $HIL = \frac{1}{2} \times 5 \times \frac{30}{8} = \frac{75}{8}$. Hence area $HLJK = 25 - \frac{75}{8} = \frac{125}{8}$.

25. C There cannot be more than 1007 knaves, for if there were, then the furthest forward knave would have at least 1007 knaves behind him and at most 1006 knights in front of him, so he would be telling the truth when he says "There are more knaves behind me than knights in front of me". Also, there cannot be more than 1007 knights, for if there were then the furthest back knight would have at least 1007 knights in front of him, and at most 1006 knaves behind him, so he would be lying when he says "There are more knaves behind me than knights in front of me". Hence there must be exactly 1007 knaves, and exactly 1007 knights. This is possible if the 1007 knights stand at the front of the queue, followed by the 1007 knaves.

(b) *The IMOK Olympiad*

The United Kingdom Mathematics Trust

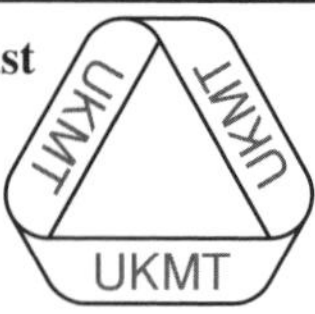

Intermediate Mathematical Olympiad and Kangaroo (IMOK)

Olympiad Cayley/Hamilton/Maclaurin Papers

Thursday 20th March 2014

READ THESE INSTRUCTIONS CAREFULLY BEFORE STARTING

1. Time allowed: 2 hours.
2. **The use of calculators, protractors and squared paper is forbidden.** Rulers and compasses may be used.
3. Solutions must be written neatly on A4 paper. Sheets must be STAPLED together in the top left corner with the Cover Sheet on top.
4. Start each question on a fresh A4 sheet.
   You may wish to work in rough first, then set out your final solution with clear explanations and proofs. ***Do not hand in rough work.***
5. Answers must be FULLY SIMPLIFIED, and EXACT. They may contain symbols such as π, fractions, or square roots, if appropriate, but NOT decimal approximations.
6. Give full written solutions, including mathematical reasons as to why your method is correct.
   Just stating an answer, even a correct one, will earn you very few marks; also, incomplete or poorly presented solutions will not receive full marks.
7. **These problems are meant to be challenging!** The earlier questions tend to be easier; the last two questions are the most demanding.
   Do not hurry, but spend time working carefully on one question before attempting another. Try to finish whole questions even if you cannot do many: you will have done well if you hand in full solutions to two or more questions.

DO NOT OPEN THE PAPER UNTIL INSTRUCTED BY THE INVIGILATOR TO DO SO!

The United Kingdom Mathematics Trust is a Registered Charity.
Enquiries should be sent to: Maths Challenges Office,
School of Mathematics, University of Leeds, Leeds, LS2 9JT.
(Tel. 0113 343 2339)
http://www.ukmt.org.uk

2014 Olympiad Cayley Paper

All candidates must be in *School Year 9 or below* (England and Wales), *S2 or below* (Scotland), or *School Year 10 or below* (Northern Ireland).

1. The two-digit integer '19' is equal to the product of its digits (1×9) plus the sum of its digits $(1 + 9)$.

   Find all two-digit integers with this property.

2. Six pool balls numbered 1–6 are to be arranged in a triangle, as shown. After three balls are placed in the bottom row, each of the remaining balls is placed so that its number is the difference of the two below it.

   Which balls can land up at the top of the triangle?

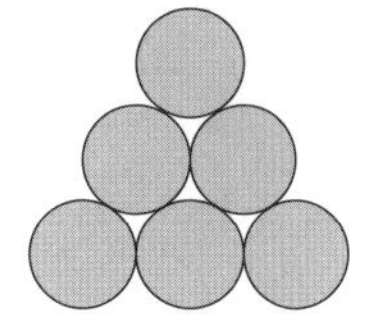

3. Rachel gave half of her money to Howard. Then Howard gave a third of all his money to Rachel. They each ended up with the same amount of money.

   Find the ratio

   amount that Rachel started with : amount that Howard started with.

4. The square $ABIJ$ lies *inside* the regular octagon $ABCDEFGH$. The sides of the octagon have length 1.

   Prove that $CJ = \sqrt{3}$.

5. Four types of rectangular tile have sizes 300 mm × 300 mm, 300 mm × 600 mm, 600 mm × 600 mm and 600 mm × 900 mm. Equal numbers of each type of tile are used, without overlaps, to make a square.

   What is the smallest square that can be made?

6. A couple own a circular piece of land that has area 2500 m^2. The land is divided into four plots by two perpendicular chords that intersect at X. Their rectangular house H has diagonally opposite corners at X and at the centre of the circle O, as shown. The two plots A and B have a combined area of 1000 m^2.

   What is the area occupied by the house?

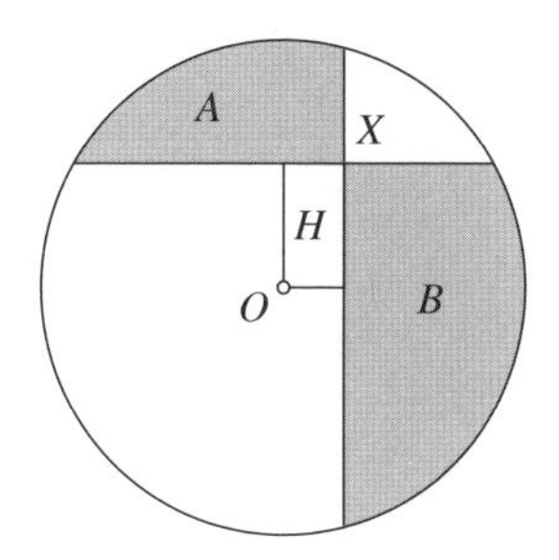

2014 Olympiad Hamilton Paper

All candidates must be in *School Year 10* (England and Wales), *S3* (Scotland), or *School Year 11* (Northern Ireland).

1. Consider five-digit integers that have the following properties. Each of the digits is 1, 2 or 3, and each of 1, 2, 3 occurs at least once as a digit; also, the number is not divisible by 2 nor divisible by 3.

   What is the difference between the largest and the smallest of these integers?

2. A rectangle has area 20 cm^2. Reducing the 'length' by $2\frac{1}{2}$ cm and increasing the 'width' by 3 cm changes the rectangle into a square.

   What is the side length of the square?

3. A regular heptagon is sandwiched between two circles, as shown, so that the sides of the heptagon are tangents of the smaller circle, and the vertices of the heptagon lie on the larger circle. The sides of the heptagon have length 2.

   Prove that the shaded *annulus*—the region bounded by the two circles—has area π.

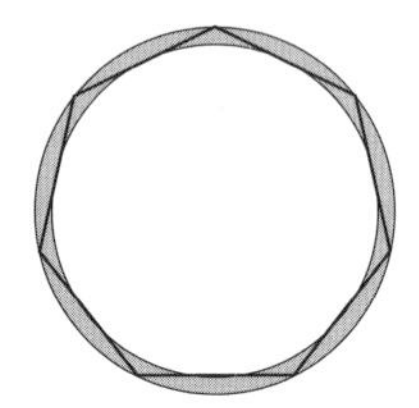

4. On Monday in the village of Newton, the postman delivered either one, two, three or four letters to each house. The number of houses receiving four letters was seven times the number receiving one letter, and the number receiving two letters was five times the number receiving one letter.

   What was the mean number of letters that each house received?

5. Two of the angles of triangle ABC are given by $\angle CAB = 2\alpha$ and $\angle ABC = \alpha$, where $\alpha < 45°$. The bisector of angle CAB meets BC at D. The point E lies on the bisector, but outside the triangle, so that $\angle BEA = 90°$. When produced, AC and BE meet at P.

   Prove that $\angle BDP = 4\alpha$.

6. Anna and Daniel play a game. Starting with Anna, they take turns choosing a positive integer less than 31 that is not equal to any of the numbers already chosen. The loser is the first person to choose a number that shares a factor greater than 1 with any of the previously chosen numbers.

   Does either player have a winning strategy?

2014 Olympiad Maclaurin Paper

All candidates must be in *School Year 11* (England and Wales), *S4* (Scotland), or *School Year 12* (Northern Ireland).

1. What is the largest three-digit prime number 'abc' whose digits a, b and c are different prime numbers?

2. Nine buns cost £11 + a pence and 13 buns cost £15 + b pence, where $0 < a < 100$ and $0 < b < 100$.

   What is the cost of a bun?

3. A regular hexagon, with sides of length 2 cm, is cut into two pieces by a straight line parallel to one of its sides. The ratio of the area of the smaller piece to the area of the larger piece is 1 : 5.

   What is the length of the cut?

4. In the diagram, RAQ is the tangent at A to the circle ABC, and $\angle AQB$, $\angle CRA$ and $\angle APC$ are all right angles.

   Prove that $BQ \times CR = AP^2$.

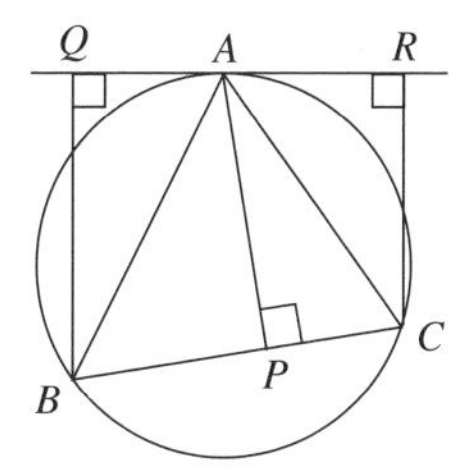

5. Kim and Oli played nine games of chess, playing alternately with the white and black pieces. Exactly five games were won by whoever was playing with the black pieces, Kim won exactly six games, and no game was drawn.

   With which colour pieces did Kim play the first game?

6. The T-tetromino T is the shape made by joining four 1×1 squares edge to edge, as shown. The rectangle R has dimensions $2a \times 2b$, where a and b are integers. The expression 'R can be tiled by T' means that R can be covered exactly with identical copies of T without gaps or overlaps.

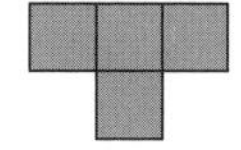

   (a) Prove that R can be tiled by T when both a and b are even.

   (b) Prove that R cannot be tiled by T when both a and b are odd.

Solutions to the 2014 Olympiad Cayley Paper

C1. The two-digit integer '19' is equal to the product of its digits (1×9) plus the sum of its digits $(1 + 9)$. Find all two-digit integers with this property.

Solution

If such a two-digit number has first digit a and second digit b, then its value is $10a + b$. The given condition then says that the product ab of the digits, plus the sum $a + b$ of the digits, is equal to $10a + b$, in other words,

$$ab + a + b = 10a + b.$$

Subtracting b from both sides, we obtain

$$ab + a = 10a.$$

Since a two-digit number cannot have first digit zero, we have $a \neq 0$ and we can divide both sides by a to get $b + 1 = 10$, that is, $b = 9$. This shows that a number with this property has second digit 9.

We therefore check the numbers 19, 29, 39, …, 89 and 99, and find that all of them have the required property.

C2. Six pool balls numbered 1–6 are to be arranged in a triangle, as shown. After three balls are placed in the bottom row, each of the remaining balls is placed so that its number is the difference of the two below it.

Which balls can land up at the top of the triangle?

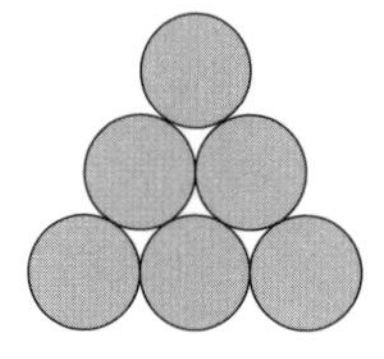

Solution

First we observe that the ball numbered 6 is on the bottom row of the triangle, since there are no permitted numbers which differ by 6 (because the furthest apart are 1 and 6 itself, and they differ by only 5).

This tells us not only that 6 cannot appear at the top, but also that 5 cannot. Indeed, if 5 is at the top, then the middle row is 1 and 6 in some order, and that means 6 is not on the bottom row.

If 4 is at the top, then the numbers below are either 2 and 6 (which, as above, is not permitted), or 1 and 5. In the latter case, the numbers below the 5 have to be 1 and 6, but we have already used the 1, so this cannot happen.

That just leaves three possibilities for the top number: 1, 2 and 3. The following examples show that they can all be achieved.

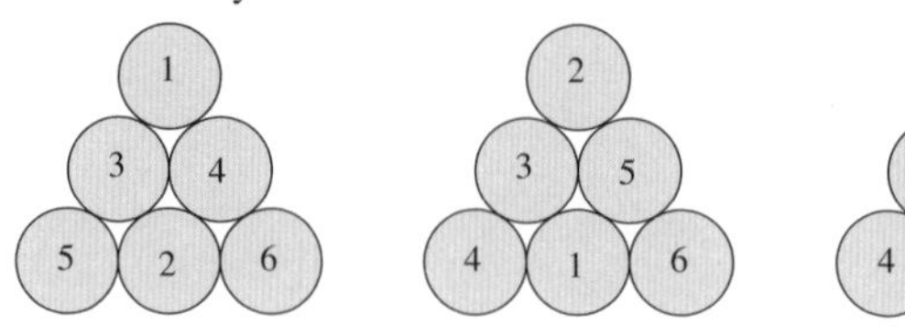

C3. Rachel gave half of her money to Howard. Then Howard gave a third of all his money to Rachel. They each ended up with the same amount of money.

Find the ratio

amount that Rachel started with : amount that Howard started with.

Solution

Suppose Howard starts with h pence and Rachel with r pence. Then Rachel gives $\frac{r}{2}$ to Howard; so after this Howard has $h + \frac{r}{2}$.

Next, Howard gives one third of his money to Rachel, so he has two thirds left. Thus he now has

$$\frac{2}{3}\left(h + \frac{r}{2}\right), \text{ that is, } \frac{2h}{3} + \frac{r}{3}.$$

We are told that they then have the same amount of money, and so each of them has half the total amount. Therefore

$$\frac{2h}{3} + \frac{r}{3} = \frac{h}{2} + \frac{r}{2}.$$

Multiplying both sides by 6, we get

$$4h + 2r = 3h + 3r,$$

and subtracting $3h + 2r$ from both sides we get $h = r$ or, in words, Howard and Rachel started with the same amount of money. So the ratio we were asked to find is 1 : 1.

C4. The square $ABIJ$ lies *inside* the regular octagon $ABCDEFGH$. The sides of the octagon have length 1.

Prove that $CJ = \sqrt{3}$.

Solution

The exterior angles of any polygon add up to 360°, so for a regular octagon they are 45° each. That means the interior angles are 180° – 45° = 135° each.

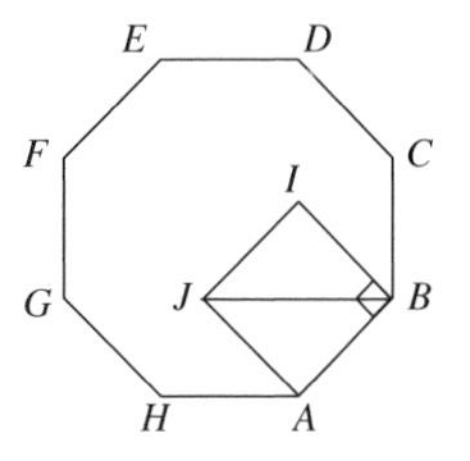

Since the angle ABI is a right angle, the angle IBC is $135° - 90° = 45°$.

Consider now the line JB.

This is the diagonal of the unit square $ABIJ$, and so

$$JB^2 = 1^2 + 1^2 = 2,$$

by Pythagoras' theorem for the triangle ABJ.

Also, $\angle JBI = 45°$, so $\angle JBC = \angle JBI + \angle IBC = 45° + 45° = 90°$.

This means that triangle JBC is right-angled at B. We have computed JB^2 and we know $BC = 1$, so, applying Pythagoras' theorem to triangle JBC, we now get

$$\begin{aligned} CJ^2 &= JB^2 + 1^2 \\ &= 2 + 1, \end{aligned}$$

that is, $CJ = \sqrt{3}$, as required.

C5. Four types of rectangular tile have sizes 300 mm × 300 mm, 300 mm × 600 mm, 600 mm × 600 mm and 600 mm × 900 mm. Equal numbers of each type of tile are used, without overlaps, to make a square.

What is the smallest square that can be made?

Solution

Let us say that one unit is 300 mm, so that the permitted tiles are 1 × 1, 1 × 2, 2 × 2 and 2 × 3.

Since the sides of all the tiles have lengths that are a whole number of units, any square made out of them will have sides of length N that is a whole number of units. This square has area N^2.

Also, the total area of one tile of each type is $1 + 2 + 4 + 6 = 13$, so N^2 is a multiple of 13. The smallest such N is 13 itself, so we ask ourselves if such a tiling is possible with 13 copies of each tile. It can indeed be done, as the example in the figure shows.

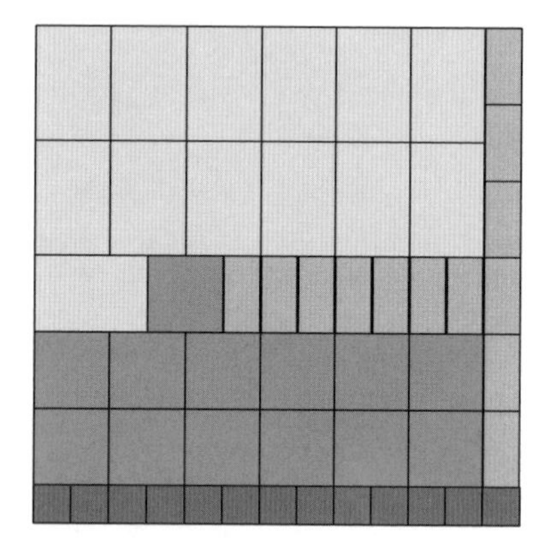

This square, which we have proved to be the smallest possible, measures 13 units on each side, or 3.9 m × 3.9 m.

C6. A couple own a circular piece of land that has area 2500 m^2. The land is divided into four plots by two perpendicular chords that intersect at X. Their rectangular house H has diagonally opposite corners at X and at the centre of the circle O, as shown. The two plots A and B have a combined area of 1000 m^2.

What is the area occupied by the house?

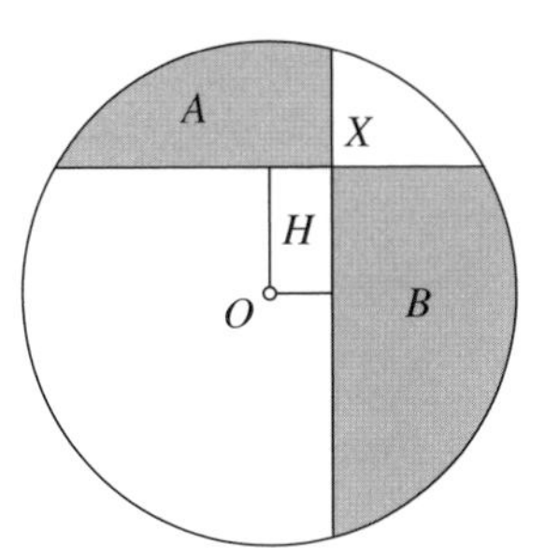

Solution

Suppose the couple construct two new fences, by reflecting the two given perpendicular chords in the lines through the walls of their house.

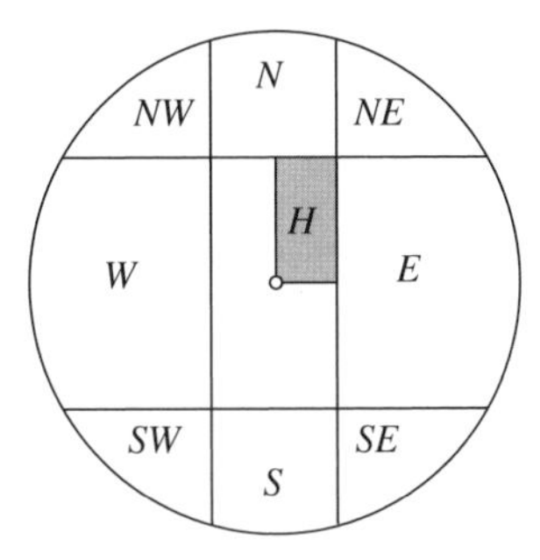

This creates a symmetric configuration, as shown, so that their piece of land now consists of:

(i) one central plot, containing the couple's house;

(ii) two plots W and E, of the same size and shape, at the west and east;

(iii) two plots N and S, of the same size and shape, at the north and south;

(iv) four plots NW, NE, SW and SE, all of the same size and shape, in each corner, at the northwest, northeast, southwest and southeast.

The original two plots A and B, with the combined area 1000 m^2, now consist of N and NW, and E and SE.

But those areas are equal, respectively, to S and SW, and W and NE, so those have a combined area of 1000 m^2. That means that all the regions, apart from the central one, have a combined area of 2000 m^2, leaving 500 m^2 inside the central region.

Of this, one quarter is the couple's house, since the couple's house consists of everything in the central region northeast of the centre of the circle. So their house occupies 125 m^2.

Solutions to the 2014 Olympiad Hamilton Paper

H1. Consider five-digit integers that have the following properties. Each of the digits is 1, 2 or 3, and each of 1, 2, 3 occurs at least once as a digit; also, the number is not divisible by 2 nor divisible by 3.
What is the difference between the largest and the smallest of these integers?

Solution

There are four conditions on the five-digit integer:

A each digit is 1, 2 or 3;

B there is at least one occurrence of each of 1, 2 and 3;

C it is not divisible by 2, and so the final digit is either 1 or 3;

D it is not divisible by 3, and so the sum of its digits is not divisible by 3.

The largest and smallest five-digit integers that satisfy both condition A and condition B are 33 321 and 11 123, respectively. Each of these numbers satisfies condition C.

Now $1 + 1 + 1 + 2 + 3 = 8$, which is not divisible by 3, so that 11 123 also satisfies condition D. Therefore 11 123 is the smallest five-digit integer of the required form.

However, $3 + 3 + 3 + 2 + 1 = 12$, which *is* divisible by 3, and hence 33 321 does *not* satisfy condition D. We deduce that, in order to satisfy condition D, a smaller number is required, whose digit sum is not a multiple of 3. The largest such integer less than 33 321 and satisfying all of conditions A, B and C is 33 221, with digit sum $3 + 3 + 2 + 2 + 1 = 11$. It follows that 33 221 is the largest five-digit integer of the required form.

Hence the required answer is 33 221 − 11 123, which equals 22 098.

Alternative

Each integer under consideration is not divisible by 3, and therefore its digit sum is not divisible by 3. But the only digits are 1, 2 and 3, so the number of digits 1 is different from the number of digits 2.

In the smallest such number the digits will be arranged in increasing order from left to right (as far as possible); in the largest such number the digits will be be arranged in decreasing order (as far as possible). Since all three digits 1, 2 and 3 occur, the smallest such number is therefore 11 123 and the largest is 33 221.

We observe that neither of these integers is divisible by 2, so they actually have all four desired properties.

Therefore the difference between the largest and smallest integers with the required properties is 33 221 − 11 123, which equals 22 098.

H2. A rectangle has area $20\,\text{cm}^2$. Reducing the 'length' by $2\frac{1}{2}$ cm and increasing the 'width' by 3 cm changes the rectangle into a square.
What is the side length of the square?

Solution

Let the length of each side of the square be s cm.
Then the rectangle has length $\left(s + \frac{5}{2}\right)$ cm and width $(s - 3)$ cm. From the information about the area of the rectangle, we therefore have

$$\left(s + \tfrac{5}{2}\right)(s - 3) = 20,$$

which we may expand to obtain

$$s^2 - \frac{s}{2} - \frac{15}{2} = 20,$$

or, on multiplying by 2 and subtracting 40 from both sides,

$$2s^2 - s - 55 = 0.$$

Factorising the left-hand side, we obtain

$$(2s - 11)(s + 5) = 0,$$

from which it follows that $s = \frac{11}{2}$ or $s = -5$. Since negative s has no meaning here, we conclude that the length of each side of the square is $5\frac{1}{2}$ cm.

H3. A regular heptagon is sandwiched between two circles, as shown, so that the sides of the heptagon are tangents of the smaller circle, and the vertices of the heptagon lie on the larger circle. The sides of the heptagon have length 2.

Prove that the shaded *annulus*—the region bounded by the two circles—has area π.

Solution

Let the radius of the larger circle be R and the radius of the smaller circle be r, so that the area of the shaded annulus is $\pi R^2 - \pi r^2$.

Since the heptagon is regular, the two circles have the same centre. The figure shows the common centre O of the two circles, a point of contact T of a side of the heptagon with the smaller circle, and the two vertices U and V of the heptagon adjacent to T. Then $OU = OV = R$ and $OT = r$.

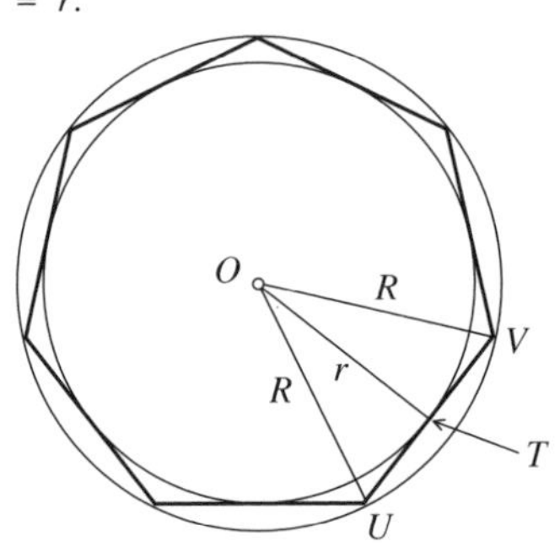

Now $\angle UTO = 90°$ because UV is a tangent and OT is the radius to the point of contact. Thus OT is perpendicular to the base UV of the isosceles triangle OUV, and therefore T is the midpoint of UV. But $UV = 2$, so that $UT = 1$.

By Pythagoras' theorem in triangle OUT, we have $R^2 = r^2 + 1^2 = r^2 + 1$. Hence

$$\begin{aligned}\pi R^2 - \pi r^2 &= \pi\left(R^2 - r^2\right)\\ &= \pi\left(r^2 + 1 - r^2\right)\\ &= \pi,\end{aligned}$$

so that the area of the shaded annulus is π.

Note: There is nothing special about heptagons; the result is true for any regular polygon.

H4. On Monday in the village of Newton, the postman delivered either one, two, three or four letters to each house. The number of houses receiving four letters was seven times the number receiving one letter, and the number receiving two letters was five times the number receiving one letter.

What was the mean number of letters that each house received?

Solution

Let the number of houses receiving one letter on Monday be m, and let the number receiving three letters be n.

Hence, the number of houses receiving four letters was $7m$ and the number of houses receiving two letters on Monday was $5m$.

Thus, the total number of letters delivered was

$$m \times 1 + 7m \times 4 + 5m \times 2 + n \times 3 = 39m + 3n.$$

These letters were delivered to $7m + 5m + m + n = 13m + n$ houses, so the mean number of letters that each house received was

$$\frac{39m + 3n}{13m + n} = \frac{3(13m + n)}{13m + n} = 3.$$

H5. Two of the angles of triangle ABC are given by $\angle CAB = 2\alpha$ and $\angle ABC = \alpha$, where $\alpha < 45°$. The bisector of angle CAB meets BC at D. The point E lies on the bisector, but outside the triangle, so that $\angle BEA = 90°$. When produced, AC and BE meet at P. Prove that $\angle BDP = 4\alpha$.

Solution

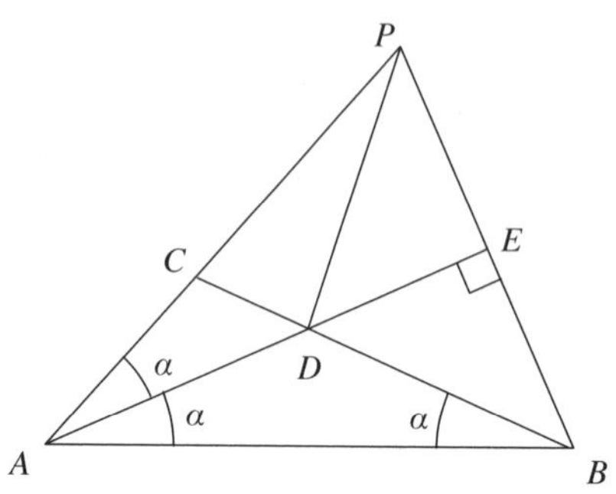

We are given that $\angle CAB = 2\alpha$ and the bisector of angle CAB meets BC at D, that is, $\angle CAD = \angle BAD = \alpha$.

An external angle of a triangle equals the sum of the two interior opposite angles, so that $\angle BDE = \angle DAB + \angle DBA = \alpha + \alpha = 2\alpha$.

In the triangles ABE and APE:

(i) $\angle BAE = \angle BAD = \alpha = \angle CAD = \angle PAE$;

(ii) $\angle BEA = 90° = \angle PEA$ (since the sum of the angles on a straight line equals 180°);

(iii) AE is common.

Thus triangles ABE and APE are congruent (AAS). Hence, $EP = EB$.

Now in triangles PED and BED:

(i) $PE = BE$;

(ii) $\angle PED = 90° = \angle BED$;

(iii) ED is common.

Thus triangles PED and BED are congruent (SAS). Hence $\angle PDE = \angle BDE$.

Therefore $\angle BDP = \angle BDE + \angle PDE = 2 \times \angle BDE = 2 \times 2\alpha = 4\alpha$.

H6. Anna and Daniel play a game. Starting with Anna, they take turns choosing a positive integer less than 31 that is not equal to any of the numbers already chosen. The loser is the first person to choose a number that shares a factor greater than 1 with any of the previously chosen numbers.
Does either player have a winning strategy?

Solution

Anna has a winning strategy: she chooses 30 on her first turn. Now $30 = 2 \times 3 \times 5$, so that in order not to lose, neither player can ever select a number not in the list

$$1, 7, 11, 13, 17, 19, 23 \text{ and } 29,$$

since all other positive integers less than 31 are multiples of 2, 3 or 5.

Because no two numbers in this list share a factor greater than 1, whichever number Daniel selects on his turn, Anna may select another one on her next turn, then Daniel may select another one, and so on.
Since eight is an even number, this process can continue for four turns in all by each player, after which all of the numbers will have been selected. At that point Daniel will be forced to select one of the other numbers, which all share a factor greater than 1 with 30, and hence Daniel will lose.

Therefore Anna has a winning strategy.

Solutions to the 2014 Olympiad Maclaurin Paper

M1. What is the largest three-digit prime number '*abc*' whose digits a, b and c are different prime numbers?

Solution

The primes available as digits are 2, 3, 5 and 7.

The three-digit prime p sought cannot end in 2 or 5, since then it would be divisible by 2 or 5. Also, p cannot consist of the digits 2, 3 and 7 or the digits 3, 5 and 7 since it would then be divisible by 3.

Hence p is composed either of 2, 3 and 5 or of 2, 5 and 7.

Now p cannot begin with 7 since it would then end in 2 or 5. The next biggest candidate is 527. But 527 is not a prime because $527 = 17 \times 31$.

However, the next biggest candidate 523 *is* prime. We can confirm this by showing that 523 has no factors less than 23, which is sufficient since $23^2 = 529 > 523$. Our evidence for this is that

$$\begin{aligned} 523 &= 7 \times 75 - 2 \\ &= 11 \times 47 + 6 \\ &= 13 \times 40 + 3 \\ &= 17 \times 30 + 13 \\ &= 19 \times 27 + 10. \end{aligned}$$

M2. Nine buns cost £11 + a pence and 13 buns cost £15 + b pence, where $0 < a < 100$ and $0 < b < 100$.

What is the cost of a bun?

Solution

Let a bun cost x pence.

Since $9x = 1100 + a$ and $0 \leqslant a < 100$, we have $1100 \leqslant 9x < 1200$. Therefore $123 \leqslant x \leqslant 133$.

Similarly, since $13x = 1500 + b$ and $0 \leqslant b < 100$, we have $1500 \leqslant 13x < 1600$. Therefore $116 \leqslant x \leqslant 123$.

It follows that $x = 123$ (and $a = 7$, $b = 99$). Hence the cost of a bun is £1.23.

M3. A regular hexagon, with sides of length 2 cm, is cut into two pieces by a straight line parallel to one of its sides. The ratio of the area of the smaller piece to the area of the larger piece is 1 : 5.

What is the length of the cut?

Solution

For convenience, we omit units throughout our working: all lengths are measured in cm, and all areas in cm^2.

The hexagon may be divided into six equilateral triangles with sides of length 2, as shown in

Figure 1. Each triangle has area $\frac{1}{2} \times 2 \times \sqrt{3} = \sqrt{3}$, so the area of the hexagon is $6\sqrt{3}$

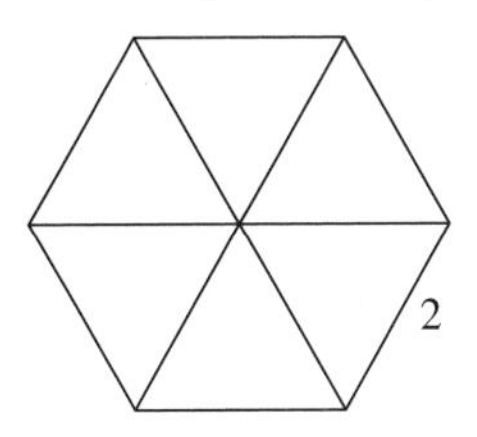

Figure 1

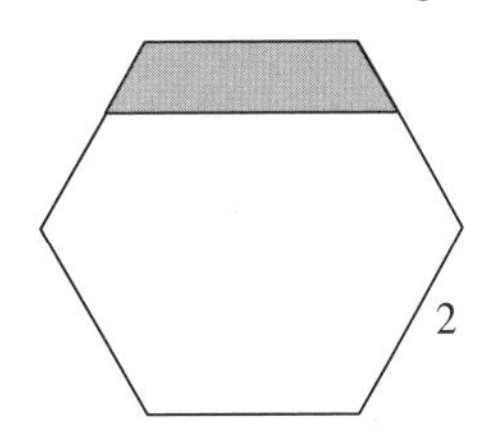

Figure 2

Figure 2 shows the hexagon cut into two pieces by the straight line parallel to a side. The ratio of the areas of the two pieces is 1 : 5, so that the shaded area is equal to $\sqrt{3}$.

Now the shaded region is a trapezium, which we may divide into an equilateral triangle of side d and a parallelogram, as shown below.

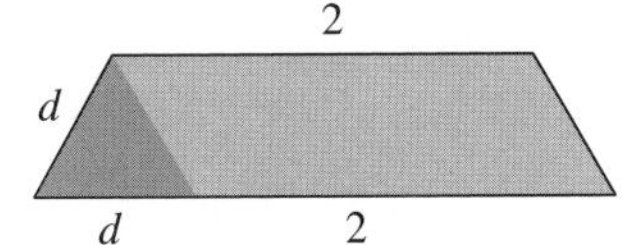

The height of the trapezium is equal to the height of the triangle, which is $\dfrac{\sqrt{3}}{2}d$.

Therefore the area of the trapezium is

$$\frac{1}{2}(2 + 2 + d) \times \frac{\sqrt{3}}{2}d = \frac{\sqrt{3}d\,(4 + d)}{4}.$$

Thus we have

$$\frac{\sqrt{3}d\,(4 + d)}{4} = \sqrt{3},$$

that is,

$$4d + d^2 = 4.$$

Hence

$$(2 + d)^2 = 8,$$

so that, because d is positive and therefore $2 + d$ is,

$$2 + d = \sqrt{8}.$$

In other words, the length of the cut is $\sqrt{8}$, which equals $2\sqrt{2}$.

M4. In the diagram, RAQ is the tangent at A to the circle ABC, and $\angle AQB$, $\angle CRA$ and $\angle APC$ are all right angles.

Prove that $BQ \times CR = AP^2$.

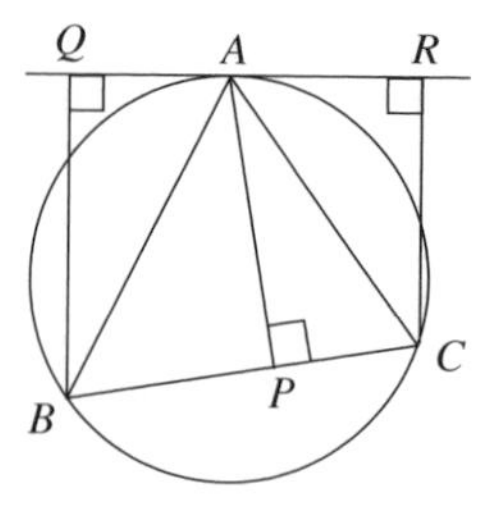

Solution

By the alternate segment theorem, since RAQ is a tangent we have $\angle QAB = \angle BCA$. Also $\angle AQB = 90° = \angle APC$. Hence the triangles QAB and PCA are similar (AA), so that

$$\frac{BQ}{AP} = \frac{BA}{AC}. \qquad (1$$

Furthermore, $\angle RAC = \angle ABC$ (again by the alternate segment theorem) and $\angle ARC = 90° = \angle BPA$. Hence the triangles ARC and BPA are also similar (AA), so that

$$\frac{CR}{AP} = \frac{AC}{BA}. \qquad (2$$

From equations (1) and (2), we obtain

$$\begin{aligned} \frac{BQ}{AP} \times \frac{CR}{AP} &= \frac{BA}{AC} \times \frac{AC}{BA} \\ &= 1 \end{aligned}$$

and so

$$BQ \times CR = AP^2,$$

as required.

M5. Kim and Oli played nine games of chess, playing alternately with the white and black pieces. Exactly five games were won by whoever was playing with the black pieces, Kim won exactly six games, and no game was drawn.

With which colour pieces did Kim play the first game?

Solution

Suppose that Kim wins b games playing Black. Then Kim wins $6 - b$ playing White. Now Oli wins $5 - b$ games playing Black, therefore Kim loses $5 - b$ games playing White. Hence altogether the number of games when Kim plays White is $(6 - b) + (5 - b) = 11 - 2b$, which is an odd integer. But the only possibilities for the number of games of either colour played by either player are 4 or 5. It follows that Kim plays 5 games as White. Thus Kim starts by playing with the white pieces.

(Since $11 - 2b = 5$, we have $b = 3$. So to summarise, Kim wins 3 games as Black and 3 games as White, and Oli wins 2 games as Black and 1 game as White. Hence Kim wins the series 6 games to 3, and Black wins 5 games with White winning 4.)

M6. The T-tetromino T is the shape made by joining four 1×1 squares edge to edge, as shown. The rectangle R has dimensions $2a \times 2b$, where a and b are integers. The expression 'R can be tiled by T' means that R can be covered exactly with identical copies of T without gaps or overlaps.

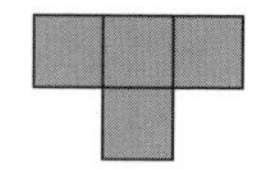

(a) Prove that R can be tiled by T when both a and b are even.

(b) Prove that R cannot be tiled by T when both a and b are odd.

Solution

(a) Four tetrominos can be fitted together to form a 4×4 square, as shown alongside, and these can be tessellated inside a $4m \times 4n$ board.

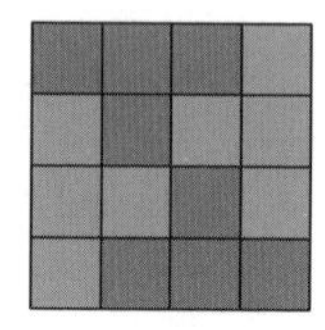

(b) Colour the board like a chessboard. Then a tetromino covers either three white squares and one black square, or one white and three black.

Let there be m of the first type of tetromino and n of the second. Then the total number of black squares they cover is $m + 3n$ and the total number of white squares is $3m + n$.

But the numbers of squares of each colour are equal, so $m + 3n = 3m + n$ and therefore $m = n$. Hence there are $4m$ squares of each colour, making $8m$ altogether.

It follows that $2a \times 2b = 8m$ and so $ab = 2m$. In other words, ab is even. Hence it is impossible to tile the board when both a and b are odd.

Alternative

Colour the board like a chessboard. Then a tetromino covers either one white square, or three white squares. So each tetromino covers an odd number of white squares.

Suppose that the board can be tiled. The board has $2a \times 2b = 4ab$ squares and each tetromino covers four of them, so there are ab tetrominos. Thus when both a and b are odd, there is an odd number of tetrominos.

Therefore, together the tetrominos cover an odd number of white squares—there is an odd number of them, and each of them covers an odd number of white squares. But the number of white squares is half the total number of squares, which is $2ab$, an even number.

Hence it is impossible to tile the board when both a and b are odd.

Comments on the IMOK Olympiad Papers and Scripts

General comments (Gerry Leversha)

Both candidates and their teachers will find it helpful to know something of the general principles involved in marking Olympiad-type papers. These preliminary paragraphs therefore serve as an exposition of the 'philosophy' which has guided both the setting and marking of all such papers at all age levels, both nationally and internationally.

What we are looking for, essentially, is solutions to problems. This approach is therefore rather different from what happens in public examinations such as GCSE, AS and A level, where credit is given for the ability to carry out individual techniques regardless of how these techniques fit into a protracted argument. Such marking is cumulative; a candidate may gain 60% of the available marks without necessarily having a clue about how to solve the final problem. Indeed, the questions are generally structured in such a way as to facilitate this approach, divided into many parts and not requiring an overall strategy for tackling a multi-stage argument.

In distinction to this, Olympiad-style problems are marked by looking at each question synoptically and deciding whether the candidate has some sort of overall strategy or not. An answer which is essentially a solution, but might contain either errors of calculation, flaws in logic, omission of cases or technical faults, will be marked on a '10 minus' basis. One question we often ask is: if we were to have the benefit of a two-minute interview with this candidate, could they correct the error or fill the gap? On the other hand, an answer which shows no sign of being a genuine solution is marked on a '0 plus' basis; up to 3 marks might be awarded for particular cases or insights. It is therefore important that candidates taking these papers realise the importance of the rubric about trying to finish whole questions rather than attempting lots of disconnected parts.

Cayley (comments from James Cranch)

IMOK Cayley is the UKMT's hardest individual competition targeted at students up to Year 9 in England and Wales, Year S2 in Scotland and Year 10 in Northern Ireland. About 500 students participate annually. The format consists of one paper, providing two hours in which to tackle six tough problems.

Even the easier problems at the beginning are intended to be nonstandard, and the problems at the end should be beyond the reach of all but a small minority of eligible students. In marking, we seek good ideas and clear thinking and reward them with more than we reward a correct final answer, or even unmotivated calculation leading to such a correct answer.

As such, every mark is a genuine credit to the student who obtains it.

At the marking weekend in Leeds, my diligent and hard-working team were refreshed by the evident strength and variation of ideas they saw. What follows are my personal comments on the problems, as suggested by the scores of students' scripts that I was able to inspect personally.

1. A few students simply checked all ninety possible two-digit integers by hand. Of course this is quite tedious but not nearly beyond the reach of a student willing to spend a few minutes doing so. However, it is a bad method: a suitably long string of explicit checks is nearly bound to go wrong, and the process does not generate any insight into the problem.

   A much better effort involves actually thinking about what would cause this to arise. Quite the cleanest way is to write the two-digit number as $10x + y$, where the two digits are x and y. This results in a tidy equation, which can readily be solved (if one is careful to use only fully-justified steps, particularly when cancelling).

   We were also perfectly prepared to attempt non-algebraic approaches, which described the process verbally. The danger with these is that it is quite easy to persuade the reader that numbers ending in a '9' work, but quite hard to persuade them in a clear fashion that no other number will.

2. If simply given the task of placing balls into the grid in a legal fashion so as to have 1, 2, or 3 at the top, I suspect most students would not be detained for long by the puzzle.

   The hardest part, therefore, is producing some convincing reason why, of the many (in fact, 360) ways of arranging six balls in a triangle so that 4, 5, or 6 is at the top, not a single one can be a valid arrangement. In fact, this can be done very briefly, but to do so is evidence of a lot of clear thinking, leading to a good understanding of how the balls can legally be placed. It was thus possible to gain all the marks in only a few lines of writing (plus three examples, with 1, 2 and 3 at the top), but this does not make this an easy problem, and students who managed to do this should feel proud.

3. The main difficulty with this problem perhaps lay not in the details, but in understanding what kind of reasoning would constitute a full solution.

   On its own, it is not much use to give a worked example showing that it is possible that Rachel and Howard each started with some given sum of money as chosen by the student: the challenge is to prove that they *can only* have started with the same sum of money.

   Perhaps the most obvious method is to choose variables representing Rachel and Howard's initial wealth, and study how their wealth changes with each transaction and thus form an equation. One impressively clever alternative, favoured by a few, was to choose a variable for the common equal final wealth, and to work backwards through the transactions in order to find expressions for their initial wealth.

4. We found this question more challenging than any other to mark. One cause for this was the format: students were asked not to calculate an unknown value, but were given the value and asked to *prove* it correct.

   A few students simply presented rough working arriving at the desired answer. Even if, as in many cases, we suspected that their technique of calculation was sound, we were frequently unable to reward it highly since the whole aim is that they describe their technique to us in a manner which convinces us of its validity.

   Then there were some scripts which largely adopted the desired format, but which were mysteriously incoherent or evasive at some key point: we usually decided that the student had worked hard from both ends to meet in the middle, but were aware they had not quite succeeded in doing so.

   A particularly common inadequacy was to do the problem with a series of uses of Pythagoras' theorem, but not to attempt to justify that the triangles used were indeed right-angled as would be needed. This always resulted in a penalty.

   Finally, one unfortunate error, which occurred a handful of times, was in not understanding that polygons are traditionally labelled in a cyclic fashion, and hence drawing a square which we would denote $ABJI$, rather than $ABIJ$ as asked. This changes the details of the problem considerably.

5. The situation here is somewhat like that in question 2: if asked to slot 13 complete sets of tiles into a square grid of side length 13×300 mm, a student would very likely succeed in doing so. The principal challenge is to eliminate all smaller side lengths and all smaller numbers of tiles, so as to be sure that this check is the right check.

   Most students who managed to describe their reasoning in a clear fashion began by normalising the units of length. One fine example was the student who chose to call 300 mm a *voot*, since it approximates a foot. Often in mathematics, a good choice of notation can help and a poor choice (or no choice at all) can hinder.

   Among students who did manage to show that numbers smaller than 13 could not work, many lost a few marks by failing to show that 13 was in fact possible. This was a shame.

6. This question was found very difficult, and with good reason. As stated, it requires some preparation before it is tractable. The first important thing is to make some construction that enables sizes of regions to be compared. One popular choice was to extend the walls which meet at the centre so as to form diameters. Even having done so, it is not quite obvious how to form equations which provide useful information about areas, and solving them to find the desired result is similarly impressive work.

Hamilton (comments from Dean Bunnell)

1. The integers considered by most candidates were 11 123, 33 321 and 33 221; all of these are odd, so divisibility by 2 was not relevant to the arguments of these candidates. Whilst this is fine, it is necesssary to check that the integers obtained do satisfy all the conditions given in the question, so a mark was deducted when a candidate failed to mention that both 11 123 and 33 221 are not divisible by 2.

   In order to qualify for the '10 minus' category, candidates had to explain, with reason, that 11 123 is *not* divisible by 3 and that 33 321 *is* divisible by 3. Just asserting that this was true, rather than giving evidence, was penalised. Suitable evidence included calculating the digit sum, or doing a division. In order to progress further, candidates had to prove that 33 221 is not divisible by 3.

   Only about half of the candidates managed to obtain the correct answer of 22 098 satisfactorily.

2. This question was started fairly successfully by the majority of candidates. The most popular approach was to use variables representing the length and width of the triangle. A more succinct method was to use just one variable to represent the side length of the square. In both cases, setting up a quadratic equation caused little problem.

   A major stumbling block was an inability to solve a quadratic equation using a method, such as factorisation, that finds all possible solutions. Just identifying one value that works is not sufficient. Though some candidates used the quadratic formula in order to make further progress, unfortunately many of these were unable to simplify their answer, because they did not realise that $\sqrt{441} = 21$.

3. Setting up terms for the areas of both the smaller and larger circles was straightforward for all those who attempted this question. One way is to let the radii be R and r; many did this, and then expressed the area of the annulus correctly as $\pi R^2 - \pi r^2$.

From then on, too many candidates assumed, or asserted rather than proved, some handy geometrical fact—usually that each side of the heptagon touches the inner circle at its midpoint.

Using Pythagoras' theorem to form the equation $R^2 = r^2 + 1$ saw the candidate 'home and dry'.

4. Both the total number of letters and the total number of houses needed to be considered in order to qualify for the '10 minus' category.

   Candidates who set up some algebraic notation to deal with this were often successful. Those who worked with ratios had more work to do, in order to explain why ratios, rather than absolute numbers, can be used when finding the mean.

   It was pleasing to see some candidates realise that they had basically solved the question once they had found a value of 3 for the mean number of letters for the houses receiving 1, 2 and 4 letters. They went on to argue that including houses receiving 3 letters would not change the mean.

5. This question was the least popular on the Hamilton paper.

   Most candidates who attempted it used appropriate reasoning to prove that:

   (a) $\angle CAD = \angle BAD = \alpha$ (bisector of $\angle CAB$);

   (b) $\angle PEA = 90°$ (angles on a straight line add up to 180°); and

   (c) $\angle BDE = 2\alpha$ (the external angle of triangle *BDE* is equal to the sum of the two interior angles *DAB* and *DBA*).

   The key to completing a solution is to find a way to involve the other side of the diagram, such as using congruent triangles. Many of the submitted proofs failed to do this, or did not do so with the required level of formality, which meant that they did not qualify for the '10 minus' category.

6. The essence of this question was to realise that numbers that do not share a factor other than 1 with any other number are prime. This concept was seen by most candidates attempting this question. However, the question states 'a number that shares a factor *greater than* 1' and, unfortunately, many did not appreciate the significance of this: as well as primes, the number 1 has to be considered, because it does not share a factor greater than 1 with any other number.

   Nevertheless, the fact that Anna has a winning strategy—choosing the number 30 first—was deduced, and explained, by a pleasing number of candidates.

Maclaurin (comments from Gerry Leversha)

1. Theoretically you could answer this question by checking three-digit numbers in descending order from 999 until you find the first which satisfies the criteria. This would be very time-consuming since you would need to give reasons for each rejection, so clearly it is better to begin by cutting down the possibilities.

   There are only four primes available, so we need only consider the 24 permutations of these. Again you could look at these in descending order, but it is better to use some insight. A number has a divisor of 3 exactly when its digit sum is a multiple of 3, and primes cannot end in 2 or 5. This reduces the possibilities to four, which can be checked in order.

   A common error was to think that 527 is prime when it is in fact 17×31. It was necessary to ensure that 523 is prime, but, since the square of 23 is 529, it is enough to check prime divisors less than 23.

   A surprising number of candidates thought that 1 is prime. This trivialises the problem since the largest possibility, 753, is divisible by 3 and then 751 is prime, and such attempts were marked on the '0 plus' basis. Teachers explain why 1 is not counted as a prime when they are discussing prime factorisation.

2. This question is really about inequalities, since the two conditions can be used to show that the cost is at least £1.23 and at most £1.23, and any method which used this method carefully was going to succeed. However, it is alarming how many candidates were unable to deal with the relationship between pounds and pence or to define a variable, such as x, properly. It is quite inadequate to say 'Let x be buns', and it was clear that some candidates who did this went on to think that their variable was the number of buns.

   It is best to define x as the cost of a bun in pence, and then form statements such as $1100 \leqslant x \leqslant 1199$ to express the information in the problem. Modular arithmetic was also useful. Solutions which reached the correct answer by means of arguments which effectively treated x as a number to two decimal places were treated tolerantly, but it is much better to be clear about what is happening and define the variable to be a positive integer.

3. The usual first step was to calculate the area of the trapezium to be $\sqrt{3}$ and then use algebra to determine either its height or base. This gave a quadratic equation which could be solved using the formula. The negative solution is rejected and then a little manipulation of surds yielded the answer $2\sqrt{2}$. There were many variations possible and the criterion for a '10 minus' was setting up a single variable equation which evaluated an area.

There were some original solutions using similar triangles, but also some bogus arguments – note that if you cut a trapezium into two using a line parallel to the base, the resulting trapezia are not similar to each other or to the original one. In general, quadrilaterals are not similar if they have the same angles; you must also check that the sides are in proportion.

A few candidates were unable to solve the quadratic either by formula (which is in the GCSE syllabus) or completing the square, but if they had a correct equation they would have scored 7 marks.

4. This was a simple geometry question but it required the use of the alternate segment theorem and similar triangles, and the response was a little disappointing. Common mistakes were to state that ΔAQB was similar to ΔBPA (rather than ΔCPA) or that AP was perpendicular to QR.

   It is possible to use the sine rule twice and multiply to obtain the desired relationship. Candidates for Maclaurin should be aware that they will need to use theorems in GCSE geometry without being told exactly which ones are needed.

5. This was an intriguing question and there was a big response to it. The key step is to appreciate that every game which Kim wins as White is a game which Oki loses as Black, since this forms a sort of bridge between counting the number of games won by an individual player and the number of games won by an individual colour.

   There is a lovely argument using parity but very few candidates saw that. Surprisingly few used algebra, setting up a statement such as 'Let Kim play b games as Black, winning x of them', which would have shown that, in order for x to be an integer, b had to be 4 and so Kim started with White.

   What the markers were looking for was a lucid argument showing that the stated outcome would follow if Kim won 3 out of 4 games as Black and 3 out of 5 as White, but also that there was no such strategy if Kim started playing Black. It was therefore necessary for candidates to express themselves clearly and not to write 'essay-type' answers.

6. This question divided into two parts, with 2 marks being awarded for (a) and the remaining 8 for (b). There were many correct solutions to (a) which showed how to place the T-tetrominos, either in 4 by 4 squares or in an arrangement around the border. However, it is not enough to say that, since these methods do not work when a and b are both odd, it is impossible to tile the board with T-tetrominos. There might be other ways to tile the board which do not involve squares or bordering.

The key to part (b) is to colour the board like a chessboard and notice that a T-tetromino will always cover three squares of one colour and one of the other. A parity argument then leads to the conclusion that the tiling is impossible.

Marking

The marking was carried out on the weekend of 28th – 30th March in Leeds. There were three marking groups led by James Cranch, Dean Bunnell and Gerry Leversha. The other markers are listed later in this book.

IMOK certificates

All participating students who qualified automatically were awarded a certificate. These came in three varieties: Participation, Merit and Distinction.

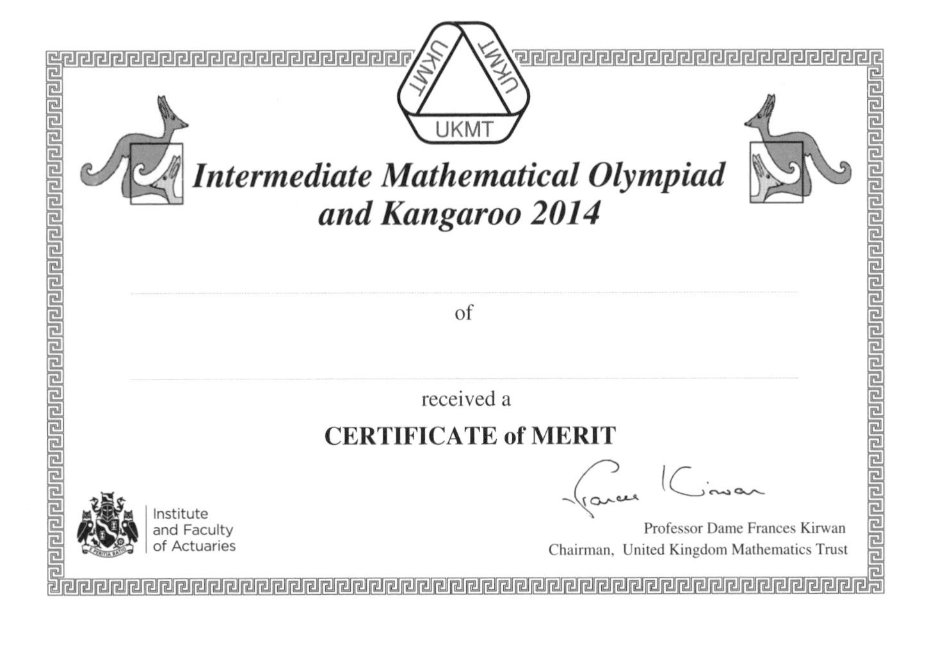

THE UKMT INTERMEDIATE MATHEMATICAL OLYMPIAD AND KANGAROO

The IMOK is the follow-on round for the Intermediate Mathematical Challenge and is organised by the UK Mathematics Trust. For each year group, the top scoring 500 or so IMC pupils are invited to participate in the Olympiad, and the next 2500 are invited to participate in the European Kangaroo. Schools may also enter additional pupils to the Olympiad upon payment of a fee; the Kangaroo is by invitation only.

The Olympiad is a two-hour examination which includes six demanding questions requiring full written solutions. The problems are designed to include interesting and attractive mathematics and may involve knowledge or understanding beyond the range of normal school work.

The one-hour multiple choice European Kangaroo requires the use of logic as well as mathematical understanding to solve amusing and thought-provoking questions. The 'Kangourou sans Frontières' is taken by students in over forty countries in Europe and beyond.

The UKMT is a registered educational charity. See our website www.ukmt.org.uk for more information. Donations would be gratefully received and can be made at www.donate.ukmt.org.uk if you would like to support our work in this way.

IMOK Olympiad awards

As in recent years, medals were awarded in the Intermediate Mathematical Olympiad. Names of medal winners are listed below. Book prizes were awarded to the top 50 or so in each age group. The Cayley prize was *Numbers: A Very Short Introduction* by Peter M. Higgins; the Hamilton prize was *Euler's Gem* by David S. Richeson; and for Maclaurin, *The Big Questions: Mathematics* by Tony Crilly.

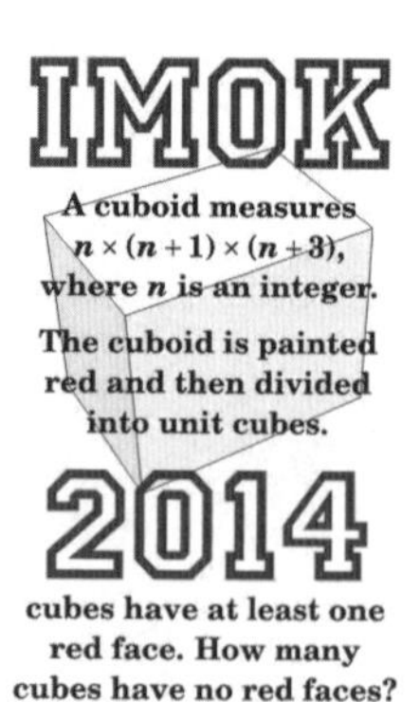

IMOK medal winners

Cayley

Jonathan Aizlewood	Watford Grammar School for Boys
Najeeb Alshabibi	Bootham School, York
GianFranco Ameri	Westminster Under School
Luke Barratt	Backwell School, North Somerset
Sam Bealing	Bridgewater High School, Warrington
Connor Bennett	William Brookes School, Shropshire
Jonathan Bostock	Eltham College, London
Joshua Bridges	Penistone Grammar School, South Yorks
Matthew Bullock	Heckmondwike Gr. Sch., West Yorkshire
Ivy Cai	Beijing Dulwich International School
Gabriel Cairns	Wilson's School, Surrey
Thomas Campbell	St Nicholas High School, Northwich
Yifei Chen	Cardiff High School
Alex Chen	Westminster School
Soren Choi	Westminster Under School
Jongihn Chung	Perse School, Cambridge
George Clements	Norwich School
Louisa Cullen	Pocklington School, nr York
Alex Darby	Sutton Grammar School for Boys, Surrey
Chiara Darnton	Stanwell School, Vale of Glamorgan
Stanley Dodds	Weydon School, Farnham, Surrey
Raymond Douglas	Magdalen College School, Oxford
Andrew Ejemai	Brentwood School

Mila Feldman	The Stephen Perse Foundation, Cambridge
Chris Finn	The Royal Grammar Sch., High Wycombe
Arul Gupta	Eltham College, London
Freddie Hand	Cage Green Primary School, Kent
Alice Harray	St Paul's Girls' School, Hammersmith
Ruiyang He	Glasgow Academy
Aaron Heighton	Aylesbury Grammar School
Thomas Hillman	Beechwood Park School, St Albans
Alec Hong	St Olave's Grammar School, Kent
Katherine Horton	All Hallows Catholic School, Farnham
Samuel Howard	Stockport Grammar School
Charlie Hu	City of London School
Dion Huang	Westminster Under School
Isuru Jayasekera	Wilson's School, Surrey
Joris Josiek	Caerleon Comprehensive School, Newport
Om Kanchanasakdich	Bangkok Patana School
Ryan Kang	Westminster School
Basim Khajwal	Heckmondwike Gr. Sch., West Yorkshire
Chanho Kim	British School of Paris
Kyowon Koo	UWCSEA Dover Campus, Singapore
Mantra Kusumgar	Wembley High Academy
Timothy Lavy	Magdalen College School, Oxford
Adrian Law	Winchester College
Ryan Lee	Magdalen College School, Oxford
Shi Hao Lee	Anglo-Chinese School, Singapore
Shri Lekkala	Westminster School
Ryan Leung	Renaissance College, Hong Kong
Joshua Lim	Anglo-Chinese School, Singapore
Dmitry Lubyako	Eton College, Windsor
Shaun Marshall	Shelley College, Huddersfield
Fraser Mason	St Mary's Music School, Edinburgh
Peter Mathieson	Judd School, Tonbridge, Kent
Laurence Mayther	John Roan School, London
Liam McKnight	Magdalen College School, Oxford
Meera Murali	Bancroft's School, Essex
Leo Nam	Ewell Castle School, Surrey
Andy Nam	North London Coll. Sch. Jeju, South Korea

Joseph Nash	Abingdon School
Karthikeya Neelamegam	Reading School
Navonil Neogi	Tiffin School, Kingston-upon-Thames
Shintaro Nishijo	St George's School, Germany
Oliver Normand	Winchester College
Yuji Okitani	Tapton School, Sheffield
Sooyong Park	North London Coll. Sch. Jeju, South Korea
Luke Parry	Merchant Taylors' School, Middlesex
Tanish Patil	Institut International de Lancy, Switzerland
Robert Perry	Sevenoaks School, Kent
Benedict Randall Shaw	Westminster Under School
Alex Root	Immanuel College, Bushey, Herts
Joshua Rowe	St John Fisher High School, Harrogate
Sam Rudd Jones	Stamford School, Lincs
Mayuka Saegusa	Henrietta Barnett School, London
Zacharie Sciamma	St Paul's School, Barnes, London
Yasith Senanayake	Sutton Grammar School for Boys, Surrey
Amri Shakir	Dr Challoner's Grammar Sch., Amersham
Andrew Shaw	Verulam School, St Albans
Phoenix Sremcevic	The Cherwell School, Oxford
Felix Stocker	Eton College, Windsor
Pasa Suksmith	Harrow International School, Bangkok
James Sun	Reading School
Emma Sun	Henrietta Barnett School, London
Samuel Sutherland	Wells Cathedral School, Somerset
Daniel Townsend	Colchester Royal Grammar School
Yuriy Tumarkin	Durham Johnston School
Laurence Van Someren	Eton College, Windsor
Prashast Vir	Kings College School, Wimbledon
Lauren Weaver	St Paul's Girls' School, Hammersmith
Naomi Wei	City of London Girls' School
Nicholas West	Alleyn's School, Dulwich
Sean White	City of London School
Nicholas Wiseman	City of London School
Ryan Wong	Reading School
Yuqing Wu	Bangkok Patana School
Harvey Yau	Ysgol Dyffryn Taf, Carmarthenshire

Hyunji You	Bangkok International School
Daniel Yue	King Edward's School, Birmingham

Hamilton

Hugo Aaronson	St Paul's School, Barnes, London
Samuel Ahmed	Kings College School, Wimbledon
Haroon Ahmed	Manchester Grammar School
Anusha Ashok	Durham High School for Girls
Anirudh Baddepudi	UWCSEA Dover Campus, Singapore
John Bamford	The Fernwood School, Nottingham
Joe Benton	St Paul's School, Barnes, London
Patrick Bevan	Perse School, Cambridge
Adit Bhansali	BD Somani International School, Mumbai
Colin Brown	Winchester College
Eric Canavan	Wanstead High School, London
Rosie Cates	Perse School, Cambridge
Ron Cheng	City of London Freemen's School, Surrey
Jacob Chevalier Drori	Highgate School, London
Wei Chin	Wycombe Abbey School, High Wycombe
Tek Kan Chung	Colchester Royal Grammar School
Nathaniel Cleland	Gillingham School, Dorset
Jacob Coxon	Magdalen College School, Oxford
Benjamin Dayan	Westminster School
Alexander Dergachev	Concord College, Shrewsbury
Richard Efezeybek	Bournemouth School
Philip Fernandes	St Paul's School, Barnes, London
Thomas Foster	St Paul's School, Barnes, London
Alex Fruh	St Aloysius College, Glasgow
Isabella Fulford	St Paul's Girls' School, Hammersmith
Quentin Gueroult	St Paul's School, Barnes, London
Peter Hicks	Magdalen College School, Oxford
Curtis Ho	Harrow School
Matthew Hutton	Royal Grammar School (Newcastle)
Nanako Ishikawa	UWCSEA Dover Campus, Singapore
Gyuhyun Jung	North London Coll. Sch. Jeju, South Korea
Ragyeom Kim	British International School of Shanghai
Seung Joo Kim	Eton College, Windsor
Jia Kim	Wycombe Abbey School, High Wycombe

Kohdai Komoriya	Southbank International School, London
Sophie Kuang	The Royal Latin School, Buckingham
Tommy Lam	Warwick School
Beom Jia Lee	Overseas Family School, Singapore
Kyung Chan Lee	Garden International School, Malaysia
Theo Lewy	Haberdashers' Aske's Sch. for Boys, Herts
Meng Liao	Anglo-Chinese School, Singapore
Anthony Lim	King Edward VI Camp Hill Boys' School
Luozhiyu Lin	Anglo-Chinese School, Singapore
Sichen Liu	Malvern St James, Worcestershire
Xing Liu	Beijing New Talent Academy
Asa Macdermott	Judd School, Tonbridge, Kent
Diamor Marke	Wallington County Grammar Sch., Surrey
Andrew Martin	King William's College, Isle of Man
Rory McLaurin	Hampstead School, London
Jake Mendel	City of London School
Ben Morris	City of London School
Protik Moulik	Westminster School
Lamisah Mukta	City of London Girls' School
Neel Nanda	Latymer School, London
Michael Ng	Aylesbury Grammar School
Josh Oliver	St Albans School
Nicholas Palmer	St Paul's School, Barnes, London
Thomas Pycroft	Whitchurch High School, Cardiff
Peter Rae	St Paul's School, Barnes, London
Nathan Rastogi	Eton College, Windsor
Mukul Rathi	Nottingham High School
Thomas Read	Perse School, Cambridge
Henry Sainsbury	King Edward VI Gr. Sch., Chelmsford
Suphanat Sangwongwanich	Harrow International School, Bangkok
Denys Seleznov	Hedingham School, Essex
Pratap Singh	Perse School, Cambridge
Jeongmin Song	North London Coll. Sch. Jeju, South Korea
Momoko Sumida	Royal Russell School, Croydon
Earth Tachatirakul	Shrewsbury International School, Thailand
Celine Tae	North London Coll. Sch. Jeju, South Korea
Jesse Tan	Chauncy School, Hertfordshire
Zheng Tao Li	D'Overbroeck's College, Oxford

Euan Tebbutt	Twycross House School, Warks
Lawrence Tray	St Paul's School, Barnes, London
Jim Tse	Tiffin School, Kingston-upon-Thames
Yuta Tsuchiya	Queen Elizabeth's School, Barnet
Bhurichaya Tuksinwarajarn	Harrow International School, Bangkok
Saurav Vashisht	Sir Joseph Williamson's Maths Sch., Rochester
Alice Vaughan William	Nailsea School, North Somerset
David Veres	King Edward VI School, Southampton
Xingyu Wang	Jinan Foreign Language School, China
Alex Wang	Eton College, Windsor
Henry Wang	Christ's Hospital, Horsham
Lennie Wells	St Paul's School, Barnes, London
Thomas Wilkinson	Lambeth Academy
Edwin Winata Hartanto	Anglo-Chinese School, Singapore
Bill Xuan	King Edward's School, Birmingham
Minghua Yin	Reading School
Harry Yoo	St James School, Grimsby
Jack You	Eton College, Windsor
Zhiqiu Yu	Anglo-Chinese School, Singapore
Sechan Yun	Perse School, Cambridge
James Zhang	Hutchesons' Grammar School, Glasgow
Litian Zhang	Jinan Foreign Language School, China
Liam Zhou	Westminster School
Shirley Zhou	Clifton College, Bristol
Yanshen Zhou	West Buckland School, Devon

Maclaurin

Howard Au	Winchester College
George Bateman	Marlborough School, Oxon
Ben Beardsley	Seisen International School, Tokyo
Jamie Bell	King Edward VI Five Ways Sch., B'ham
Lydia Buckingham	Wellington School, Somerset
Henrik Burton	Perse School, Cambridge
Matthew Chaffe	Littleover Community School, Derby
Jensen Chan	Anglo-Chinese School, Singapore
Euijin Choi	Wilson's School, Surrey
Jeffrey Chu	Tonbridge School, Kent
Edmund Coke	Eton College, Windsor
Clarissa Costen	Altrincham Girls' Grammar School

Esha Dasgupta	Sutton Coldfield Grammar School for Girls
John Dawson	Friends' School Lisburn
Stewart Feasby	Hazelwick School, Crawley
Yu Fu	Anglo-Chinese School, Singapore
Harry Goodburn	Wilson's School, Surrey
Charlotte Grayson	Watford Grammar School for Girls
Reuben Green	Culloden Academy, nr Inverness
Abdul Hadi Khan	Haileybury Almaty School, Kazakhstan
Joshua Hampson	St Paul's School, Barnes, London
Qiwei Han	Sidcot School, Somerset
Alex Harris	Perse School, Cambridge
Robert Harvey Wood	Highgate School, London
Lars Heidrich	St Paul's School, Barnes, London
Alfred Hewes	Magdalen College School, Oxford
Donald Hobson	Webster's High School, Angus
Matthias Hoffman Vagenheim	Manchester Grammar School
Lawrence Hollom	Churcher's College, Hampshire
Michael Hu	Bristol Grammar School
Lucas Huysmans	Beaumont School, St Albans
Kiwan Hyun	North London Coll. Sch. Jeju, South Korea
Alfred Jacquemot	St Paul's School, Barnes, London
Jaehwan Jeong	UWCSEA Dover Campus, Singapore
Matthew Johnson	Whitgift School, Surrey
Jeon Jongheon	Winchester College
Tomoka Kan	St Paul's Girls' School, Hammersmith
Annanay Kapila	Nottingham High School
Anthony Kattuman	Perse School, Cambridge
Muhammed Khan	King Edward VI Camp Hill Boys' School
David Ko	North London Coll. Sch. Jeju, South Korea
John Kwon	Winchester College
Alan Lai	Overseas Family School, Singapore
Kirsten Land	Hornsey School for Girls, London
Daiwei Lang	Tapton School, Sheffield
Chong Hou Lao	Ashford School, Kent
Filipp Lavrentiev	Magdalen College School, Oxford
June Whee Lee	Norwich School
Jinju Lee	Badminton School, Bristol
Yuri Lee	British International School of Shanghai
Jackie Li	St Paul's Girls' School, Hammersmith

Jaeyeon Lim	Epsom College, Surrey
Sophie Maclean	Watford Grammar School for Girls
Oleg Malanyuk	English College in Prague
Annabel Manley	Pate's Grammar School, Cheltenham
Calum McCain	Colchester Royal Grammar School
Callum Mclean	Harrow School
Jacob Menkus	Eton College, Windsor
Stephen Mitchell	St Paul's School, Barnes, London
Conor Murphy	Eltham College, London
Arvind Narayan	The Grammar School at Leeds
Krit Patarapak	Charterhouse, Godalming, Surrey
Philip Peters	Haberdashers' Aske's Sch. for Boys, Herts
Daniel Remo	Highgate School, London
Edward Rong	Westminster School
Asees Sachdev	Garden International School, Malaysia
Sam Seo	North London Coll. Sch. Jeju, South Korea
Ben Sharples	Tadcaster Grammar School, N. Yorks
Bemin Sheen	Tiffin School, Kingston-upon-Thames
Amritpal Singh	Myton School, Warwick
Daniel Smith	King Henry VIII School, Coventry
Finlay Stafford	Newfield School, Sheffield
Alan Sun	City of London School
Adrian Tang	West Island School (ESF), Hong Kong
Charles Thomas	St Paul's School, Barnes, London
Jacob Thorn	Winchester College
Kent Vainio	Westminster School
Hanno Von Bergen	Giggleswick School, N. Yorks
Bill Wang	King Edward's School, Birmingham
Sam Watt	Monkton Combe School, Bath
Rebecca Weare	The Romsey School, Hampshire
Cao Wenbo	Highgate School, London
Dmitri Whitmore	King's School Macclesfield
Alfred Wong	Reading School
Kieran Woodcock	Ripon Grammar School, Skipton, N. Yorks
Leonie Woodland	The Stephen Perse Foundation, Cambridge
Jiaqi Wu	Anglo-Chinese School, Singapore
Rusi Xu	Malvern St James, Worcestershire
Ziming Xue	Anglo-Chinese School, Singapore
Jiwon You	Haileybury Almaty School, Kazakhstan

Cindy Yu	Wycombe Abbey School, High Wycombe
Jingwei Zhang	Concord College, Shrewsbury
Mengchun Zhang	Jinan Foreign Language School, China
Kejing (Linda) Zhong	Wellington School, Somerset
Renzhi Zhou	Perse School, Cambridge
Mike Zhou	Rossall School, Lancashire
Joseph Zhu	Oxford Spires Academy

UKMT Summer Schools 2014

Introduction

The first Summer School was held in The Queen's College, Oxford in July 1994. It was the brainchild of Dr Tony Gardiner (University of Birmingham) who ran the first five, from 1994 to 1998. UKMT then took over the organisation. From 1997 to 2012 the Summer Schools were held in Queen's College, Birmingham; from 2013 the Summer Schools have been held at Woodhouse Grove School, West Yorkshire.

Initially there was a single Summer School each year, with the second National Mathematics Summer School being introduced in 2007. Three further Summer Schools were introduced in Oxford from 2013.

Attendance at the UKMT Summer Schools is by invitation only, and selection of students to invite is based on performance in UKMT Intermediate Maths Challenge and follow-on rounds. Invitations are normally sent to students via their school in May.

Summer Schools 2013-14

At the beginning of the year, in August 2013, the Trust organised and ran three new week-long residential schools in Oxford. Two of these were supported by the Department for Education (DfE) and the third, a new summer school for girls, was supported by a number of Oxford Colleges. Our thanks go to Balliol, Somerville, St Anne's and Christchurch Colleges for their support of our summer schools in Oxford.

All three schools were accommodated at Balliol College, however the Girls' Summer School took their evening meal at Christchurch College. Lunches were taken at either St Anne's College or Somerville College. Teaching was held in the Mathematical Institute building.

The first DfE supported summer school was held between 18 – 23 August and was overseen by Dr Anne Andrews (ex Royal Latin School, Bucks) and the second DfE week (25 – 30 August) by Philip Coggins (ex Bedford School). The Summer School for Girls (SSFG) was at the same time as the first of the DfE weeks and Dr Elizabeth Kimber (Chetham's School Manchester) ran this.

Each of the schools in Oxford was attended by forty students from school years 10 and 11 (and equivalent), along with five older senior students, and a number of staff and visiting speakers.

Two National Mathematics Summer Schools were held in July 2014 at Woodhouse Grove School, West Yorkshire. On these weeks there were 42 attending students, assisted by six senior students. These two weeks were held between 6th – 11th July, and 13th – 18th July.

The first week was run by Dr. Steven O'Hagan (Hutchesons' Grammar School) and the second week by James Gazet (Eton College).

All younger students were invited to attend a summer school based on their performance in the Intermediate Mathematical Challenge or Intermediate follow-on competitions. The senior students had previously attended a summer school as a junior and were present to assist and guide the younger pupils as well as to participate in sessions. The senior girls attending the SSFG had all been members of the UK team for the European Girls' Mathematical Olympiad 2013.

The academic timetable for all the UKMT Summer Schools was full and challenging, with masterclasses and group sessions on a whole host of mathematical topics, including number theory, geometry and combinatorics. The students also enjoyed an evening social calendar, including quizzes, talks, a boat or bowling trip, and the traditional UKMT summer school concert.

Typical timetable

For example, in the first of the DfE Summer Schools, after breakfast, there were two sessions in the mornings with a short break in between. There was a break for lunch of just over an hour. In the afternoon, the two sessions were split by a short break. Dinner started at 6 pm and was followed by organised activities.

The first morning session was related to algebra and the second morning session included such topics as: Square roots and 17-gons; Numbers and codes. The afternoon topics were more varied and included: Combinatorics; Pigeonhole principle; Continued fractions; Modular arithmetic; Conics; Combinatorics; Triangles; Catalan numbers; and, Inequalities. The titles of the after dinner activities were: Pennies; Conway's Soldiers; FLT film; a concert; and, a boat trip.

Students attending Summer Schools in 2013/14

DfE Summer School: Oxford 18 – 23 August 2013

Hader Ali Dar (St Joseph's College), Jowan Atkinson (Romsey School), Shanon Bernard Healey (Dorothy Stringer High School), Meghan Bird (Bourne Grammar School), Natalie Carter (Ecclesbourne School), Benjamin Chant (Kenilworth School), Hannah Charman (Ripley St Thomas High School), Reetobrata Chatterjee (Portsmouth Grammar School), Wesley Chow (Haughton Academy), Dominic Clark (Abbeyfield School), Alexander Cliffe (Casterton Business and Enterprise College), James Cooper (Thomas Hardye School), Barnaby Fogg (Queen Elizabeth High School), Sam Gregson (Clitheroe Royal Grammar School), William Harris (Ashcombe School), Byron Hemingway (Birkdale School), Robert Keen (The Priory Academy LSST), Shanghav Loganathan (Parkstone Grammar School), Katie Manns (Hardenhuish School), Calum McCain (Colchester Royal Grammar School), Katherine Mellor (Fulford School), Natalie Nguyen (Northampton High School), Helen Ockenden (Lancaster Girls' Grammar School), Ben Pace (Chetham's School of Music), Isabel Parsons (Rugby High School), Ben Pease (Ripon Grammar School), Sooria Rajakanthan (Wallington County Grammar School), George Robinson (Brooke Weston Academy), Sam Rowell (Herschel Grammar School), Saira Safeer (Henrietta Barnett School), Daniel Silber (St John the Baptist School), Chris Spence (The Clere School), Michael Swain (St Clement Danes School), Kieran Tarry (Kennet School), Tom Uden (St Bartholomew's School), Edwin Watson-Miller (Richard Hale School), Adam Whitehouse (Sir Thomas Wharton Community College), Matthew Wilson (St Edmund's College), Esmae Woods (Marlwood School), Gillian Yu (Oakgrove School).

Seniors: Miriam Apsley (Cheadle and Marple Sixth Form College), Jiali Gao (Wolverhampton Girls' High School), James Hodgson (St Bernard's Convent School), Ramsay Pyper (Eton College), Iain Timmins (Wyggeston and Queen Elizabeth 1 College).

DfE Summer School: Oxford 25 – 30 August 2013

Shayan Ahmed (Queen Mary's Grammar School), Cecilie Andersen (Gordano School), Joel Baruch (Hasmonean High School), Melissa Bucknor (Seven Kings High School), Jack Cavender (Thomas Deacon Academy), Orlando Chan (Old Swinford Hosptial School), Jessica Cheung (Wetherby High School), Philip Christian (Gosforth Academy), Daniel Clark (Woodhouse Grove School), Sophie Crane (Stroud High School), Adam Dadvar (Conyers School), Hugh Duff (Harris City Academy Crystal Palace), Edmund Evans (Weydon School), Thomas Furber (Royal

Latin School), Joseph Glynn (Chellaston Academy), Elizabeth Hawkins (Redhill School), Jessica Holding (Trinity School), Lawrence Hollom (Churcher's College), Rashmi Jeyasanker (Feltham Community College), Alice Lake (Alcester Grammar School), Jennifer Lawmon (Chipping Norton School), Rowan Lee (Nottingham High School), Uthman Mahmud (Al-Furqan Community College Boys Section), Annabel Manley (Pate's Grammar School), Ben Mason (Roundwood Park School), Robin McCorkell (Dover Grammar School for Boys), Sean Middlehurst (Tytherington High School), Joseph Moss (Jews' Free School), Nathan Peters (The King's School), Ivan Pilfold (Oakwood Park Grammar School), Ethan Ren (Cardiff High School), Daniel Reynolds (Aston Academy), Ben Sharples (Tadcaster Grammar School), Amritpal Singh (Myton School), James Timmins (Durham Johnston School), Xudan Wang (Southend High School for Girls), Michael Wang (Royal Grammar School), Oliver Woollard (Robert May's School), Rusi Xu (Malvern St James), Joseph Zivny (Malvern College).

Seniors: George Fortune (Altrincham Grammar School for Boys), Maria Holdcroft (Willink School), Remy Naylor (Durrington High School), Rachel Newhouse (Skipton Girls' High School), Linden Ralph (Comberton Village College).

Summer School for Girls: 18 – 23 August 2013

Sophie Andrews (Guildford High School), Lucy Biddle (Purcell School), Amy Boyd (The Mirus Academy), Hazel Browne (Lancaster Girls' Grammar School), Charlotte Caplan (North London Collegiate School), Mrinalin Chakrabarty (Newport Girls' High School), Eleanor Chapman (Dr Challoner's High School), Joanna Chen (Hinchingbrooke School), Heidi Chiu (Badminton School), Megan Cryer (Newcastle under Lyme School), Katharine Curran (City of London Freemen's School), Grace Curtis (Blundell's School), Poppy Duncan (Bedales School), Tegan Forbes (Simon Langton Girls' School), Surina Fordington (Norwich High School), Catalina Garcia (St Paul's Girls' School), Charlotte Hallam (St Alban's High School for Girls), Emily Hampson (Court Moor School), Sophie Humphrey (Harrogate Grammar School), Ingrid Jiang (Arnewood School), Nithya Kadiyala (Kendrick School), Anna Knight (Bablake School), Charmain Lai, (Cheltenham Ladies College), India Mackay (St Swithun's School), Xanthe Malcolm (West Kirkby Grammar School), Lucie Mathison (Cannock Chase High School), Emma Morrison (St Francis Xavier School), Lauren Muir (St Aidan's High School), Dionne O'Brien (Chelmsford County High School), Rachel O'Connor (Wallace High School), Annie Paine (Cockermouth School), Kira Pandya (Croydon High School), Drishti Sharma (Wycombe High School), Ji yao Tang

(Gordano School), Lara Tritton (Alleyn's School), Jessica Wang (Watford Grammar School for Girls), Siyang Wei (Withington Girls' School), Maddie Wigmore Sykes (Princethorpe College), Catherine Wooller (Downlands School).

Seniors: Maria Holdcroft (Willink School), Eleanor Holderness (Latymer Upper School), Elizabeth Lee (Loughborough High School), Katya Richards (School of St Helen and St Katharine), Kasia Warburton (Reigate Grammar School).

Leeds Summer School: 6 July – 11 July 2014

Samuel Ahmed (Kings College School, Wimbledon), James Aiken (St Gregory's School), Thomas Baycroft (Notre Dame High School), Daniel Berenson (Immanuel College), Michael Berry (Boroughmuir High School), James Blake (St Mark's RC School), Emma Brown (St Helen's School), George Brown (Beverley Grammar School), Sarah Buddle (Backwell School), Jacob Campbell (Mayville High School), Serene Chongtrakul (St Mary's School Ascot), Jake Clement-Jones (Wirral Grammar School for Boys), Alexander Cook (Adams Grammar School), Mark Cooper (Westwood College), John Dawson (Friends' School Lisburn), Riordan De Vries (Lancaster Royal Grammar School), Harry Ellison-Wright (Bryanston School), Hethvi Gada (Sevenoaks School), Thomas Gbadamosi (Harrow High School), William Holdsworth (Latymer Upper School), Amaya Jones (Blenheim High School), William Jones (Ibstock Place School), Melissa Knapton (Wakefield Girls' High School), Scott Macandrew (High School of Dundee), Andrew Martin (King William's College), Ross Martin (St Leonard's School), James Mowbray (The Norton Knatchbull School), Rachel O'Connor (Wallace High School), Yifei Painter (Nottingham Girls' High School), Frederick Robinson (The Hollyfield School), Rhianna Robinson (Rougemont School), Ryan Salter (Woodhey High School), Jonathan Sewell (Hereford Cathedral School), Oscar Simpson (Queen Elizabeth's Grammar School), Cammy Sriram (High School of Glasgow), Stephanie Stacey (Lancaster Girls' Grammar School), Zoe Xin Yu Tan (St Swithun's School), Ken Thie (The Blue School), Alex Wardle-Solano (Wellingborough School), Oliver Welsh (Benton Park School), Kaitrin Wilson (Derby High School), Yu Xiao (Sir William Perkins's School).

Seniors: Meghan Bird (Bourne Grammar School), David Clarke (Solihull School), Laura Embrey (King's School), Jack Hodkinson (Queen Elizabeth Grammar School), Henry Mckay (King's College School), Rebecca Poon (George Watson's College).

Leeds Summer School: 13 – 18 July 2014

Anusha Ashok (Durham High School for Girls), John Bamford (The Fernwood School), Tek Kan Chung (Colchester Royal Grammar School), Nathaniel Cleland (Gillingham School), Clarissa Costen (Altrincham Girls' Grammar School), Jacob Coxon (Magdalen College School), Benjamin Dayan (Westminster School), Richard Efezeybek (Bournemouth School), Alex Fruh (St Aloysius College), Charlotte Grayson (Watford Grammar School for Girls), Reuben Green (Culloden Academy), Elizabeth Hayman (Bartholomew School), Curtis Ho (Harrow School), Kate Howes (Howard of Effingham School), Matt Hutton (Royal Grammar School Newcastle), Anthony Kattuman (Perse School), Jia Kim (Wycombe Abbey School), Sophie Kuang (The Royal Latin School), June Whee Lee (Norwich School), Jackie Li (St Paul's Girls' School), Anthony Lim (King Edward VI Camp Hill Boys' School), Asa Macdermott (Judd School), Rory McLaurin (Hampstead School), Stephen Mitchell (St Paul's School), Ben Morris (City of London School), Lamisah Mukta (City of London Girls' School), Arvind Narayan (The Grammar School at Leeds), Michael Ng (Aylesbury Grammar School), Thomas Pycroft (Whitchurch High School), Mukul Rathi (Nottingham High School), Euan Tebbutt (Twycross House School), Alice Vaughan-William (Nailsea School), David Veres (King Edward VI School), Alex Wag (Eton College), Bill Wang (King Edward's School), Rebecca Weare (The Romsey School), Olivia Westwood (Wolverhampton Girls' High School), Thomas Wilkinson (Lambeth Academy), Kieran Woodcock (Ripon Grammar School), Leonie Woodland (The Stephen Perse Foundation), Minghua Yin (Reading School), Duo Zhao (Simon Langton Girls' School).

Seniors: Jongheon Jeon (Winchester College), Georgina Majury (Down High School), Katya Richards (School of St Helen and St Katharine), Marcus Roberts (The Grammar School at Leeds), Kasia Warburton (Reigate Grammar School), Sam Watt (Monkton Combe School).

Our thanks go to everyone who made the UKMT Summer Schools such as success, in particular to our supporters: the Department for Education; Balliol College; Christ Church College; Somerville College; St Anne's College; and Oxford University; and to our volunteers who helped to run each week with such efficiency and energy: in particular Anne Andrews; Philip Coggins; James Gazet; Lizzie Kimber; and Steven O'Hagan. A list of all our volunteers who assisted at the summer schools can be found at the back of the Yearbook.

Senior Mathematical Challenge and British Mathematical Olympiads

The Senior Challenge took place on Tuesday 7th November 2013. Once again it was sponsored by the Institute of Actuaries. There were 104,360 entries and around 1500 candidates took part in the next stage, British Mathematical Olympiad Round 1, held on Friday 29th November 2013. The Senior Kangaroo was held on the same day, around 3400 candidates were eligible.

UK SENIOR MATHEMATICAL CHALLENGE

Thursday 7 November 2013

Organised by the **United Kingdom Mathematics Trust**

and supported by

RULES AND GUIDELINES (to be read before starting)

1. Do not open the question paper until the invigilator tells you to do so.
2. **Use B or HB pencil only**. Mark *at most one* of the options A, B, C, D, E on the Answer Sheet for each question. Do not mark more than one option.
3. Time allowed: **90 minutes**.
   No answers or personal details may be entered on the Answer Sheet after the 90 minutes are over.
4. The use of rough paper is allowed.
   Calculators, measuring instruments and squared paper are forbidden.
5. Candidates must be full-time students at secondary school or FE college, and must be in Year 13 or below (England & Wales); S6 or below (Scotland); Year 14 or below (Northern Ireland).
6. There are twenty-five questions. Each question is followed by five options marked A, B, C, D, E. Only one of these is correct. Enter the letter A-E corresponding to the correct answer in the corresponding box on the Answer Sheet.
7. **Scoring rules**: all candidates start out with 25 marks;
   0 marks are awarded for each question left unanswered;
   4 marks are awarded for each correct answer;
   1 mark is deducted for each incorrect answer.
8. **Guessing**: Remember that there is a penalty for wrong answers. Note also that later questions are deliberately intended to be harder than earlier questions. You are thus advised to concentrate first on solving as many as possible of the first 15-20 questions. Only then should you try later questions.

The United Kingdom Mathematics Trust is a Registered Charity.

http://www.ukmt.org.uk

1. Which of these is the largest number?

A $2 + 0 + 1 + 3$ B $2 \times 0 + 1 + 3$ C $2 + 0 \times 1 + 3$ D $2 + 0 + 1 \times 3$ E $2 \times 0 \times 1 \times 3$

2. Little John claims he is 2m 8cm and 3mm tall. What is this height in metres?

A 2.83m B 2.803m C 2.083m D 2.0803m E 2.0083m

3. What is the 'tens' digit of $2013^2 - 2013$?

A 0 B 1 C 4 D 5 E 6

4. A route on the 3×3 board shown consists of a number of steps. Each step is from one square to an adjacent square of a different colour. How many different routes are there from square S to square T which pass through every other square exactly once?

A 0 B 1 C 2 D 3 E 4

5. The numbers x and y satisfy the equations $x(y + 2) = 100$ and $y(x + 2) = 60$. What is the value of $x - y$?

A 60 B 50 C 40 D 30 E 20

6. Rebecca went swimming yesterday. After a while she had covered one fifth of her intended distance. After swimming six more lengths of the pool, she had covered one quarter of her intended distance. How many lengths of the pool did she intend to complete?

A 40 B 72 C 80 D 100 E 120

7. In a 'ninety nine' shop, all items cost a number of pounds and 99 pence. Susanna spent £65.76. How many items did she buy?

A 23 B 24 C 65 D 66 E 76

8. The right-angled triangle shown has a base which is 4 times its height. Four such triangles are placed so that their hypotenuses form the boundary of a large square as shown.
What is the side-length of the shaded square in the diagram?

A $2x$ B $2\sqrt{2}x$ C $3x$ D $2\sqrt{3}x$ E $\sqrt{15}x$

9. According to a headline, 'Glaciers in the French Alps have lost a quarter of their area in the past 40 years'. What is the approximate percentage reduction in the length of the side of a square when it loses one quarter of its area, thereby becoming a smaller square?

A 13% B 25% C 38% D 50% E 65%

10. Frank's teacher asks him to write down five integers such that the median is one more than the mean, and the mode is one greater than the median. Frank is also told that the median is 10. What is the smallest possible integer that he could include in his list?

A 3 B 4 C 5 D 6 E 7

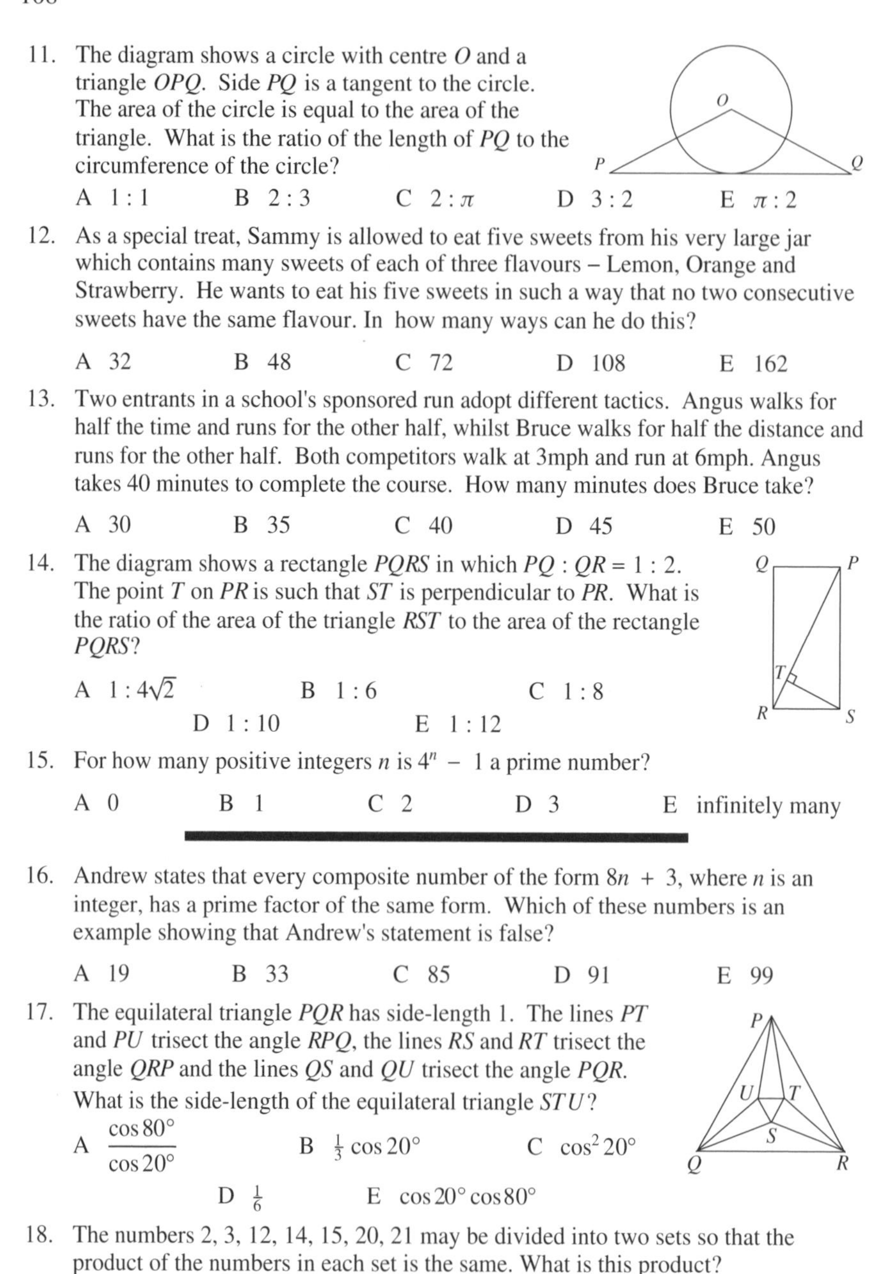

11. The diagram shows a circle with centre O and a triangle OPQ. Side PQ is a tangent to the circle. The area of the circle is equal to the area of the triangle. What is the ratio of the length of PQ to the circumference of the circle?

A $1:1$ B $2:3$ C $2:\pi$ D $3:2$ E $\pi:2$

12. As a special treat, Sammy is allowed to eat five sweets from his very large jar which contains many sweets of each of three flavours – Lemon, Orange and Strawberry. He wants to eat his five sweets in such a way that no two consecutive sweets have the same flavour. In how many ways can he do this?

A 32 B 48 C 72 D 108 E 162

13. Two entrants in a school's sponsored run adopt different tactics. Angus walks for half the time and runs for the other half, whilst Bruce walks for half the distance and runs for the other half. Both competitors walk at 3mph and run at 6mph. Angus takes 40 minutes to complete the course. How many minutes does Bruce take?

A 30 B 35 C 40 D 45 E 50

14. The diagram shows a rectangle $PQRS$ in which $PQ : QR = 1 : 2$. The point T on PR is such that ST is perpendicular to PR. What is the ratio of the area of the triangle RST to the area of the rectangle $PQRS$?

A $1:4\sqrt{2}$ B $1:6$ C $1:8$ D $1:10$ E $1:12$

15. For how many positive integers n is $4^n - 1$ a prime number?

A 0 B 1 C 2 D 3 E infinitely many

---

16. Andrew states that every composite number of the form $8n + 3$, where n is an integer, has a prime factor of the same form. Which of these numbers is an example showing that Andrew's statement is false?

A 19 B 33 C 85 D 91 E 99

17. The equilateral triangle PQR has side-length 1. The lines PT and PU trisect the angle RPQ, the lines RS and RT trisect the angle QRP and the lines QS and QU trisect the angle PQR. What is the side-length of the equilateral triangle STU?

A $\dfrac{\cos 80°}{\cos 20°}$ B $\frac{1}{3}\cos 20°$ C $\cos^2 20°$ D $\frac{1}{6}$ E $\cos 20° \cos 80°$

18. The numbers 2, 3, 12, 14, 15, 20, 21 may be divided into two sets so that the product of the numbers in each set is the same. What is this product?

A 420 B 1260 C 2520 D 6720 E 6350400

19. The 16 small squares shown in the diagram each have a side length of 1 unit. How many pairs of vertices are there in the diagram whose distance apart is an integer number of units?

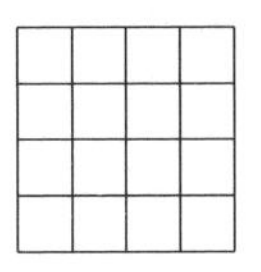

A 40 B 64 C 108 D 132 E 16

20. The ratio of two positive numbers equals the ratio of their sum to their difference. What is this ratio?

A $(1+\sqrt{3}):2$ B $\sqrt{2}:1$ C $(1+\sqrt{5}):2$ D $(2+\sqrt{2}):1$ E $(1+\sqrt{2}):1$

---

21. 

The shaded design shown in the diagram is made by drawing eight circular arcs, all with the same radius. The centres of four arcs are the vertices of the square; the centres of the four touching arcs are the midpoints of the sides of the square. The diagonals of the square have length 1.

What is the total length of the border of the shaded design?

A 2π B $\frac{5\pi}{2}$ C 3π D $\frac{7\pi}{2}$ E 4π

22. Consider numbers of the form $10n + 1$, where n is a positive integer. We shall call such a number 'grime' if it cannot be expressed as the product of two smaller numbers, possibly equal, both of which are of the form $10k + 1$, where k is a positive integer.

How many 'grime numbers' are there in the sequence 11, 21, 31, 41, ..., 981, 991?

A 0 B 8 C 87 D 92 E 99

23. *PQRS* is a square. The points *T* and *U* are the midpoints of *QR* and *RS* respectively. The line *QS* cuts *PT* and *PU* at *W* and *V* respectively. What fraction of the area of the square *PQRS* is the area of the pentagon *RTWVU*?

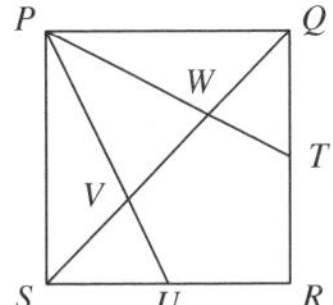
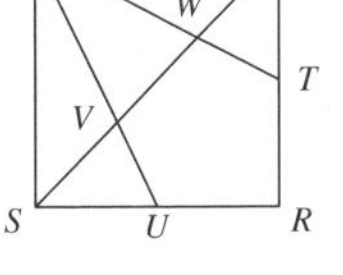

A $\frac{1}{3}$ B $\frac{2}{5}$ C $\frac{3}{7}$ D $\frac{5}{12}$ E $\frac{4}{15}$

24. The diagram shows two straight lines *PR* and *QS* crossing at *O*.

What is the value of x?

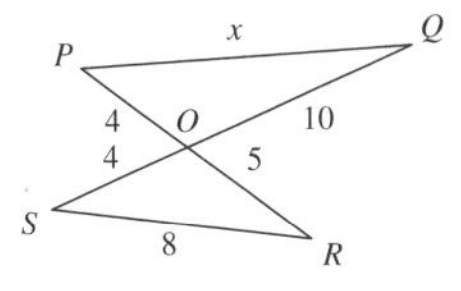

A $7\sqrt{2}$ B $2\sqrt{29}$ C $14\sqrt{2}$ D $7(1+\sqrt{13})$ E $9\sqrt{2}$

25. 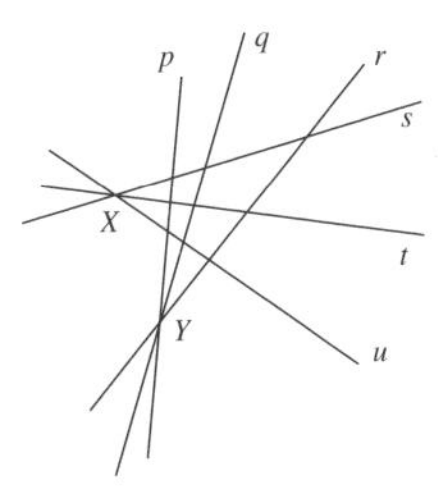

Challengeborough's underground train network consists of six lines, p, q, r, s, t, u, as shown. Wherever two lines meet there is a station which enables passengers to change lines. On each line, each train stops at every station.

Jessica wants to travel from station X to station Y. She does not want to use any line more than once, nor return to station X after leaving it, nor leave station Y having reached it.

How many different routes, satisfying these conditions, can she choose?

A 9 B 36 C 41 D 81 E 720

Further remarks

The solutions are provided in a leaflet which is also set up to facilitate marking in centres who wished to continue to mark in house.

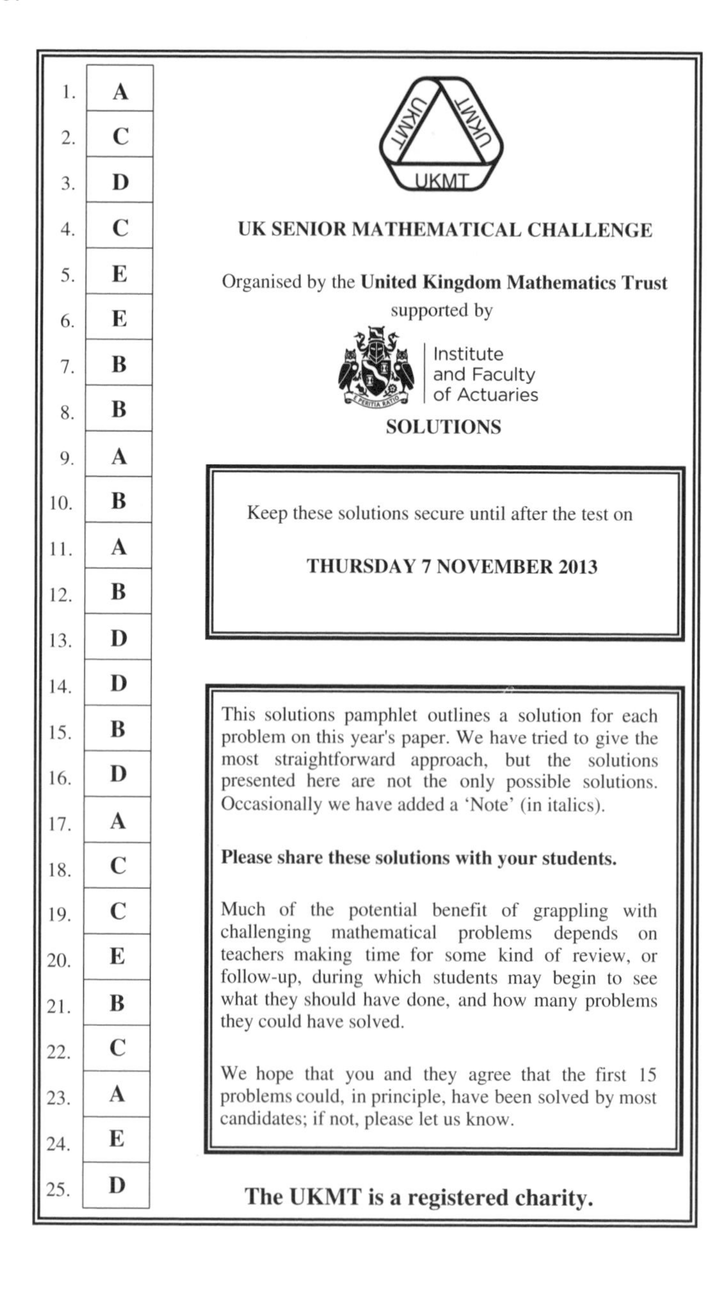

1.	A
2.	C
3.	D
4.	C
5.	E
6.	E
7.	B
8.	B
9.	A
10.	B
11.	A
12.	B
13.	D
14.	D
15.	B
16.	D
17.	A
18.	C
19.	C
20.	E
21.	B
22.	C
23.	A
24.	E
25.	D

UKMT UKMT UKMT

UK SENIOR MATHEMATICAL CHALLENGE

Organised by the **United Kingdom Mathematics Trust**

supported by

Institute and Faculty of Actuaries

SOLUTIONS

Keep these solutions secure until after the test on

THURSDAY 7 NOVEMBER 2013

This solutions pamphlet outlines a solution for each problem on this year's paper. We have tried to give the most straightforward approach, but the solutions presented here are not the only possible solutions. Occasionally we have added a 'Note' (in italics).

Please share these solutions with your students.

Much of the potential benefit of grappling with challenging mathematical problems depends on teachers making time for some kind of review, or follow-up, during which students may begin to see what they should have done, and how many problems they could have solved.

We hope that you and they agree that the first 15 problems could, in principle, have been solved by most candidates; if not, please let us know.

The UKMT is a registered charity.

1. **A** Calculating the value of each option gives $2 + 0 + 1 + 3 = 6$, $2 \times 0 + 1 + 3 = 4$, $2 + 0 \times 1 + 3 = 5$, $2 + 0 + 1 \times 3 = 5$ and $2 \times 0 \times 1 \times 3 = 0$ so $2 + 0 + 1 + 3$ is the largest.

2. **C** In metres, the height 2m 8cm and 3mm is $2 + 8 \times 0.01 + 3 \times 0.001 = 2 + 0.08 + 0.003 = 2.083$ m.

3. **D** Factorising $2013^2 - 2013$ gives $2013(2013 - 1)$ which equals 2013×2012. So the tens digit is 5 as $13 \times 12 = 156$ and only this part of the product contributes to the tens digit of the answer.

4. **C** In order to pass through each square exactly once, a route must pass in and out of both unlabelled corner squares and also pass through the middle. Passing in and out of a corner involves three squares, coloured grey, white and grey in that order. Passing in and out of the two unlabelled corners therefore accounts for six unlabelled squares, leaving only the middle square which must be in the middle of any possible route. So, there are two possible routes as shown.

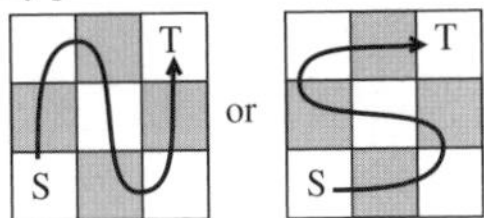

5. **E** Since $x(y + 2) = 100$ and $y(x + 2) = 60$ then $xy + 2x = 100$ and $xy + 2y = 60$. Subtracting gives $2x - 2y = 40$ and therefore $x - y = 20$.

6. **E** Let d be the number of lengths that Rebecca intended to swim. Then $6 = \frac{d}{4} - \frac{d}{5} = \frac{d}{20}$ and therefore $d = 6 \times 20 = 120$.

7. **B** The first item that Susanna buys makes her bill a number of pounds and 99 pence. Each extra item she buys after that decreases by one the number of pence in her total bill. Let n be the number of items bought. To be charged £65.76, $1 + 99 - n = 76$ so $n = 100 - 76 = 24$. Alternatives of 124 items or more are infeasible as they would each give a total greater than £65.76.

8. **B** The area of the shaded square is equal to the area of the large square minus the area of the four triangles. Thus the area of the shaded square is $(4x)^2 - 4 \times \frac{1}{2} \times 4x \times x = 16x^2 - 8x^2 = 8x^2$. So the side-length is $\sqrt{8x^2} = 2\sqrt{2}x$.

9. **A** When a square loses a quarter of its area, thereby becoming a smaller square, three quarters of its area remains. Therefore the lengths of the sides of the original square have been multiplied by $\sqrt{\frac{3}{4}} = \frac{1}{2}\sqrt{3} \approx 0.866$. This means a reduction of $(100 - 86.6)\%$ which is approximately 13%.

10. **B** The median is 10. Therefore the mode must be 11 and there must be two 11s in Frank's list. The mean is 9, so the total of the five numbers is 45. This means that the total of the two smallest integers is $45 - (10 + 2 \times 11) = 13$. The maximum size of the second largest integer is 9 so the smallest integer that Frank could include in his list is $13 - 9 = 4$.

11. **A** Let the radius of the circle be r. Then its area is πr^2. The height of the triangle is r and its area is $\frac{1}{2} \times PQ \times r$. So $\frac{1}{2} \times PQ \times r = \pi r^2$ and therefore $PQ = 2\pi r$, which is also the circumference of the circle. Therefore the ratio of the length of PQ to the circumference of the circle is $1 : 1$.

12. **B** There are three options for Sammy's first choice and then two options for each subsequent choice. Therefore the number of possible ways is $3 \times 2 \times 2 \times 2 \times 2 = 48$.

13. **D** Angus completes the course in 40 minutes, so he spends 20 minutes (which is $\frac{1}{3}$ of an hour) walking and the same time running. By using distance = speed × time, the length of the course is $3 \times \frac{1}{3} + 6 \times \frac{1}{3} = 1 + 2 = 3$ miles.
Bruce completes the course by walking for $1\frac{1}{2}$ miles and running for $1\frac{1}{2}$ miles. So, by using time $= \frac{\text{distance}}{\text{speed}}$, Bruce's total time in hours is $\frac{1\frac{1}{2}}{3} + \frac{1\frac{1}{2}}{6} = \frac{1}{2} + \frac{1}{4} = \frac{3}{4}$ of an hour. So Bruce takes 45 minutes to complete the course.

14. **D** Triangle RST is similar to triangle RPS as their corresponding angles are equal. Using Pythagoras' Theorem, the ratio of RS to RP is $1 : \sqrt{5}$. So the ratio of RT to RS is also $1 : \sqrt{5}$. Therefore the ratio of the area of the triangle RST to the area of triangle RPS is $1 : 5$. Triangle RPS is half the rectangle $PQRS$, so the ratio of the area of triangle RST to the area of rectangle $PQRS$ is $1 : 10$.

15. **B** A prime number has exactly two factors, one of which is 1. The expression $4^n - 1$ can be factorised as $4^n - 1 = (2^n + 1)(2^n - 1)$. For $4^n - 1$ to be prime, the smaller of the factors, $2^n - 1$, must equal 1.
If $2^n - 1 = 1$ then $2^n = 2$ giving $n = 1$. So there is exactly one value of n for which $4^n - 1$ is prime and this value is 1.

16. **D** By the Fundamental Theorem of Arithmetic, every positive integer greater than 1 is either prime or a product of two or more primes. A number that is the product of two or more primes is called a *composite* number.
We are looking to choose, from the options provided, a composite number which is of the form $8n + 3$ but does not have a prime factor of the form $8n + 3$.
Option A is prime, so is not possible. Options B and C are not of the form $8n + 3$. Option E is $8 \times 12 + 3 = 99$. The number 99, when expressed as a product of its prime factors, is $3 \times 3 \times 11$ and the factor 11 is of the required form as $11 = 8 \times 1 + 3$. However, option D is of the form $8n + 3$ as $8 \times 11 + 3 = 91$ but neither of the prime factors of 91, which are 7 and 13, are of the form $8n + 3$.

17. **A** Triangle PQR is equilateral so $\angle QPU = \angle UPT = \angle TPR = 20°$. Triangle PUT is isosceles, so $\angle PUT = 80°$. Let X be the midpoint of PQ and Y be the midpoint of UT.
Considering the right-angled triangle PXU gives $\cos 20° = \dfrac{PX}{PU} = \dfrac{\frac{1}{2}}{PU}$, so $PU = \dfrac{1}{2\cos 20°}$.
Considering the right-angled triangle PUY gives $\cos 80° = \dfrac{UY}{PU}$, so $UY = PU \cos 80° = \dfrac{\cos 80°}{2\cos 20°}$. Therefore $UT = 2UY = \dfrac{2\cos 80°}{2\cos 20°} = \dfrac{\cos 80°}{\cos 20°}$.
{*Note that triangle UTS is a Morley triangle, named after the mathematician Frank Morley. His 1899 trisector theorem states that in any triangle, the three points of intersection of the adjacent angle trisectors form an equilateral triangle, in this case, triangle UTS.*}

18. **C** The product of all the numbers in the list is $2 \times 3 \times 12 \times 14 \times 15 \times 20 \times 21$ which, when expressed in terms of prime factors is $2 \times 3 \times 2 \times 2 \times 3 \times 2 \times 7 \times 3 \times 5 \times 2 \times 2 \times 5 \times 3 \times 7$ which is equal to $2^6 \times 3^4 \times 5^2 \times 7^2 = (2^3 \times 3^2 \times 5 \times 7)^2 = 2520^2$. The answer 2520 is expressible as both $2 \times 3 \times 20 \times 21$ and $12 \times 14 \times 15$.

19. **C** There are 25 vertices in the diagram. Each vertex is part of a row of 5 vertices and a column of 5 vertices. Each vertex is therefore an integer number of units away from the 4 other vertices in its row and from the other 4 vertices in its column. This appears to give $25 \times (4 + 4) = 200$ pairs. However, counting in this manner includes each pair twice so there are only 100 different pairs.
By using the Pythagorean triple 3, 4, 5, each corner vertex is five units away from two other non-corner vertices, giving another 8 pairs. No other Pythagorean triples include small enough numbers to yield pairs of vertices on this grid.
Thus the total number of pairs is 108.

20. **E** Let the two positive numbers be x and y with $x > y$. The sum of the numbers is greater than their difference, so the two ratios which are equal are $x : y$ and $x + y : x - y$. Therefore $\dfrac{x}{y} = \dfrac{x+y}{x-y}$. By dividing the top and bottom of the right-hand side by y we obtain $\dfrac{x}{y} = \dfrac{\frac{x}{y}+1}{\frac{x}{y}-1}$.
Letting $k = \frac{x}{y}$ gives $k = \frac{k+1}{k-1}$ which gives the quadratic $k^2 - 2k - 1 = 0$. Completing the square gives $(k-1)^2 = 2$ whence $k = 1 \pm \sqrt{2}$. However, as x and y are both positive, $k \neq 1 - \sqrt{2}$. As the ratio $\frac{x}{y} = 1 + \sqrt{2}$, the ratio $x : y$ is $1 + \sqrt{2} : 1$.

21. **B** Let the top vertex of the square be A and the midpoints of the two lines that meet at A be B and C. The line BC is of length $\frac{1}{2}$ and is perpendicular to the diagonal of the square through A. Let the point of intersection of these two lines be D. Let the end of the uppermost arc, above B, be E. Then $ADBE$ is a rhombus, made from four radii of the arcs, AD, DB, BE and EA, each of length $\frac{1}{4}$. As $\angle ADB = 90°$, this rhombus is a square.
It then follows that the four arcs whose centres are the vertices of the original square are all semi-circles. The remaining four touching arcs are each $\frac{3}{4}$ of a circle.
In total, the length of the border is $4 \times \frac{1}{2} + 4 \times \frac{3}{4}$ times the circumference of a circle with the same radius, so is $5 \times 2\pi \times \frac{1}{4} = \frac{5}{2}\pi$.

22. **C** The numbers in the sequence 11, 21, 31, 41, ... , 981, 991 are of the form $10n + 1$ for $n = 1$ to 99. There are therefore 99 numbers in this sequence.
Twelve terms of this sequence can be expressed using factors of the form $10k + 1$. In this form, these terms are 11×11, 11×21, 11×31, ..., 11×81 and 21×21, 21×31, 21×41 and 31×31. All other pairings give products that are too large.
Hence, there are $99 - 12 = 87$ 'grime' numbers.

23. **A** The pentagon $RTWVU$ is the remainder when triangles SUV and WTQ are removed from the bottom right half of the square. Draw in the diagonal PR and consider the triangle PRS. The medians of triangle PRS join each vertex P, R and S to the midpoint of its opposite side, i.e. P to U and S to the middle of the square. The medians intersect at V and therefore the height of V above SR is $\frac{1}{3}$ of PS.
The area of triangle SUV is therefore $\frac{1}{2} \times \frac{1}{2}SR \times \frac{1}{3}PS = \frac{1}{12}$ of the area of the square. By symmetry, this is also the area of triangle WTQ. The area of the pentagon $RTWVU$ is then $\frac{1}{2} - \left(\frac{1}{12} + \frac{1}{12}\right) = \frac{1}{3}$ of the area of the square $PQRS$.

24. **E** As they are vertically opposite, $\angle POQ = \angle SOR$. Let α denote the size of each of these.
Applying the cosine rule to triangle SOR gives $8^2 = 4^2 + 5^2 - 2 \times 4 \times 5 \cos\alpha$, therefore $40 \cos\alpha = -23$.
Similarly, from triangle POQ we obtain $x^2 = 4^2 + 10^2 - 2 \times 4 \times 10 \cos\alpha$. So $x^2 = 16 + 100 - 2 \times (-23) = 162$.
Hence $x = \sqrt{162} = \sqrt{81 \times 2} = 9\sqrt{2}$.

25. **D** Jessica must travel alternately on lines which are connected to station X (i.e. s, t or u), and connected to station Y (i.e. p, q or r). In order to depart from X and end her journey at Y, she must travel along an even number of lines. This can be 2, 4 or 6 lines, making 1, 3 or 5 changes respectively.
Case A, 2 lines: Jessica leaves station X along one of the lines s, t or u, makes one change onto one of lines p, q or r and reaches station Y. Here there are 3×3 possibilities.
Case B, 4 lines: Jessica leaves station X along one of the lines s, t or u and makes her first change onto one of lines p, q or r. She then makes her second change onto either of the two lines s, t or u on which she has not previously travelled and her third change onto either of the two lines p, q or r on which she has not previously travelled and reaches station Y. Here there are $3 \times 3 \times 2 \times 2$ possibilities.
Case C, 6 lines: Her journey is as described in Case B but her fourth change is onto the last of the lines s, t or u on which she has not previously travelled and her fifth change is onto the last of the lines p, q or r on which she has not previously travelled. Here there are $3 \times 3 \times 2 \times 2 \times 1 \times 1$ possibilities.
So in total Jessica can choose $9 + 36 + 36 = 81$ different routes.

The answers

The table below shows the proportion of pupils' choices. The correct answer is shown in bold. [The percentages are rounded to the nearest whole number.]

Qn	A	B	C	D	E	Blank
1	**77**	0	1	21	0	1
2	3	3	**84**	7	2	1
3	4	8	3	**64**	17	4
4	2	3	**76**	4	9	6
5	1	3	7	4	**62**	22
6	3	4	2	2	**82**	7
7	12	**64**	3	12	2	8
8	4	**33**	16	11	5	30
9	**48**	18	8	14	3	10
10	11	**58**	6	8	4	12
11	**37**	8	16	4	6	29
12	8	**35**	11	9	4	32
13	4	3	9	**72**	3	9
14	7	9	18	**18**	4	44
15	9	**41**	7	4	25	13
16	12	6	9	**11**	8	54
17	**9**	8	3	5	4	71
18	2	5	**38**	7	2	46
19	6	11	**14**	6	4	58
20	2	3	3	4	**11**	77
21	2	**11**	3	4	3	78
22	4	5	**9**	4	8	70
23	**10**	5	4	6	3	73
24	2	4	4	2	**6**	81
25	7	13	5	**8**	2	65

SMC 2013: Some comments on the pupils' choice of answers as sent to schools in the letter with the results

It is pleasing to see that the average mark of 58 is significantly higher than last year's 53. It seems that the Problems Group's aim of making the early questions accessible to the great majority of students was achieved. The good response of the students to these questions is encouraging.

Nonetheless, we should not be complacent. You can see from the table included with your results how the national distribution of answers to the questions compares with those of your students. We hope you will find the time to go through the questions with your students, and, particularly, those questions where they were not as successful as you might have hoped.

Note that over one fifth of the students overall chose option D for Question 1. If the outcome for your students was similar, this suggests that significantly many of them are not fully aware of the standard 'multiplication before addition' convention for evaluating expressions such as $2 + 0 + 1 \times 3$. This is discussed in more detail in the Extended Solutions which may be downloaded from our website. Please note that these also include suggestions for further investigations of some of the topics covered by the questions.

More than one in five of the students did not even guess an answer to Question 5. This is a high proportion of blank answers for such an early question. If your students responded in this way, is it because they are put off by algebra?

The answers to Questions 8, 11 and 14, were left blank by rather more pupils than is usual for the earlier questions. These are all geometry questions which a low percentage of students answered correctly. Is this an area of mathematics where your students lack skills and confidence?

More positively, it is good see how many students achieved very high marks. Please make sure that the achievement of your high-scoring students is widely recognized in your school or college.

The SMC marks

The profile of marks obtained is shown below.

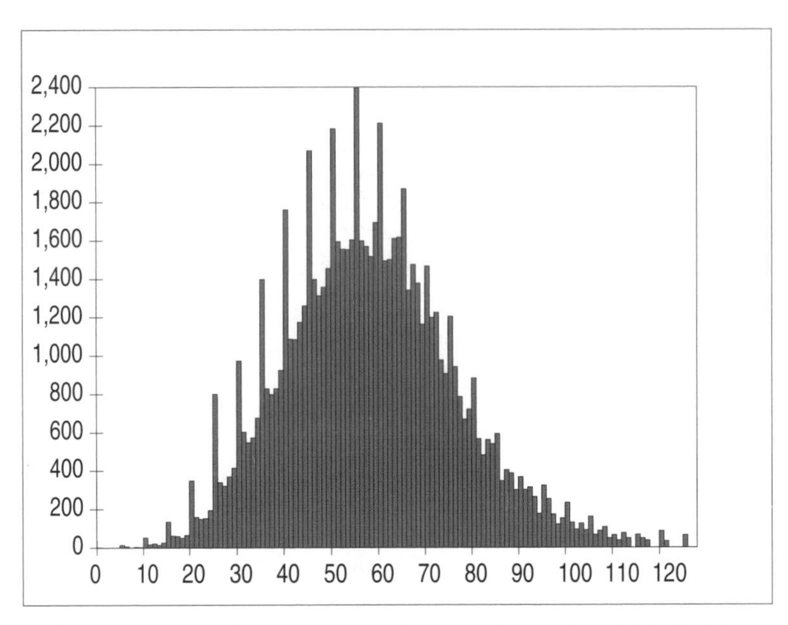

Bar chart showing the actual frequencies in the 2013 SMC

The average score increased significantly from 53 in 2012 to 58 in 2013.

Since 2012, the UKMT has awarded certificates to the top 60% of SMC students. On this basis the cut-off marks were set at

GOLD – 82 or over SILVER – 67 to 81 BRONZE – 53 to 66

Candidates who scored 100 or more were invited to take part in BMO 1 and those who scored 86 or more were invited to take part in the Senior Kangaroo.

A sample of one of the certificates is shown below.

THE UNITED KINGDOM SENIOR MATHEMATICAL CHALLENGE

The Senior Mathematical Challenge (SMC) is run by the UK Mathematics Trust. The SMC encourages mathematical reasoning, precision of thought, and fluency in using basic mathematical techniques to solve interesting problems. It is aimed at those in full-time education and with sufficient mathematical competence to undertake a post-16 course.

The problems on the SMC are designed to make students think. Most are accessible, yet still challenge those with more experience; they are also meant to be memorable and enjoyable.

Mathematics controls more aspects of the modern world than most people realise—from iPods, cash machines, telecommunications and airline booking systems to production processes in engineering, efficient distribution and stock-holding, investment strategies and 'whispering' jet engines. The scientific and industrial revolutions flowed from the realisation that mathematics was both the language of nature, and also a way of analysing—and hence controlling—our environment. In the last fifty years old and new applications of mathematical ideas have transformed the way we live.

All these developments depend on mathematical thinking—a mode of thought whose essential style is far more permanent than the wave of technological change which it has made possible. The problems on the SMC reflect this style, which pervades all mathematics, by encouraging students to think clearly about challenging problems.

The SMC was established as the National Mathematics Contest in 1961. In recent years there have been over 90,000 entries from around 2000 schools and colleges. Certificates are awarded to the highest scoring 60% of candidates (Gold : Silver : Bronze 1 : 2 : 3).

The UKMT is a registered charity. Please see our website www.ukmt.org.uk for more information. Donations to support our work would be gratefully received; a link for on-line donations is below.

www.donate.ukmt.org.uk

The next stages

Subject to certain conditions, candidates who obtained a score of 100 or over in the 2013 Senior Mathematical Challenge were invited to take the British Mathematical Olympiad Round One and those who scored from 86 to 99 were invited to take part in the Senior Kangaroo. It makes use of Kangaroo questions as well as a few others and is not a multiple choice paper but can be marked by character recognition as all the answers are three-digit numbers.

SENIOR 'KANGAROO' MATHEMATICAL CHALLENGE

Friday 29th November 2013

Organised by the United Kingdom Mathematics Trust

The Senior Kangaroo paper allows students in the UK to test themselves on questions set for the best school-aged mathematicians from across Europe and beyond.

RULES AND GUIDELINES (to be read before starting):

1. Do not open the paper until the Invigilator tells you to do so.
2. Time allowed: **1 hour**.
3. The use of rough paper is allowed; **calculators** and measuring instruments are **forbidden**.
4. **Use B or HB pencil only** to complete your personal details and record your answers on the machine-readable Answer Sheet provided. **All answers are written using three digits, from 000 to 999.** For example, if you think the answer to a question is 42, write 042 at the top of the answer grid and then code your answer by putting solid black pencil lines through the 0, the 4 and the 2 beneath.

   Please note that the machine that reads your Answer Sheet will only see the solid black lines through the numbers beneath, not the written digits above. You must ensure that you code your answers or you will not receive any marks. There are further instructions and examples on the Answer Sheet.
5. The paper contains 20 questions. Five marks will be awarded for each correct answer. There is no penalty for giving an incorrect answer.
6. The questions on this paper challenge you **to think**, not to guess. Though you will not lose marks for getting answers wrong, you will undoubtedly get more marks, and more satisfaction, by doing a few questions carefully than by guessing lots of answers.

Enquiries about the Senior Kangaroo should be sent to:

Maths Challenges Office, School of Maths Satellite,
University of Leeds, Leeds, LS2 9JT
Tel. 0113 343 2339
www.ukmt.org.uk

1. Adam, Bill and Carl have 30 sweets between them. Bill gives 5 sweets to Carl, Carl gives 4 sweets to Adam and Adam gives 2 sweets to Bill. Now each of them has the same number of sweets. How many sweets did Carl have initially?

2. An i-rectangle is defined to be a rectangle all of whose sides have integer length. Two i-rectangles are considered to be the same if they have the same side-lengths. The sum of the areas of all the different i-rectangles with perimeter 22 cm is A cm^2. What is the value of A?

3. Some historians claim that the ancient Egyptians used a rope with two knots tied in it to construct a right-angled triangle by joining the two ends of the rope and taking the vertices of the triangle to be at the two knots and at the join. The length of the rope shown is 60 m and one of the knots is at X, which is 15 m from one end of the rope. How many metres from the other end of the rope should the second knot be placed to be able to create a right-angled triangle with the right angle at X?

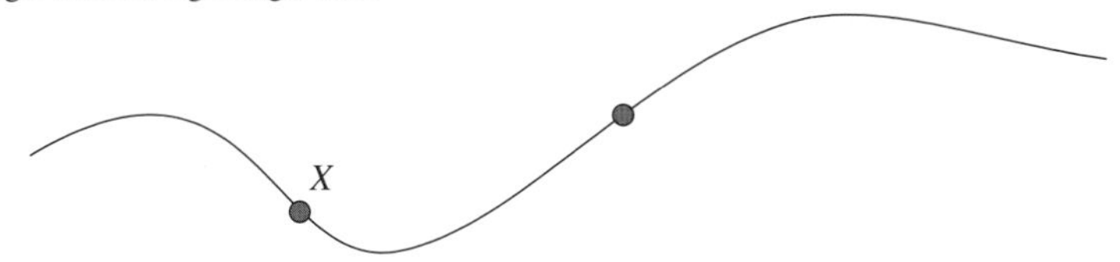

4. The height, width and length of a cube are multiplied by 2, 3 and 6 respectively to create a cuboid. The surface area of the cuboid is N times the surface area of the original cube. What is the value of N?

5. In a university admissions test, Dean gets exactly 10 of the first 15 questions correct. He then answers all the remaining questions correctly. Dean finds out he has answered 80% of all the questions correctly. How many questions are there on the test?

6. In the diagram, AE is divided into four equal parts and semicircles have been drawn with AE, AD and DE as diameters. This has created two new paths, an upper path and a lower path, from A to E. The ratio of the length of the upper path to the length of the lower path can be written as $a : b$ in its lowest terms. What is the value of $a + b$?

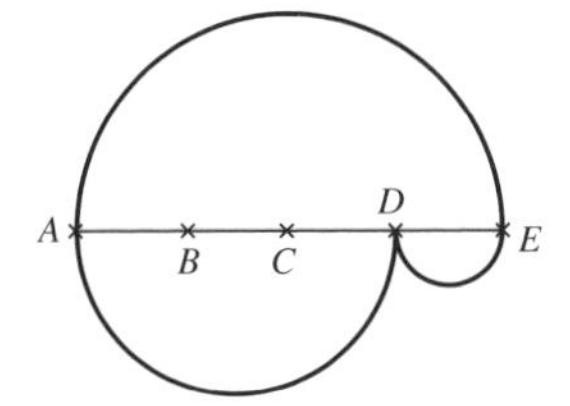

7. A mathematically skilful spider has spun a web and the lengths of some of the strands (which are all straight lines) are as shown in the diagram. It is known that x is an integer. What is the value of x?

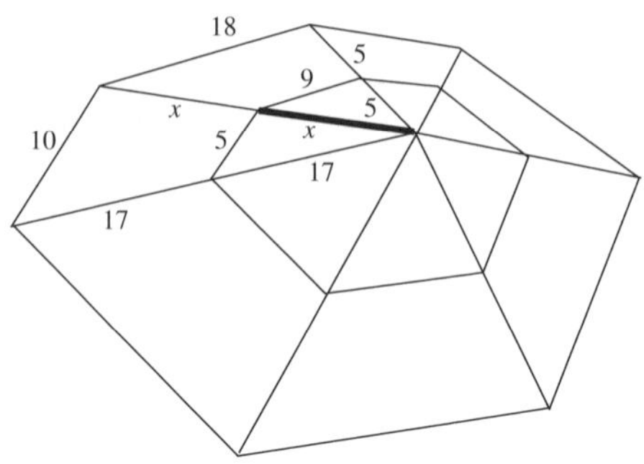

8. The square $ABCD$ has sides of length 1. All possible squares that share two vertices with $ABCD$ are drawn. The boundary of the region formed by the union of these squares is an irregular polygon. What is the area of this polygon?

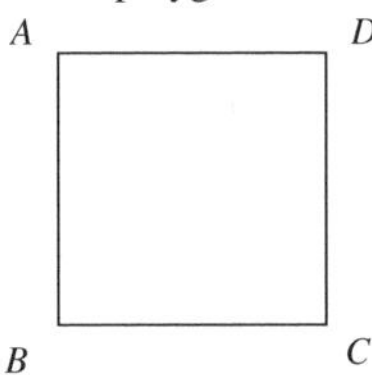

9. In triangle ABC, angle B is 25% smaller than angle C and 50% larger than angle A. What is the size in degrees of angle B?

10. In the equation $2^{m+1} + 2^m = 3^{n+2} - 3^n$, m and n are integers. What is the value of m?

11. The diagram shows two semicircles. The chord CD of the larger semicircle is parallel to AB, and touches the smaller semicircle. The length of CD is 32 m. The area of the shaded region is $k\pi$ m^2. What is the value of k?

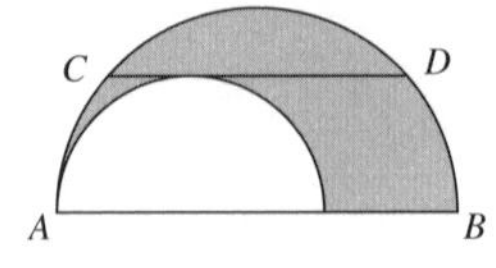

12. The sum of five consecutive integers is equal to the sum of the next three consecutive integers. What is the largest of these eight integers?

13. Zoe was born on her mother's 24th birthday so they share birthdays. Assuming they both live long lives, on how many birthdays will Zoe's age be a factor of her mother's age?

14. What is the largest three-digit integer that can be written in the form $n + \sqrt{n}$ where n is an integer?

15. How many integers a are there for which the roots of the quadratic equation $x^2 + ax + 2013 = 0$ are integers?

16. A sphere of radius 3 has its centre at the origin. How many points on the surface of the sphere have coordinates that are all integers?

17. The length of each side of the rhombus $PQRS$ is equal to the geometric mean of the lengths of its diagonals. What is the size in degrees of the obtuse angle PQR?

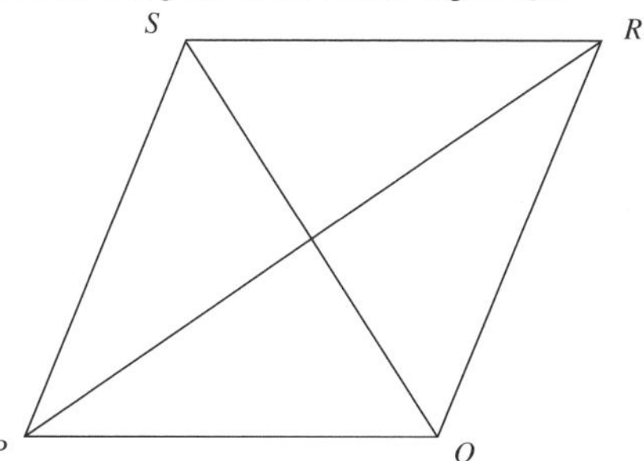

[The geometric mean of 2 values x_1 and x_2 is given by $\sqrt{x_1 x_2}$.]

18. How many of the first 2013 triangular numbers are multiples of 5?

19. The increasing sequence 1, 3, 4, 9, 10, 12, 13, … contains all the powers of 3 and all the numbers that can be written as the sum of two or more distinct powers of 3. What is the 70th number in the sequence?

20. Rachel and Nicky stand at either end of a straight track. They then run at constant (but different) speeds to the other end of the track, turn and run back to their original end at the same speed they ran before. On their first leg, they pass each other 20 m from one end of the track. When they are both on their return leg, they pass each other for a second time 10 m from the other end of the track. How many metres long is the track?

Further remarks

A solutions leaflet was provided.

SENIOR 'KANGAROO' MATHEMATICAL CHALLENGE

Friday 29th November 2013

Organised by the United Kingdom Mathematics Trust

SOLUTIONS

1. **9** There are 30 sweets in total so, since the boys all finish with the same number of sweets, they must then have $30 \div 3 = 10$ sweets. Carl gains 5 sweets from Bill and gives 4 sweets to Adam so has a net gain of 1 sweet. Since Carl finishes with 10 sweets, he must start with $10 - 1 = 9$ sweets.

2. **110** The perimeter of each *i*-rectangle is 22 cm. Therefore, the sum of the length and the width is 11 cm. All the sides of the *i*-rectangle are whole numbers so the possible *i*-rectangles are 1×10 with area 10 cm^2, 2×9 with area 18 cm^2, 3×8 with area 24 cm^2, 4×7 with area 28 cm^2 and 5×6 with area 30 cm^2. Hence the sum of the areas of all possible *i*-rectangles is $10 + 18 + 24 + 28 + 30 = 110$ cm^2. Therefore the value of A is 110.

3. **25** Let the distance of the second knot from the other end of the rope be d m.

This part of the rope will become the hypotenuse of the right-angled triangle so, on applying Pythagoras' Theorem, we have the equation $d^2 = 15^2 + (45 - d)^2$. Now expand the brackets to get $d^2 = 225 + 2025 - 90d + d^2$. This simplifies to $90d = 2250$, which has solution $d = 25$.

Hence the second knot is 25 m from the other end of the rope.

4. **12** Let each side of the original cube have length x so that the cube has surface area $6x^2$. Then the cuboid has side-lengths $2x$, $3x$ and $6x$, so has surface area $2 \times (2x \times 3x + 2x \times 6x + 3x \times 6x) = 72x^2$.

Hence the value of N is $72x^2 \div 6x^2 = 12$.

5. **25** Dean has answered 5 questions incorrectly so 5 questions must represent 20% of the questions. 20% is equivalent to $\frac{1}{5}$ so the total number of questions is $5 \times 5 = 25$.

6. **2** Let the length of AE be $4x$. Therefore, the lengths of AD and DE are $3x$ and x respectively. The length of the upper path is $\frac{1}{2} \times \pi \times 4x = 2\pi x$.
The length of the lower path is $\frac{1}{2} \times \pi \times 3x + \frac{1}{2} \times \pi \times x = 2\pi x$.

Therefore the ratio of the length of the upper path to the length of the lower path is 1 : 1. Hence the value of $a + b$ is 2.

7. **13** In any triangle, the length of the longest side is less than the sum of the lengths of the other two sides.

Apply this result (known as the triangle inequality) to the triangle BCD to obtain $x < 9 + 5$ or $x < 14$. In the same way, apply this result to triangle ABD to obtain $17 < x + 5$ or $x > 12$. But we are told that x is an integer and so $x = 13$.

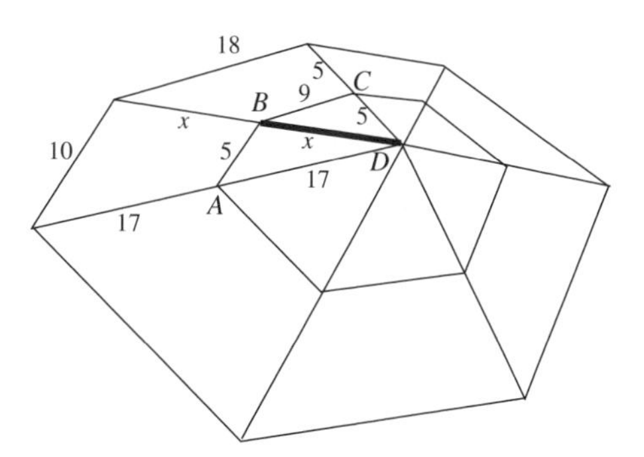

8. **7** In addition to the original square, four squares can be drawn that share two adjacent vertices of the original square and a further four squares can be drawn that share two opposite vertices of the original square. The union of these squares creates the octagon as shown.

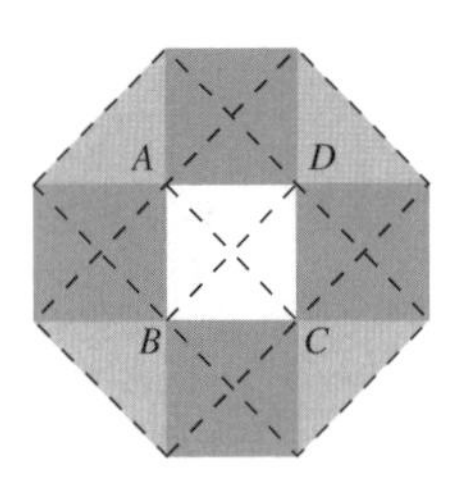

The octagon is made up of five squares of side 1 unit and four halves of a square of side 1 unit. Hence the area of the polygon is equal to $7 \times 1 \times 1 = 7$.

9. **60** Let the sizes of angles A, B and C be $a°$, $b°$ and $c°$ respectively.
From the question we have $b = 0.75 \times c$. Therefore $c = \frac{4}{3}b$.
Similarly we have $b = 1.5 \times a$. Therefore $a = \frac{2}{3}b$.
Angles in a triangle add up to 180°, so that we have $180 = \frac{2}{3}b + b + \frac{4}{3}b$, which means that $180 = 3b$. It follows that $b = 60$.

10. **3** Factorise both sides of the equation to get $2^m(2^1 + 1) = 3^n(3^2 - 1)$. Thus we have $2^m \times 3 = 3^n \times 8$ which is equivalent to $2^{m-3} = 3^{n-1}$. Since 2 and 3 have no factors in common other than 1, a power of 2 cannot equal a power of 3 unless both powers are zero when both sides of the equation equal 1. Therefore we have $m - 3 = 0$ and $n - 1 = 0$. Hence the value of m is 3 (and the value of n is 1).

11. **128** Let the radii of the larger and smaller semicircles be R and r respectively. Then the shaded area as $\frac{1}{2} \times \pi R^2 - \frac{1}{2} \times \pi r^2 = \frac{1}{2}\pi(R^2 - r^2)$.
Let X be the centre of the larger semicircle and let Y be the midpoint of CD. Since CD is parallel to AB then $XY = r$ and $\angle XYD = 90°$. Apply Pythagoras' Theorem to triangle XYD to give $R^2 = r^2 + 16^2$ or $R^2 - r^2 = 256$. Therefore the shaded area is $\frac{1}{2}\pi(R^2 - r^2) = 128\pi$. Hence the value of k is 128.

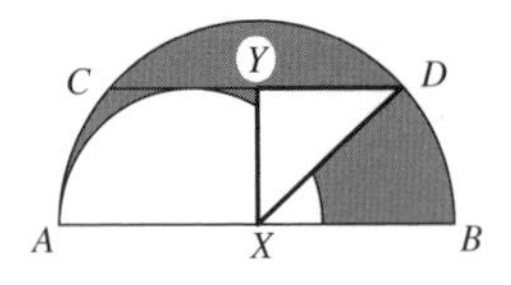

12. **11** Let the smallest number be n. From the information in the question, we obtain the equation

$$n + n + 1 + n + 2 + n + 3 + n + 4 = n + 5 + n + 6 + n + 7.$$

Therefore we get $5n + 10 = 3n + 18$, which has solution $n = 4$.
Hence the largest number is $4 + 7 = 11$.

13. **8** Let Zoe be x years old. Therefore, her mother's age is $x + 24$ years old. Now x divides $x + 24$ if and only if x divides 24. The positive factors of 24 are 1, 2, 3, 4, 6, 8, 12 and 24 and so Zoe's age is a factor of her mother's age on 8 birthdays, when her mother's age will be 25, 26, 27, 28, 30, 32, 36 and 48.

14. **992** Since $n + \sqrt{n}$ is an integer, n is a square number. The square numbers near 1000 are $30^2 = 900$, $31^2 = 961$ and $32^2 = 1024$. Clearly, if $n = 32^2$ then $n + \sqrt{n}$ is greater than 1000, so this is not possible. However, if $n = 31^2$, then $n + \sqrt{n} = 961 + 31 = 992$, which is less than 1000. Hence the largest three-digit integer than can be written in the given form is 992.

15. **8** If the equation $x^2 + ax + 2013 = 0$ has integer solutions, then it can be written in the form $(x + b)(x + c) = 0$ for integers b and c. This means that $bc = 2013$.
As the prime factorisation of 2013 is $3 \times 11 \times 61$, so the possible factor pairs of 2013 are 1 and 2013, 3 and 671, 11 and 183 and 33 and 61. However, these only take into account the cases when both b and c are positive and four further pairs are possible if both b and c are negative. Thus there are 8 distinct values of a, namely ±2014, ±674, ±194 and ±94.

16. 30 Let the coordinates of a relevant point on the sphere be (x, y, z). By the three-dimensional version of Pythagoras' Theorem, we have $x^2 + y^2 + z^2 = 3^2$. The only solutions for which x, y and z are positive integers are $(3, 0, 0)$ and $(1, 2, 2)$ in some order. There are $3 \times 2 = 6$ solutions based on the values $(3, 0, 0)$ as the 3 can go in any of the three positions and be either positive or negative. Similarly there are $3 \times 2 \times 2 \times 2 = 24$ solutions based on the values $(1, 2, 2)$ as the 1 can go in any of the three positions and all three of the values can independently be either positive or negative. This gives $6 + 24 = 30$ solutions in total.

17. 150 Let x be the length of a side of the rhombus and let a and b be the lengths of the two diagonals. The area of the rhombus is

$$\text{area}\,\Delta QRS + \text{area}\,\Delta PQS = \tfrac{1}{2}x^2 \sin \angle SRQ + \tfrac{1}{2}x^2 \sin \angle SPQ.$$

Opposite angles in a rhombus are equal so this simplifies to $x^2 \sin \angle SRQ$. However, the area of a rhombus can also be calculated in a similar way to a kite, i.e. half the product of the diagonals. This gives the equation $x^2 \sin \angle SRQ = \frac{1}{2}ab$. From the question, we know that $x = \sqrt{ab}$ so $x^2 = ab$. Hence $\sin \angle SRQ = \frac{1}{2}$ and so $\angle SRQ = 30°$. Lines SR and PQ are parallel and so, using co-interior angles, $\angle PQR + \angle SRQ = 180°$. This means $\angle PQR = 150°$.

18. 804 The triangular numbers are given by the formula $T_n = \frac{1}{2}n(n + 1)$. T_n is a multiple of 5 if, and only if, one of n or $n + 1$ is also a multiple of 5. This means that two triangular numbers in every group of 5 consecutive triangular numbers will be a multiple of 5. None of the numbers 2011, 2012, 2013 or 2014 is a multiple of 5 and so none of T_{2011}, T_{2012} or T_{2013} is a multiple of 5 either. Hence the number of multiples of 5 in the first 2013 triangular numbers is $2 \times \frac{2010}{5} = 804$.

19. 741 Consider the n numbers $3^0,\ 3^1,\ 3^2,\ \ldots,\ 3^{n-1}$. Using at most one of each of these in a sum, the number of totals we can create is $2^n - 1$ as each of the n numbers can either be included or excluded from the sum but at least one number must be included so the choice of excluding all the numbers is discounted (and they are all distinct). For $n = 6$, this is 63 and so the 64th number in the sequence will be $3^6 = 729$. Then the 70th term is equal to the 64th term + 6th term $= 729 + 12 = 741$.

20. 50 Let the distance Rachel runs before they first meet be x m. Let v_R and v_N be the respective speeds of Rachel and Nicky and let t_1 and t_2 be the times they take to get to their first and second passing points respectively (shown as P and Q on the diagram below).

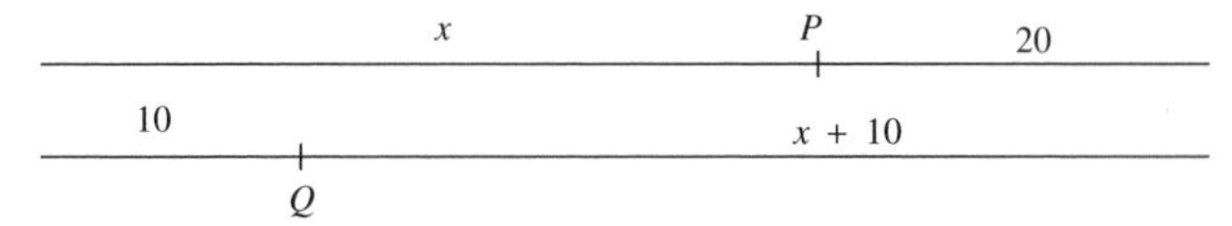

As distance = speed × time, we have the following equations:

$$x = v_R t_1 \text{ and } 20 = v_N t_1;\ 2x + 30 = v_R t_2 \text{ and } x + 30 = v_N t_2$$

where the first and second pair give the distances travelled by Rachel and Nicky from the start to P and Q respectively.

Divide each equation in the first set by the corresponding equation in the second set to eliminate v_R and v_N to obtain $\dfrac{x}{2x + 30} = \dfrac{t_1}{t_2} = \dfrac{20}{x + 30}$. Now multiply both sides by the common denominator $(x + 30)(2x + 30)$ to obtain $x(x + 30) = 20(2x + 30)$. This simplifies to $x^2 + 30x = 40x + 600$, i.e. $x^2 - 10x - 600 = 0$. This factorises to $(x - 30)(x + 20) = 0$ with solutions $x = 30$ and $x = -20$. As x is measuring a distance, it must be positive so $x = 30$. Hence the length of the track is $30 + 20 = 50$ m.

Certificates

These were awarded at two levels, Merit and Participation.

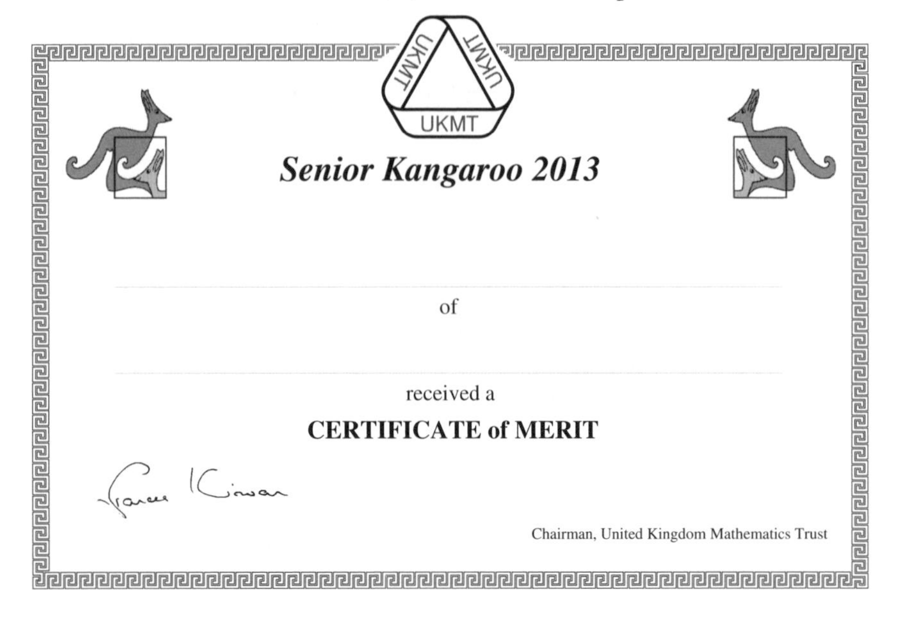

THE UKMT SENIOR KANGAROO

The Senior Kangaroo is one of the follow-on rounds for the Senior Mathematical Challenge (SMC) and is organised by the UK Mathematics Trust (UKMT). Around 3,000 high-scoring students in the SMC are invited to participate in the Senior Kangaroo and to test themselves on questions set for the best school-aged mathematicians from across Europe and beyond.

The Senior Kangaroo is a one-hour examination comprising 20 questions; all answers are written using 3 digits, from 000 to 999. The problems involve amusing and thought-provoking situations which require the use of logic as well as mathematical understanding.

The UKMT is a registered charity.
For more information please see our website www.ukmt.org.uk
Donations to support our work would be gratefully
received and can be made by visiting
www.donate.ukmt.org.uk

Mathematical Olympiad for Girls

The UK Mathematical Olympiad for Girls (UK MOG) is held annually to identify students to engage in training for EGMO. Students who are not involved in training are still eligible for selection for the team.

The 2013 MOG paper was held on 26th September. The time allowed was $2\frac{1}{2}$ hours. The question paper and solutions follow, and a list of 32 high scorers.

United Kingdom Mathematics Trust

UK Mathematical Olympiad for Girls
26 September 2013

Instructions

1. Do not turn over until told to do so.
2. Time allowed: $2\frac{1}{2}$ hours.
3. Full written solutions – not just answers – are required, with complete proofs of any assertions you may make.

   Marks awarded will depend on the clarity of your mathematical presentation. Work in rough first, and then write up your best attempt. Do not hand in rough work.
4. One complete solution will gain more credit than several unfinished attempts. It is more important to complete a small number of questions than to try all the problems.
5. Each question carries 10 marks. However, earlier questions tend to be easier. In general you are advised to concentrate on these problems first.
6. Some questions have two parts. Part (a) introduces results or ideas useful in solving part (b).
7. The use of rulers and compasses is allowed, but calculators and protractors are forbidden.
8. Start each question on a fresh sheet of paper. Write on one side of the paper only.

   On each sheet of working write the number of the question in the top left-hand corner and your name, initials and school in the top right-hand corner.
9. Complete the cover sheet provided and attach it to the front of your script, followed by your solutions in question number order.
10. Staple all the pages neatly together in the top left- hand corner.
11. To accommodate candidates sitting in other time zones, please do not discuss the paper on the internet until 08:00 BST on Friday 27th September.

1. The diagram shows three identical overlapping *right-angled* triangles, made of coloured glass, placed inside an equilateral triangle, one in each corner. The total area covered twice (dark grey) is equal to the area left uncovered (white).

   What fraction of the area of the equilateral triangle does one glass triangle cover?

2. *In triangle ABC, the median from A is the line AM, where M is the midpoint of the side BC. In any triangle, the three medians intersect at the point called the centroid, which divides each median in the ratio* 2 : 1.

   In the convex quadrilateral $ABCD$, the points A', B', C' and D' are the centroids of the triangles BCD, CDA, DAB and ABC, respectively.

   (a) By considering the triangle MCD, where M is the midpoint of AB, prove that $C'D'$ is parallel to DC and that $C'D' = \frac{1}{3}DC$.

   (b) Prove that the quadrilaterals $ABCD$ and $A'B'C'D'$ are similar.

3. (a) Find all positive integers a and b for which $a^2 - b^2 = 18$.

   (b) The diagram shows a sequence of points $P_0, P_1, P_2, P_3, P_4, \ldots$, which spirals out around the point O. For any point P in the sequence, the line segment joining P to the next point is perpendicular to OP and has length 3. The distance from P_0 to O is 29. What is the next value of n for which the distance from P_n to O is an integer?

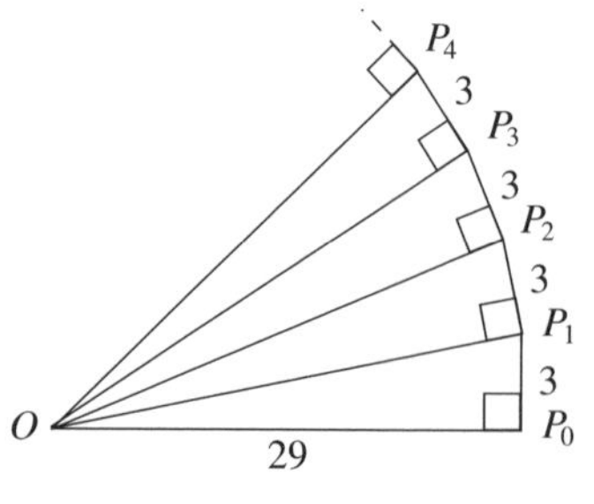

4. (a) An ant can move from any square on an 8×8 chessboard to an adjacent square. (Two squares are adjacent if they share a side).

   The ant starts in the top left corner and visits each square exactly once. Prove that it is impossible for the ant to finish in the bottom right corner.

   [*You may find it helpful to consider the chessboard colouring.*]

(b) A ladybird can move one square up, one square to the right, or one square diagonally down and left, as shown in the diagram, and cannot leave the board.

Is it possible for the ladybird to start in the bottom left corner of an 8×8 board, visit every square exactly once, and return to the bottom left corner?

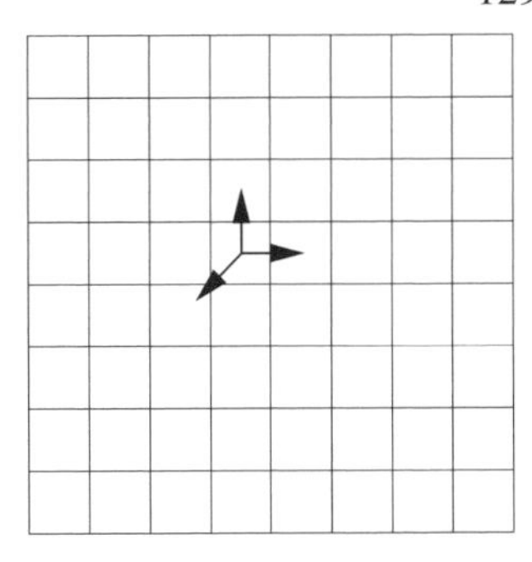

5. (a) Find an integer solution of the equation $x^3 + 6x - 20 = 0$ and prove that the equation has no other real solutions.

(b) Let x be $\sqrt[3]{\sqrt{108} + 10} - \sqrt[3]{\sqrt{108} - 10}$. Prove that x is equal to 2.

Time allowed: $2\frac{1}{2}$ hours

Mathematical Olympiad for Girls: Solutions

These are polished solutions and do not illustrate the process of failed ideas and rough work by which candidates may arrive at their own solutions. Some of the solutions include comments, which are intended to clarify the reasoning behind the selection of a particular method.

The mark allocation on Mathematics Olympiad papers is different from what you are used to at school. To get any marks, you need to make significant progress towards the solution. It is therefore important that you realise the importance of the rubric about trying to finish whole questions rather than attempting lots of disconnected parts.

3 or 4 marks roughly means that you had most of the relevant ideas, but were not able to link them into a coherent proof.

8 or 9 marks means that you have solved the problem, but have made a minor calculation error or have not explained your reasoning clearly enough. One question we often ask is: if we were to have the benefit of a two-minute interview with this candidate, could they correct the error or fill the gap?

Enquiries about the Mathematical Olympiad for Girls should be sent to: UKMT, School of Mathematics Satellite, University of Leeds, Leeds LS2 9JT. 0113 343 2339 enquiry@ukmt.org.uk

1. The diagram shows three identical overlapping *right-angled* triangles, made of coloured glass, placed inside an equilateral triangle, one in each corner. The total area covered twice (dark grey) is equal to the area left uncovered (white).

   What fraction of the area of the equilateral triangle does one glass triangle cover?

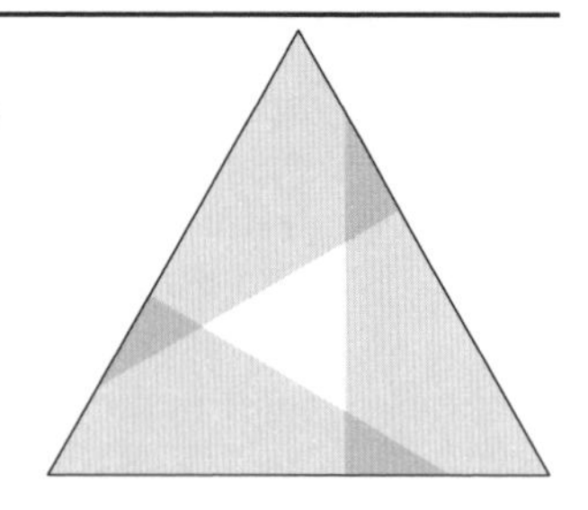

Solution

Commentary: It is possible to solve this problem by calculating the sides of the dark grey area and the glass triangles in terms of the side of the equilateral triangle. However, it turns out that we can find the ratio of areas without calculating the sides first.

Here is one possible argument: As the dark grey area is covered twice, if we 'take off' one layer and use it to cover the white area, then the whole equilateral triangle will be covered once. This means that the glass from all three glass triangles exactly covers the equilateral triangle, so one glass triangle covers one-third of the equilateral triangle. But is this explanation mathematically rigorous? To make it clearer, it is very useful to give names and labels to the important quantities in the question.

Denote the whole area by E, the area of one glass triangle by T, the white area by W, one light grey part by A and one dark grey part by B.

From the given information, we have $W = 3B$.

From the diagram, we have $E = W + 3A + 3B$ and $T = A + 2B$. Using the given information, we get $E = 3A + 6B$, and now we see that $T = \frac{1}{3}E$.

So one glass triangle covers one third of the area of the equilateral triangle.

Alternative

Let E be the whole area, T the area of one glass triangle, D the dark grey area, and W the white area.

Since each dark grey area is covered twice, $E = 3T - D + W$.

But from the information given $D = W$, so $T = \frac{1}{3}E$.

2. *In triangle ABC, the median from A is the line AM , where M is the midpoint of the side BC. In any triangle, the three medians intersect at the point called the centroid, which divides each median in the ratio* 2 : 1.

   In the convex quadrilateral $ABCD$, the points A', B', C' and D' are the centroids of the triangles BCD, CDA, DAB and ABC, respectively.

   (a) By considering the triangle MCD, where M is the midpoint of AB, prove that $C'D'$ is parallel to DC and that $C'D' = \frac{1}{3}DC$.

   (b) Prove that the quadrilaterals $ABCD$ and $A'B'C'D'$ are similar.

Solution

Commentary: When a diagram is not given in the question it is always worth drawing one, if only to have something you can refer to in your explanation. The purpose of a diagram is to convey information, so be sure to draw diagrams clearly, don't make them too small, and label them carefully.

(a) We are given that M is the midpoint of AB, so that CM is a median of triangle ABC. Since D' is the centroid of triangle ABC, it lies on CM, and $CD' : D'M = 2 : 1$. Similarly, $DC' : C'M = 2 : 1$. This means that $MD' = MC$ and $MC' = MD$, so the triangles MCD and $MD'C'$ have two pairs of sides in the same ratio, namely 3 : 1. The angle CMD is also common to both triangles. Hence the triangles are similar (they have two pairs of sides in the same ratio and the angles between those sides are equal).

It follows that the third sides are also in the ratio 3 : 1, so that $C'D' = \frac{1}{3}DC$, as required. Furthermore, corresponding angles in the two triangles are equal, so that $\angle MD'C' = \angle MCD$. We conclude that $C'D'$ and DC are parallel.

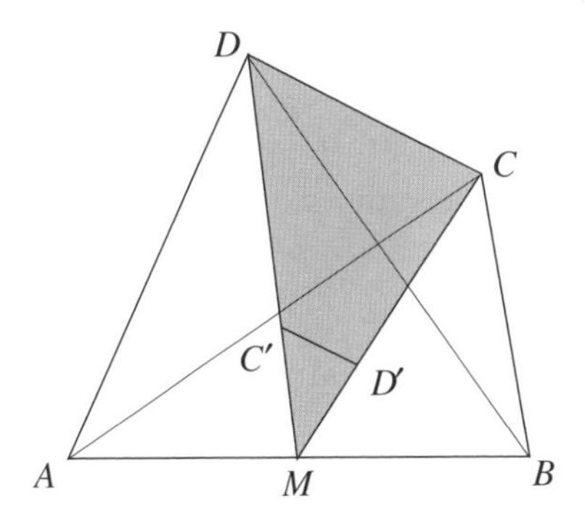

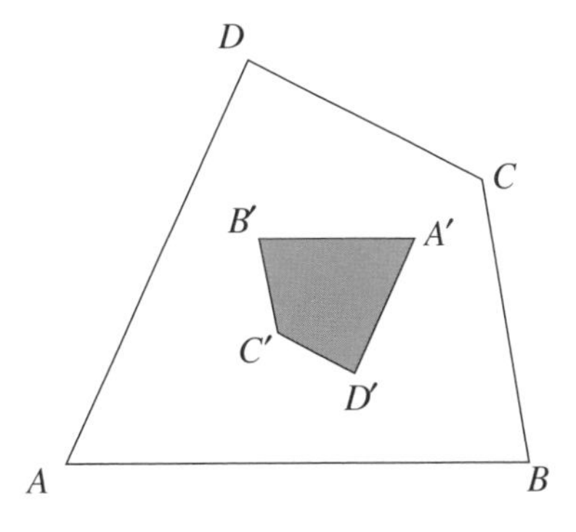

(b) *Commentary*: How can we prove that two quadrilaterals are similar? There are some tests for similar triangles, such as AAA, but do they work for quadrilaterals? For example, two rectangles have all corresponding angles equal, but they are not necessarily similar. It is helpful, therefore, to recall the definition of similar figures. Loosely speaking, two figures are similar if they are of the same shape, but of different sizes. More precisely, two figures are similar if all pairs of corresponding sides are in the same ratio, *and* all pairs of corresponding angles are equal.

We proved in part (a) that $D'C'$ is parallel to CD. Similarly, $D'A'$ is parallel to AD. Hence $\angle A'D'C' = \angle ADC$. It can be shown analogously that the other corresponding angles in the two quadrilaterals are equal. Also from part (a), the corresponding sides of the two quadrilaterals are all in the ratio 3 : 1. Hence the two quadrilaterals are similar.

Remarks: The result still holds when $ABCD$ is not convex, or even if it is self-intersecting.

---

3. (a) Find all positive integers a and b for which $a^2 - b^2 = 18$.

   (b) The diagram shows a sequence of points $P_0, P_1, P_2, P_3, P_4, \ldots$, which spirals out around the point O. For any point P in the sequence, the line segment joining P to the next point is perpendicular to OP and has length 3. The distance from P_0 to O is 29. What is the next value of n for which the distance from P_n to O is an integer?

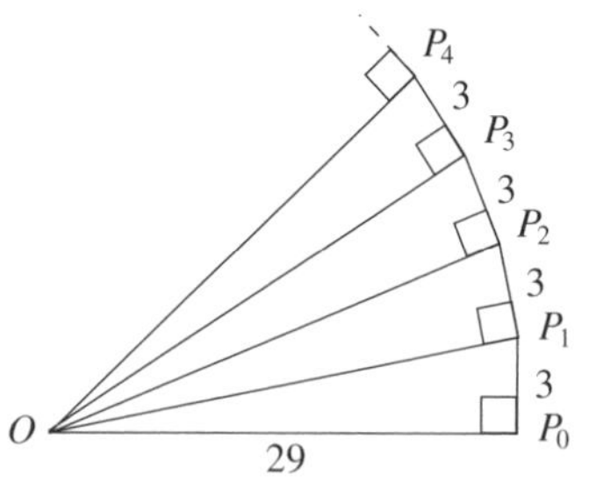

Solution

(a) Notice that the left-hand side is a difference of two squares and hence can be factorised as $(a - b)(a + b)$. We are looking for integer solutions, so that $a - b$ and $a + b$ have to be factors of 18. Since a and b are positive, and $a^2 > b^2$, it follows that $a - b$ and $a + b$ are both positive, and $a + b > a - b$. Hence we need to consider only the following three possibilities:

$$a - b = 1 \text{ and } a + b = 18; \quad \text{or} \quad a - b = 2 \text{ and } a + b = 9; \quad \text{or} \quad a - b = 3 \text{ and } a + b = 6.$$

Solving each pair of simultaneous equations, we get

$$a = \tfrac{19}{2}, b = \tfrac{17}{2} \text{ or } a = \tfrac{11}{2}, b = \tfrac{7}{2} \text{ or } a = \tfrac{9}{2}, b = \tfrac{3}{2}.$$

Since none of the solutions are integers, the original equation has no solutions when a and b are positive integers.

Alternative: It is in fact not necessary to consider all possible factors of 18. Notice that $a - b$ and $a + b$ differ by an even number ($2b$), so they are either both odd or both even. Since their product is 18 they both have to be even. But then their product would be a multiple of 4, which 18 is not. Hence the equation has no solutions.

(b) *Commentary*: We are interested in an expression for OP_n, so consider the first few points:

$$OP_1^2 = 29^2 + 3^2$$

$$OP_2^2 = OP_1^2 + 3^2 = 29^2 + 2 \times 3^2$$

$$OP_3^2 = OP_2^2 + 3^2 = 29^2 + 3 \times 3^2$$

This suggests that $OP_n^2 = 29^2 + n \times 3^2$. Noticing the squares in this equation, and remembering that factorising the difference of two squares was a useful idea in part (a), we are tempted to rewrite this equation in the form $OP_n^2 - 29^2 = 9n$.
We have $OP^2 = 29^2 + 3^2$ and $OP_n^2 = OP_{n-1}^2 + 3^2$, so $OP_n^2 = 29^2 + n \times 3^2$.

Commentary: If we were being really careful, we would use mathematical induction to prove the last assertion.

Therefore

$$OP_n^2 - 29^2 = 9n.$$

Write $OP_n = K$, where K is an integer. Our equation becomes

$$(K - 29)(K + 29) = 9n,$$

for some positive integer K.

Commentary: Since we do not know what n is, we cannot write out all possible factorisations of $9n$. However, we can think about factors of 9. One possibility is that both the factors $(K - 29)$ and $(K + 29)$ are multiples of 3. But they differ by 58, which is not a multiple of 3, so this situation is impossible. It follows that one of these factors is a multiple of 9. (This is a similar argument to that used in the alternative solution to part (a). Notice that they cannot both be multiples of 9, since they differ by 58.)

Now 58 is not a multiple of 3, so $K - 29$ and $K + 29$ cannot both be multiples of 3. Therefore either 9 divides $K - 29$ or 9 divides $K + 29$. We also know that $K > 29$, because $OP_n > OP_0$.

Suppose that 9 divides $K - 29$. In this case the least possible value of K is 38, leading to $n = 67$.

Suppose instead that 9 divides $K + 29$. In that case the least possible value of K is 34, leading to $n = 35$.

So the next value of n for which OP_n is an integer is 35.

---

4. (a) An ant can move from any square on an 8×8 chessboard to an adjacent square. (Two squares are adjacent if they share a side).

   The ant starts in the top left corner and visits each square exactly once. Prove that it is impossible for the ant to finish in the bottom right corner.

   [*You may find it helpful to consider the chessboard colouring.*]

   (b) A ladybird can move one square up, one square to the right, or one square diagonally down and left, as shown in the diagram, and cannot leave the board.

   Is it possible for the ladybird to start in the bottom left corner of an 8×8 board, visit every square exactly once, and return to the bottom left corner?

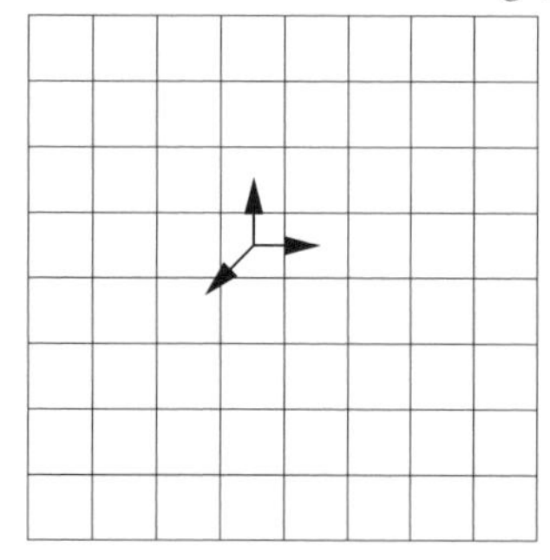

Solution

(a) *Commentary*: The question suggests that we consider a chessboard colouring, but how does that help? Each square on a chessboard has one of two colours, black or white, and adjacent squares have different colours. This means that the ant always moves from a square of one colour to a square of the other colour. This in turn tells us something about the colours of the start and end squares, depending on how many moves the ant makes.

Consider the colours of the squares on the board.

Each move changes the colour and there are 63 moves, so the start and end squares have different colours.

But the top left corner and the bottom right corner have the same colour. Hence the bottom right corner cannot be the final square.

(b) *Commentary*: Part (a) suggests that looking at the colour of the squares may be useful. However, if we just colour the squares black and white, then the up and right moves are onto a different colour, but the diagonal move is onto the same colour. Since there are three types of move, it seems sensible to use three colours, and ensure that every move changes the colour of the square.

Consider a colouring with three colours (red, blue, green, represented by R,B,G), in which all the squares in a diagonal stripe (running from top left to bottom right) have the same colour, but squares in adjacent stripes have different colours (see diagram).

R	B	G	R	B	G	R	B
G	R	B	G	R	B	G	R
B	G	R	B	G	R	B	G
R	B	G	R	B	G	R	B
G	R	B	G	R	B	G	R
B	G	R	B	G	R	B	G
R	B	G	R	B	G	R	B
G	R	B	G	R	B	G	R

Then the ladybird always moves from green to red, from red to blue and from blue to green. To return to the starting square (which is green) she needs to make 64 moves. But the moves which end on a green square are the moves numbered 3, 6, 9, and so on. Since 64 is not a multiple of 3, the final move cannot be onto a green square.

Alternative:

Suppose that the ladybird makes a tour starting and ending in the bottom left corner.

Let u, r and d be the numbers of each type of move (up, right and diagonal, respectively). Because she returns to the starting point the number of moves right must equal the number of moves left. But the only moves left are the diagonal ones, so $r = d$. Similarly, $u = d$.

Hence the total number of moves is $u + r + d = 3d$ which cannot equal 64, and thus the required tour is impossible.

---

5. (a) Find an integer solution of the equation $x^3 + 6x - 20 = 0$ and prove that the equation has no other real solutions.

   (b) Let x be $\sqrt[3]{\sqrt{108} + 10} - \sqrt[3]{\sqrt{108} - 10}$. Prove that x is equal to 2.

Solution

(a) *Commentary*: Any integer solution of this equation has to be a factor of 20. This is because, if we write the equation in factorised form, the product of the constant terms will be −20. So we can find the solution by trying some factors of 20.

A direct check shows that $x = 2$ satisfies the equation. Therefore the cubic expression can be factorised as $(x - 2)(x^2 + bx + c)$. Comparing coefficients gives $x^3 + 6x - 20 = (x - 2)(x^2 + 2x + 10)$.

Hence any other solution of the equation satisfies $x^2 + 2x + 10 = 0$. But the discrimant of this quadratic is $22 - 4 \times 1 \times 10$ which is negative, so there are no other real solutions.

(b) *Commentary*: Since x involves cube roots, it seems like a good idea to consider x^3. Moreover, the part (a) involved a cubic equation with root $x = 2$, so we can hope to find a connection between the two. It is certainly helpful here to know the expansion

$$(a - b)^3 = a^3 - 3a^2b + 3ab^2 - b^3.$$

Setting $a = \sqrt[3]{\sqrt{108} + 10}$ and $b = \sqrt[3]{\sqrt{108} - 10}$ we can use this to find an expression for x^3. The terms a^2b and ab^2 require some thought; for example,

$$\begin{aligned}(\sqrt{108} + 10)^2(\sqrt{108} - 10) &= \left(\sqrt{108}^2 - 10^2\right)\left(\sqrt{108} + 10\right)\\ &= 8\left(\sqrt{108} + 10\right).\end{aligned}$$

However, we can make the working neater by using the fact that $(a - b)^3 = a^3 - b^3 - 3ab(a - b)$.

Let $a = \sqrt[3]{\sqrt{108} + 10}$ and $b = \sqrt[3]{\sqrt{108} - 10}$. Then

$$a - b = x$$

$$a^3 - b^3 = (\sqrt{108} + 10) - (\sqrt{108} - 10) = 20$$

$$\text{and } ab = \sqrt[3]{(\sqrt{108} + 10)(\sqrt{108} - 10)} = \sqrt[3]{108 - 10^2} = 2.$$

Hence $x^3 = (a - b)^3 = a^3 - b^3 - 3ab(a - b) = 20 - 6x$, which is equivalent to $x + 6x - 20 = 0$. Since we have proved in part (a) that this equation has only one real solution, it follows that $x = 2$.

British Mathematical Olympiads

Within the UKMT, the British Mathematical Olympiad Subtrust has control of the papers and everything pertaining to them. The BMOS produces an annual account of its events which, for 2013-2014, was edited by James Aaronson (of Trinity College, Cambridge) and Tim Hennock. Much of this report is included in the following pages.

United Kingdom Mathematics Trust

British Mathematical Olympiad

Round 1 : Friday, 29 November 2013

Time allowed *Three and a half hours.*

Instructions

- *Full written solutions – not just answers – are required, with complete proofs of any assertions you may make. Marks awarded will depend on the clarity of your mathematical presentation. Work in rough first, and then write up your best attempt.*

  Do not hand in rough work.
- *One* **complete** *solution will gain more credit than several unfinished attempts. It is more important to complete a small number of questions than to try all the problems.*
- *Each question carries 10 marks. However, earlier questions tend to be easier. In general you are advised to concentrate on these problems first.*
- *The use of rulers, set squares and compasses is allowed, but calculators and protractors are forbidden.*
- *Start each question on a fresh sheet of paper. Write on one side of the paper only. On each sheet of working write the number of the question in the top* **left***-hand corner and your name, initials and school in the top* **right***-hand corner.*
- *Complete the cover sheet provided and attach it to the front of your script, followed by your solutions in question number order.*
- *Staple all the pages neatly together in the top* **left***- hand corner.*
- *To accommodate candidates sitting in other time zones, please do not discuss the paper on the internet until 8am GMT on Saturday 30 November.*

Do not turn over until told to do so.

United Kingdom Mathematics Trust

2013/14 British Mathematical Olympiad
Round 1: Friday, 29 November 2013

1. Calculate the value of

$$\frac{2014^4 + 4 \times 2013^4}{2013^2 + 4027^2} - \frac{2012^4 + 4 \times 2013^4}{2013^2 + 4025^2}.$$

2. In the acute-angled triangle ABC, the foot of the perpendicular from B to CA is E. Let l be the tangent to the circle ABC at B. The foot of the perpendicular from C to l is F. Prove that EF is parallel to AB.

3. A number written in base 10 is a string of 3^{2013} digit 3s. No other digit appears. Find the highest power of 3 which divides this number.

4. Isaac is planning a nine-day holiday. Every day he will go surfing, or water skiing, or he will rest. On any given day he does just one of these three things. He never does different water-sports on consecutive days. How many schedules are possible for the holiday?

5. Let ABC be an equilateral triangle, and P be a point inside this triangle. Let D, E and F be the feet of the perpendiculars from P to the sides BC, CA and AB respectively. Prove that

   a) $AF + BD + CE = AE + BF + CD$, and

   b) $[APF] + [BPD] + [CPE] = [APE] + [BPF] + [CPD]$.

   The area of triangle XYZ is denoted by $[XYZ]$.

6. The angles A, B and C of a triangle are measured in degrees, and the lengths of the opposite sides are a, b and c respectively. Prove that

$$60 \leqslant \frac{aA + bB + cC}{a + b + c} < 90.$$

The British Mathematical Olympiad 2013-2014

The Round 1 paper was marked by volunteers in December. Below is a list of the prize winners.

Round 1 Prize Winners

The following contestants were awarded prizes:

Gold Medals

Joe Benton	St Paul's School, Barnes, London
Jacob Coxon	Magdalen College School, Oxford
George Fortune	Priestley College, Warrington
Tsz Hin Fung	Colchester Royal Grammar School
Gabriel Gendler	Queen Elizabeth's School, Barnet
Qiang Ha	Ruthin School, Denbighshire
Frank Han	Dulwich College, London
Lawrence Hollom	Churcher's College, Hampshire
Liam Hughes	Robert Smyth Academy, Market Harborough, Leics
Freddie Illingworth	Magdalen College School, Oxford
Warren Li	Fulford School, York
Tian Bei Li	Concord College, Shrewsbury
Jared Low Jia Yi	Anglo-Chinese School, Singapore
Ramsay Pyper	Eton College, Windsor
Ashkat Sarkeev	Caterham School, Surrey
Wu Shengyang	Anglo-Chinese School, Singapore
Eloise Thuey	Caistor Grammar School, Lincs
Harvey Yau	Ysgol Dyffryn Taf, Carmarthenshire

Silver medals:

Olivia Aaronson	St Paul's Girls' School, Hammersmith
Rosie Cates	Perse School, Cambridge
Wan Fung Chui	West Island School (ESF), Hong Kong
Madhi Elango	Queen Elizabeth's School, Barnet
Ben Grant	Tapton School, Sheffield
Jongheon Jeon	Winchester College
Tomoka Kan	St Paul's Girls' School, Hammersmith
Andrew Kenyon-Roberts	Aberdeen Grammar School
Edward Kirkby	Alton College, Hampshire
Samuel Kittle	Simon Langton Boys' Grammar School
Tim Lennox	King Edward VII School, Sheffield

Jiani Li	Ruthin School, Denbighshire
Changshuo Liu	Anglo-Chinese School, Singapore
Akuan Liu	The Cherwell School, Oxford
Chen Lu	Eton College, Windsor
Roi Makov	Winchester College
Bhavik Mehta	Queen Elizabeth's School, Barnet
Harry Metrebian	Winchester College
Conor Murphy	Eltham College, London
Neel Nanda	Latymer School, London
Rachel Newhouse	Skipton Girls' High School, N. Yorks
Marcus Roberts	The Grammar School at Leeds
Andrew Ronan	Rickmansworth School, Herts
Hoseong Seo	Perse School, Cambridge
Marius Tirlea	Woking College, Surrey
Harvey Uy	British School Manila, Phillipines
Kavin Vijayakumar	Bancroft's School, Essex
Phi Bang Vo	Ashbourne Independent College, London
Yiqin Wang	Davies Laing and Dick College, London
Adam Weller	Reading School
Jessica Yung	Westminster School
Danshu Zhang	Eltham College, London

Bronze medals:

Samuel Banks	King Henry VIII School, Coventry
Oliver Bel	Loreto College, Manchester
Samuel Bodansky	The Grammar School at Leeds
Clement Chan	King Edward's School, Birmingham
Alex Cooke	South Island School, Hong Kong
Michael Cui	Magdalen College School, Oxford
Zipeng Fu	Cambridge International Exam Centre in Shanghai Experimental School
Joshua Garfinkel	Latymer School, London
Esteban Gomezllata	Ibstock Place School, Roehampton, Surrey
Harry Goodburn	Wilson's School, Surrey
Quanzhen Guo	Ashbourne Independent College, London
Alex Harris	Perse School, Cambridge
Curtis Ho	Harrow School
Vo Hoang Khai	Anglo-Chinese School, Singapore
Edward Ingram	St George's School, Harpenden
Soomin Jang	Badminton School, Bristol

Ben Jarman	Ryde School with Upper Chine, Isle of Wight
Julie Jouas	Marymount International School, Kingston-upon-Thames
Suyi Li	Langley Grammar School, Berkshire
Norman MacGregor	Bell Baxter High School, Fife
William Manson	The Henley College, Oxon
William Mateer	Norton Hill School, Bath
Callum McLean	Harrow School
Arkan Megraoui	Woodhouse College, London
Yuen Ng	Rainham Mark Grammar School, Gillingham
Philip Peters	Haberdashers' Aske's School for Boys, Herts
Noah Porcelli	The Cherwell School, Oxford
Linden Ralph	Hills Road VI Form College, Cambridge
Alice Rao	Royal High School, Bath
Bryony Richards	South Wilts Grammar School, Salisbury
Katya Richards	School of St Helen and St Katharine
Morgan Rogers	Shrewsbury VI Form College
Liangchao Shi	Abbey College, Cambridge
Alex Song	St Olave's Grammar School, Kent
Hugo Strauss	Harrogate Grammar School, N. Yorks
Alan Sun	City of London School
Juliana Tang	King Edward's School, Bath
Chris Turner	Sir William Borlase's Grammar School, Buckinghamshire
Zuyu Wang	Dalian No. 24 Senior High School, China
Kasia Warburton	Reigate Grammar School, Surrey
Clifford Wilmot	Kingston Grammar School, Surrey
Zimo Yang	Charterhouse, Godalming, Surrey
Yang Yaqiao	RDFZ, Beijing
Yatkwan Yeung	Colchester Royal Grammar School
Gloria Yin	St Paul's Girls' School, Hammersmith
Bohan Yu	The Cherwell School, Oxford
Gao Yuan	Anglo-Chinese School, Singapore
Yiteng (Ayden) Zhang	Wuxi Number 1 High School, China
Daniel Zhang	King Edward VI School, Southampton
Tingqu Zhou	Ruthin School, Denbighshire

United Kingdom Mathematics Trust

British Mathematical Olympiad

Round 2: Thursday, 30 January 2014

Time allowed *Three and a half hours.*

Each question is worth 10 marks.

Instructions

- *Full written solutions – not just answers – are required, with complete proofs of any assertions you may make. Marks awarded will depend on the clarity of your mathematical presentation. Work in rough first, and then draft your final version carefully before writing up your best attempt.*

  Rough work **should** *be handed in, but should be clearly marked.*
- *One or two* **complete** *solutions will gain far more credit than partial attempts at all four problems.*
- *The use of rulers and compasses is allowed, but calculators and protractors are forbidden.*
- *Staple all the pages neatly together in the top* **left**-*hand corner, with questions 1, 2, 3, 4 in order, and the cover sheet at the front.*
- To accommodate candidates sitting in other time zones, please do not discuss any aspect of the paper on the internet until 8am GMT on Friday 31 January.

  In early March, twenty students eligible to represent the UK at the International Mathematical Olympiad will be invited to attend the training session to be held at Trinity College, Cambridge (3-7 April). At the training session, students sit a pair of IMO-style papers and eight students will be selected for further training. Those selected will be expected to participate in further correspondence work and to attend further training sessions. The UK Team of six for this summer's International Mathematical Olympiad (to be held in Cape Town, South Africa, 3-13 July 2014) will then be chosen.

Do not turn over until told to do so.

United Kingdom Mathematics Trust

2013/14 British Mathematical Olympiad
Round 2: Thursday, 30 January 2014

1. Every diagonal of a regular polygon with 2014 sides is coloured in one of n colours. Whenever two diagonals cross in the interior, they are of different colours. What is the minimum value of n for which this is possible?

2. Prove that it is impossible to have a cuboid for which the volume, the surface area and the perimeter are numerically equal.
   The perimeter of a cuboid is the sum of the lengths of all its twelve edges.

3. Let $a_0 = 4$ and define a sequence of terms using the formula $a_n = a_{n-1}^2 - a_{n-1}$ for each positive integer n.
   a) Prove that there are infinitely many prime numbers which are factors of at least one term in the sequence.
   b) Are there infinitely many prime numbers which are factors of no term in the sequence?

4. Let ABC be a triangle and P be a point in its interior. Let AP meet the circumcircle of ABC again at A'. The points B' and C' are similarly defined. Let O_A be the circumcentre of BCP. The circumcentres O_B and O_C are similarly defined. Let O'_A be the circumcentre of $B'C'P$. The circumcentres O'_B and O'_C are similarly defined. Prove that the lines $O_AO'_A$, $O_BO'_B$ and $O_CO'_C$ are concurrent.

The British Mathematical Olympiad 2013-2014
Round 2

The second round of the British Mathematical Olympiad was held on Thursday 30th January 2014. Some of the top scorers from this round were invited to a residential course at Trinity College, Cambridge.

Leading Scorers

39	Linden Ralph	Hills Road VI Form College, Cambridge
38	Freddie Illingworth	Magdalen College School, Oxford
	Chen Lu	Eton College, Windsor
	Harvey Yau	Ysgol Dyffryn Taf, Carmarthenshire
37	Joe Benton	St Paul's School, Barnes, London
	Andrew Kenyon-Roberts	Aberdeen Grammar School
34	Changshuo Liu	Anglo-Chinese School, Singapore
	Katya Richards	School of St Helen and St Katharine
33	Harry Metrebian	Winchester College
32	Edward Kirkby	Alton College, Hampshire
	Ramsay Pyper	Eton College, Windsor
30	Olivia Aaronson	St Paul's Girls' School, Hammersmith
	Liam Hughes	Robert Smyth Academy, Market Harborough
	Samuel Kittle	Simon Langton Boys' Grammar School
	Neel Nanda	Latymer School, London
29	Esteban Gomezllata	Ibstock Place School, Roehampton
	Ben Grant	Tapton School, Sheffield
	Warren Li	Fulford School, York
	Askhat Sarkeev	Caterham School, Surrey
	Adam Weller	Reading School
28	James Davies	Fearnhill School, Letchworth
	Gareth Jones	Clifton College, Bristol
27	Gabriel Gendler	Queen Elizabeth's School, Barnet
25	Callum McLean	Harrow School

IMO 2014

The 2014 International Mathematical Olympiad took place in Cape Town, South Africa from 3 - 13 July 2014. The Team Leader was Dr Geoff Smith (University of Bath) and the Deputy Leader was Dominic Yeo (Worcester College, Oxford). A full account of the 2014 IMO and the UK preparation for it appears later in the book. The members of the team were Joe Benton, Gabriel Gendler, Frank Zhenyu Han, Freddie Illingworth, Warren Li and Harvey Yau. The first reserve was Neel Nanda. In addition to the Leader and Deputy Leader, the team were accompanied by Jill Parker, formerly of the University of Bath, to deal with pastoral aspects.

Introduction to the BMO problems and full solutions

The ‘official’ solutions are the result of many hours' work by a large number of people, and have been subjected to many drafts and revisions. The contestants' solutions included here will also have been redrafted several times by the contestants themselves, and also shortened and cleaned up somewhat by the editors. As such, they do not resemble the first jottings, failed ideas and discarded pages of rough work with which any solution is started.

Before looking at the solutions, pupils (and teachers) are encouraged to make a concerted effort to attack the problems themselves. Only by doing so is it possible to develop a feel for the question, to understand where the difficulties lie and why one method of attack is successful while others may fail. Problem solving is a skill that can only be learnt by practice; going straight to the solutions is unlikely to be of any benefit.

It is also important to bear in mind that solutions to Olympiad problems are not marked for elegance. A solution that is completely valid will receive a full score, no matter how long and tortuous it may be. However, elegance has been an important factor influencing our selection of contestants' answers.

Further, from this year, there was a new annual prize available to entrants of BMO2, in memory of Christopher Bradley. This award, known as the ‘Christopher Bradley elegance prize’, is awarded to the candidate or candidates who, in the opinion of the markers, submitted the most elegant solution or solutions. The Christopher Bradley elegance prize was awarded this year to Edward Kirkby (of Alton College) and Linden Ralph (of Hills Road VI Form College) for their solutions to problem 4.

BMO Round 1 – Questions and Solutions

1. Calculate the value of

$$\frac{2014^4 + 4 \times 2013^4}{2013^2 + 4027^2} - \frac{2012^4 + 4 \times 2013^4}{2013^2 + 4025^2}.$$

(Proposed by Andrew Jobbings)

The key to this problem was to realise that one could write the whole expression in terms of a single 'variable', 2013 (or, equivalently, 2012 or 2014). Once the expression is in an algebraic form it is much more natural to expand out the terms and simplify. We present two ways in which the resulting expression can be shown to vanish.

Solution 1 by Eoghan McDowell, Silverdale School: Let $a = 2013$. Then the given expression can be written as

$$\frac{(a+1)^4 + 4a^4}{a^2 + (2a+1)^2} - \frac{(a-1)^4 + 4a^4}{a^2 + (2a-1)^2}$$

$$= \frac{a^4 + 4a^3 + 6a^2 + 4a + 1 + 4a^4}{a^2 + 4a^2 + 4a + 1} - \frac{a^4 - 4a^3 + 6a^2 - 4a + 1 + 4a^4}{a^2 + 4a^2 - 4a + 1}$$

which can then be simplified to

$$\frac{5a^4 + 4a^3 + 6a^2 + 4a + 1}{5a^2 + 4a + 1} - \frac{5a^4 - 4a^3 + 6a^2 - 4a + 1}{5a^2 - 4a + 1}$$

$$= \frac{a^2(5a^2 + 4a + 1) + 5a^2 + 4a + 1}{5a^2 + 4a + 1} - \frac{a^2(5a^2 - 4a + 1) + 5a^2 - 4a + 1}{5a^2 - 4a + 1}$$

$$= (a^2 + 1) - (a^2 + 1)$$

and so the answer is 0.

Solution 2 by Rory Boath, The Grange School, Hartford (slightly edited):
Let $n = 2013$. We can then write

$$\frac{(n+1)^4 + 4n^4}{n^2 + (2n+1)^2} - \frac{(n-1)^4 + 4n^4}{n^2 + (2n-1)^2}$$
$$= \frac{[(n+1)^4 + 4n^4][n^2 + (2n-1)^2] - [(n-1)^4 + 4n^4][n^2 + (2n+1)^2]}{[n^2 + (2n+1)^2][n^2 + (2n-1)^2]}.$$

We then focus on expanding out the numerator. The first part of this is equal to

$$n^2(n+1)^4 + 4n^6 + 4n^4(2n-1)^2 + (n+1)^4(2n-1)^2.$$

Expanding the brackets and grouping like terms, this is equal to

$$25n^6 + 19n^4 - 5n^2 + 1.$$

On the other hand, expanding out the second pair of brackets gives us

$$n^2(n-1)^4 + 4n^6 + 4n^4(2n+1)^2 + (n-1)^4(2n+1)^2.$$

Once again, we can expand out the brackets further and group like terms, to yield

$$25n^6 + 19n^4 - 5n^2 + 1.$$

So the above expression is equal to

$$\frac{[25n^6 + 19n^4 - 5n^2 + 1] - [25n^6 + 19n^4 - 5n^2 + 1]}{[n^2 + (2n+1)^2][n^2 + (2n-1)^2]}$$

which is equal to 0.

2. In the acute-angled triangle ABC, the foot of the perpendicular from B to CA is E. Let l be the tangent to the circle ABC at B. The foot of the perpendicular from C to l is F. Prove that EF is parallel to AB.

(*Proposed by David Monk*)

Most successful solutions to this problem involved the alternate segment theorem together with some results about angles in a cyclic quadrilateral.

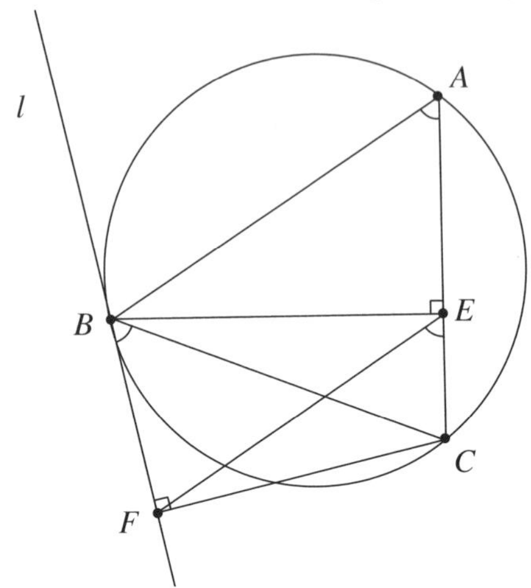

Solution by Balaji Krishna, Stanwell School: First notice that $BECF$ is a cyclic quadrilateral since $\angle CEB + \angle BFC = 180°$. Therefore, $\angle CEF = \angle CBF$ by the theorem of angles in the same segment.

Also, by the alternate segment theorem, $\angle CAB = \angle CBF$. Thus $\angle CAB = \angle CEF$.

So by the converse of the corresponding angles theorem, lines EF and AB are parallel.

3. A number written in base 10 is a string of 3^{2013} digit 3s. No other digit appears. Find the highest power of 3 which divides this number.

(*Proposed by Jeremy King*)

Most solutions to this problem involved a method similar to the first solution presented: recursively breaking the number down into a product of many terms, each divisible by 3 but not by 9. The second solution is an unusual but neat alternative.

Solution 1 by Frank Han, Dulwich College: Let the number in question be A. Notice that $\frac{1}{3}A$ is a string of 3^{2013} 1s. Consider more generally the number B_n which consists of a string of 3^n digit 1s.

Let M_n be the number formed of a digit 1, $(3^n - 1)$ consecutive digits 0, another digit 1, another $(3^n - 1)$ consecutive digits 0 and then another 1. Notice that $B_n \times M_n = B_{n+1}$.

Since the digital sum of M_n is 3, it is divisible by 3. However, since this is not divisible by 9, M_n is not divisible by 9. So B_{n+1} is divisible by exactly one higher power of 3 than B_n.

Now $B_1 = 111$ is divisible by 3^1 but not by 3^2, and so B_n is divisible by 3^n but not by 3^{n+1}. In particular, this means that $\frac{1}{3}A$ is divisible by 3^{2013} but not by 3^{2014}. Hence A is divisible by 3^{2014}, but by no higher power of 3.

Solution 2 by Kasia Warburton, Reigate Grammar School: Call the number in question N. Then

$$\begin{aligned} 3N + 1 &= 10^{3^{2013}} \\ &= \left(3^2 + 1\right)^{3^{2013}} \\ &= \left(3^2\right)^{3^{2013}} + \binom{3^{2013}}{1}\left(3^2\right)^{3^{2013} - 1} + \ldots \\ &\quad + \binom{3^{2013}}{3^{2013} - 2}\left(3^2\right)^2 + \binom{3^{2013}}{3^{2013} - 1}3^2 + 1 \end{aligned}$$

and so

$$3N = (3^2)^{3^{2013}} + \binom{3^{2013}}{1}(3^2)^{3^{2013}-1} + \ldots$$

$$+ \binom{3^{2013}}{3^{2013}-2}(3^2)^2 + \binom{3^{2013}}{3^{2013}-1}3^2.$$

Now consider the individual terms

$$\begin{aligned}
A_n &= \binom{3^{2013}}{3^{2013}-n}(3^2)^n \\
&= \frac{(3^{2013})(3^{2013}-1)\ldots(3^{2013}-n+1)}{n(n-1)(n-2)\ldots 1} \times 3^{2n} \\
&= \frac{(3^{2013}-1)\ldots(3^{2013}-n+1)}{(n-1)(n-2)\ldots 1} \times \frac{3^n}{n} \times 3^n \times 3^{2013} \\
&= \frac{(3^{2013}-1)}{1} \times \frac{(3^{2013}-2)}{2} \times \ldots \times \frac{(3^{2013}-(n-1))}{(n-1)} \times \frac{3^n}{n} \times 3^n \times 3^{2013}.
\end{aligned}$$

We will investigate which powers of 3 divide A_n.
For each $k < n$, $3^{2013} - k$ is divisible by at least as many powers of 3 as k is. Therefore none of the terms $\frac{3^{2013}-k}{k}$ has any powers of 3 in the denominator. So A_n is divisible by at least as great a power of 3 as $\frac{3^n}{n} \times 3^n \times 3^{2013}$ is. However, 3^n is divisible by at least as great a power of 3 as n is, and so A_n is divisible by at least as great a power of 3 as 3^{2013+n}.
We can check that $A_1 = 3^{2015}$ and that $3^{2016}|A_2$. By the above result, $3^{2016}|A_n$ for all $n > 2$, and so

$$3N = A_1 + A_2 + \ldots + A_{3^{2013}}$$

is divisible by 3^{2015}, but not by 3^{2016}. So the highest power of 3 that divides N is 3^{2014}.

4. Isaac is planning a nine-day holiday. Every day he will go surfing, or water-skiing, or he will rest. On any given day he does just one of these three things. He never does different water-sports on consecutive days. How many schedules are possible for the holiday?

(Proposed by Jeremy King)

There are a variety of ways of approaching this problem. Amongst successful solutions, one of the most common was to set up a recurrence, calculating the numbers of ways that Isaac could spend the first n days of his holiday. A second approach involved splitting the holiday up into blocks of three days, and counting the number of ways that these blocks could be pieced together.

Solution 1 by the setters: Denote by $f(n)$ the number of possible holidays that conform to Isaac's rules, and last n days. We are asked to find $f(9)$.

If he rests on the nth day, then he can surf, ski or rest on the $(n+1)$th day; three choices. If he water-skis on the nth day, then he can rest or water-ski on the $(n+1)$th day; two choices. Similarly if he surfs, then he can either surf or rest. So the number of possible holidays of length $n+1$ is equal to three times the number of holidays of length n that end with a rest day, plus two times the number of holidays of length n that end with surfing, plus two times the number of holidays of length n that end with water-skiing.

Thus the number of holidays over $(n+1)$ days is equal to twice the number of holidays over n days, plus the number of holidays of n days that end with a rest day. However, the number of holidays with n days that end with a rest is equal to the number of holidays of length $(n-1)$. That is to say that

$$f(n+1) = 2f(n) + f(n-1).$$

We can find directly that $f(1) = 3$ and $f(2) = 7$. Thereafter, we can calculate $f(3) = 17$, $f(4) = 41$, $f(5) = 99$, $f(6) = 239$, $f(7) = 577$, $f(8) = 1393$ and $f(9) = 3363$.

So the answer is 3363.

Solution 2 by Alexander Ma, Harrow School: Split the 9 days into three sets of 3. Writing 'R' for resting, 'S' for surfing and 'W' for water-skiing, there are 17 possible schedules for a three-day stretch, namely

SSS, SSR, SRR, SRS, SRW,
WWW, WWR, WRR, WRW, WRS,
RRR, RRS, RSR, RSS, RRW, RWR, RWW

How many ways can we piece three of these together? If we specify the last day of each of the first two sets of three, then we can calculate the number of possible ways. The restrictions are that if the first set ends in an S, then the second set must begin S or R, and if it ends in W, then the second set must begin W or R.

First set ends in S, second in S:	$5 \times 4 \times 12 = 240.$
First set ends in S, second in R:	$5 \times 5 \times 17 = 425.$
First set ends in S, second in W:	$5 \times 3 \times 12 = 180.$
First set ends in R, second in S:	$7 \times 5 \times 12 = 420.$
First set ends in R, second in R:	$7 \times 7 \times 17 = 833.$
First set ends in R, second in W:	$7 \times 5 \times 12 = 420.$
First set ends in W, second in S:	$5 \times 3 \times 12 = 180.$
First set ends in W, second in R:	$5 \times 5 \times 17 = 425.$
First set ends in W, second in W:	$5 \times 4 \times 12 = 240.$

The total number of possible schedules is the sum of these nine numbers, namely

$$240 + 425 + 180 + 420 + 833 + 420 + 180 + 425 + 240 = 3363.$$

5. Let ABC be an equilateral triangle, and P be a point inside this triangle. Let D, E and F be the feet of the perpendiculars from P to the sides BC, CA and AB respectively. Prove that

   a) $AF + BD + CE = AE + BF + CD$, and

   b) $[APF] + [BPD] + [CPE] = [APE] + [BPF] + [CPD]$.

   The area of triangle XYZ is denoted by $[XYZ]$.

   (*Proposed by Karthik Tadinada*)

The most common approach to this problem was to observe that the required equalities hold when P is some natural point such as the centre of the triangle, and then show that as P moves around, the two sides of the equalities are unaffected. We also present a very different, clean approach that avoids any need for calculation.

Solution 1 by Tian Bei Li, Concord College: If P is the centre of triangle ABC, then the result holds by symmetry. We can reach an arbitrary point P inside ABC by starting at the centre P_0 and moving along the line PD and then along the line PE (for some distance in either direction). We will prove that the equality a) holds by proving that it is preserved by such movements of P.

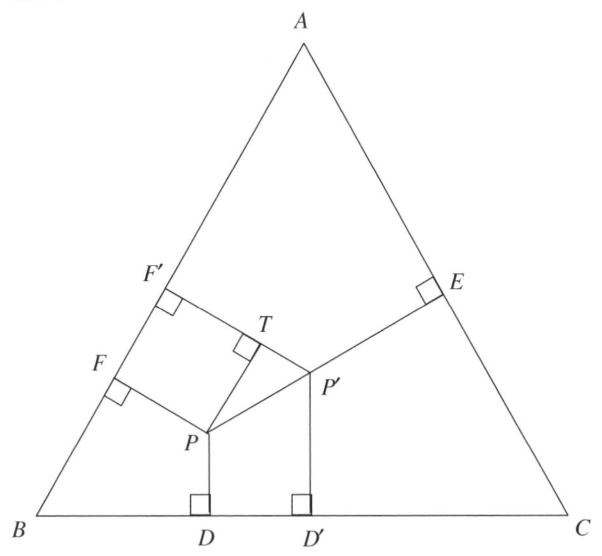

Consider points P and P' such that P' lies on the segment PE, as shown in the diagram above. Let the feet of the perpendiculars from P' to BC and AB be D' and F' respectively. Also let T be the foot of the perpendicular from P to $P'F'$.

By considering quadrilateral $P'EAF'$, $\angle TP'P = \angle EAF' = 60°$. So $PT = PP' \sin 60°$. But $PTF'F$ is a rectangle and so $FF' = PP' \sin 60°$. But by symmetry, $DD' = PP' \sin 60° = FF'$.

Thus

$$\begin{aligned} AF' + BD' + CE &= AF - FF' + BD + DD' + CE \\ &= AF + BD + CE \end{aligned}$$

and

$$\begin{aligned} AE + BF' + CD' &= AE + BF + FF' + CD - DD' \\ &= AE + BF + CD \end{aligned}$$

and so if $AF + BD + CE = AE + BF + CD$ then also $AF' + BD' + CE = AE + BF' + CD'$.

This equality is also preserved when moving along the line PE *away* from E, by considering the same situation with P and P' reversed. Similarly it is preserved when moving along the line PD. Since it holds when P is the centroid of ABC, it holds for all points P inside ABC.

To prove part b), we will use the same method; the result is clearly true when P is the centroid of the triangle, and we will show that the equality is preserved by movements along the lines PD and PE.

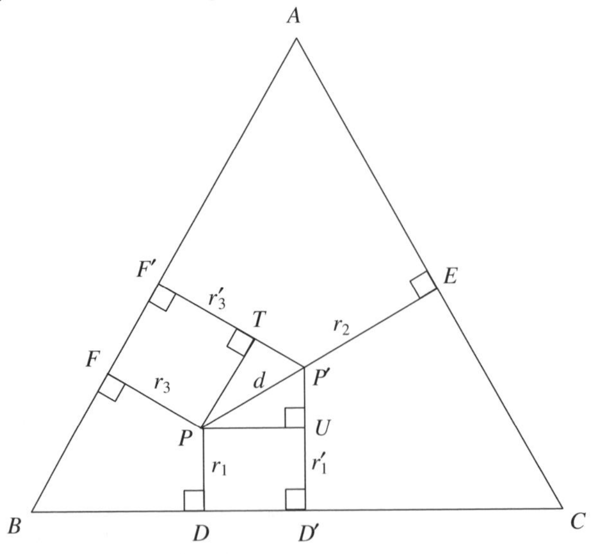

For ease of notation, we will call the lengths $PD = r_1$, $P'D' = r_1'$, $PE = r_2$ and so on as indicated in the second diagram. Also, let $PP' = d$. First of all note that, as $\angle PP'T = 60°$, $P'T = P'U = \frac{1}{2}d$ and

so $r_1' - r_1 = \frac{1}{2}d = r_3' - r_3$. (Note that it follows from this that $r_1 + r_2 + r_3 = r_1' + r_2' + r_3'$, but we shall not actually use this fact.)
By repeatedly using the formula 'area $= \frac{1}{2}$ base × height',

$$\begin{aligned}
&[AP'F'] + [BP'D'] + [CP'E] - [APF] - [BPD] - [CPE] \\
&= \tfrac{1}{2}\left(r_3'AF' + r_1'BD' + r_2CE - r_3AF - r_1BD - r_2CE\right) \\
&= \tfrac{1}{2}\Big[\left(r_3 + \tfrac{1}{2}d\right)\left(AF - \tfrac{1}{2}d\cos 30°\right) - r_3AF\Big] \\
&\quad + \left(r_1 + \tfrac{1}{2}d\right)\left(BD - d\cos 30°\right) - r_1BD \\
&\quad + \left(r_2 - d\right)CE - r_2CE \\
&= \tfrac{1}{4}d\left(AF + BD - 2CE + \sqrt{3}\left(r_1 - r_3\right)\right). \qquad (1)
\end{aligned}$$

We will aim to unpick this last term, $r_1 - r_3$. From our earlier work, $r_1 - r_3 = r_1' - r_3'$. This holds for all P' along the line PE, and so we could pick $P'' = E$.

Thus, when r_1'' is the perpendicular distance from E to BC and r_3'' is the perpendicular distance from E to AB, we have $\left(r_1 - r_3\right) = \left(r_1'' - r_3''\right)$.

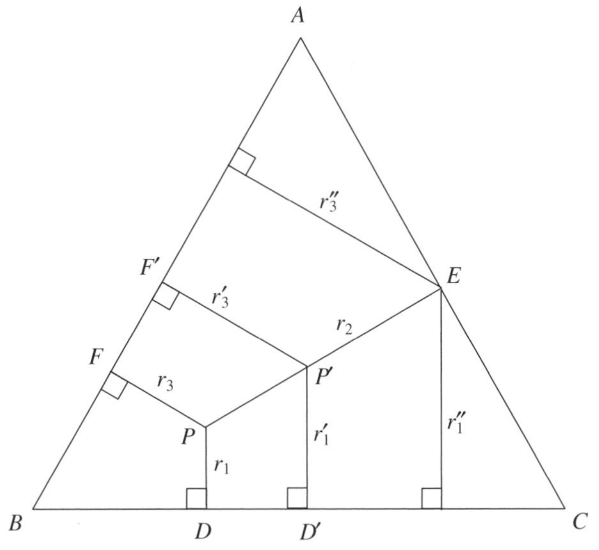

Now since $\angle D'CE = 60°$, we know that $r_1'' = CE\sin 60°$ and similarly $r_3'' = EA\sin 60°$. So

$$\left(r_1 - r_3\right) = \frac{\sqrt{3}}{2}\left(CE - (AC - CE)\right) = \sqrt{3}CE - \frac{\sqrt{3}}{2}AC.$$

We know from part a) that $AF + BD = \frac{3}{2}AC - CE$, and so we have that (1) is equal to

$$\tfrac{1}{4}d\left(\tfrac{3}{2}AC - 3CE + 3CE - \tfrac{3}{2}AC\right) = 0.$$

Thus

$$[AP'F'] + [BP'D'] + [CP'E] = [APF] + [BPD] + [CPE]$$

and so

$$[AP'E] + [BP'F] + [CP'D] = [APE] + [BPF] + [CPD].$$

Combining these two, we see that if the desired equality holds for P, then it also does for P'. As before, it follows then that it holds for any choice P' on the line PE, and then for any P' inside ABC by moving along the line AE and then the line AD.

Solution 2 by the setters: Start off by drawing three lines through P, parallel to each of the three sides; UX parallel to BC, VY parallel to CA and WZ parallel to AB. (The six points U, V, W, X, Y and Z are on the sides of the triangle as shown in the diagram.)

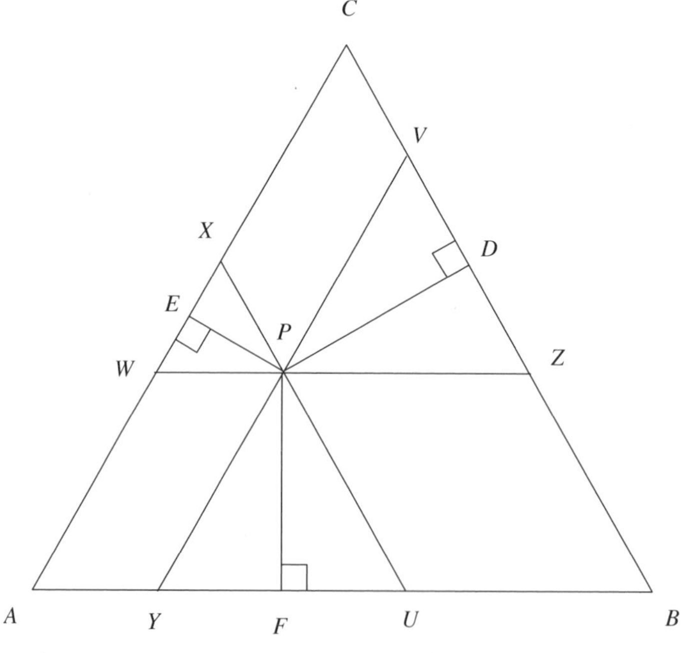

Since ABC is equilateral, each of these three lines meets the sides of the triangle at a 60° angle. So the triangles PZV, PXW and PYU are all equilateral. As a result, the perpendicular PD cuts the line segment ZV in half, and similarly for PE and PF. We thus have

$$VD = DZ, \quad (2)$$

$$WE = EX, \text{ and} \quad (3)$$

$$UF = FY. \quad (4)$$

However we also know that $BUXC$ is an isoceles trapezium. So BU and XC are the same length. Applying the same logic to the trapezia $CVYA$ and $AWZB$ gives us

$$BU = XC, \tag{5}$$
$$CV = YA, \text{ and} \tag{6}$$
$$AW = ZB. \tag{7}$$

We can divide up each of the six lengths in question as follows:

$$AF = AY + YF$$
$$BD = BZ + ZD$$
$$CE = CX + XE$$
$$AE = AW + WE$$
$$BF = BU + UF$$
$$CD = CV + VD.$$

Thus the combination of (2), (3), (4), (5), (6) and (7) tells us exactly that

$$AF + BD + CE = AE + BF + CD,$$

as the question required.

For part b), we will add the lines AP, BP and CP to the diagram.

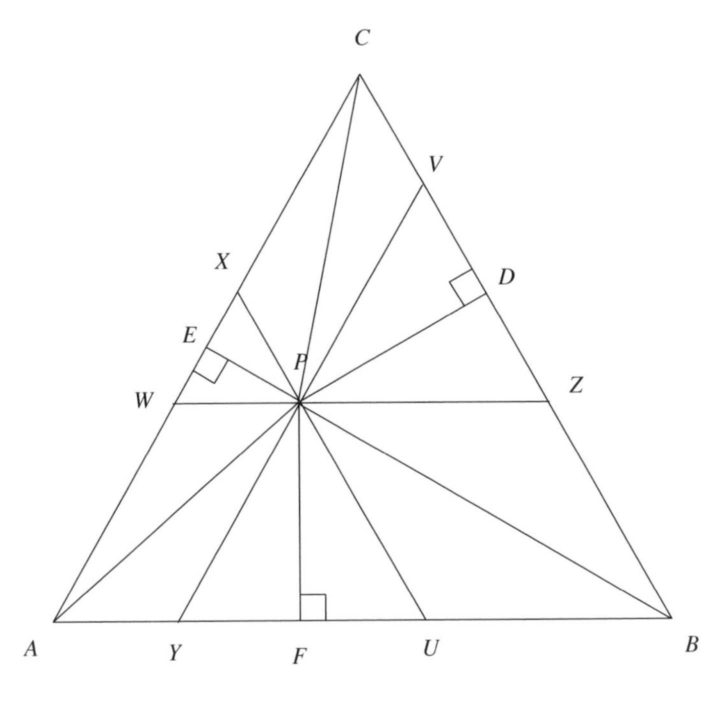

The quadrilateral $AYPW$ is a parallelogram. Therefore, the two triangles PAW and APY are congruent. Similarly, the triangles PBU and BPZ are congruent, and the triangles PCV and CPX are congruent.

Exactly as in part a), we know that the line PD splits the triangle PVZ in half, and so triangles PDV and PDZ are congruent. Similarly, triangles PEW and PEX are congruent, and triangles PFU and PFY are congruent.

We have learnt that six pairs of triangles are congruent, and so each pair has equal area:

$$[PAW] = [APY], \tag{8}$$

$$[PBU] = [BPZ], \tag{9}$$

$$[PCV] = [CPX], \tag{10}$$

$$[PDV] = [PDZ], \tag{11}$$

$$[PEW] = [PEX], \text{ and} \tag{12}$$

$$[PFU] = [PFY]. \tag{13}$$

Totalling the left sides and right sides of (8), (9), (10), (11), (12) and (13) tells us

$$[APF] + [BPD] + [CPE] = [APE] + [BPF] + [CPD],$$

as required.

6. The angles A, B and C of a triangle are measured in degrees, and the lengths of the opposite sides are a, b and c respectively. Prove that

$$60 \leqslant \frac{aA + bB + cC}{a + b + c} < 90.$$

(*Proposed by Graham Hoare*)

The two parts of the inequality can be tackled separately. Most successful solutions used the rearrangement inequality for the left side, and the triangle inequality for the right side, as the solution presented below does.

Solution by Freddie Illingworth, Magdalen College School: Without loss of generality we may assume that $a \geqslant b \geqslant c$. Since the largest angle is opposite the longest side in any triangle, and the smallest angle is opposite the shortest side, we then also have $A \geqslant B \geqslant C$.
That is to say, that a, b, c and A, B, C are both non-increasing sequences. Then it follows from the rearrangement inequality that

$$aA + bB + cC \geqslant aB + bC + cA$$

$$aA + bB + cC \geqslant aC + bA + cB.$$

Summing these two inequalities, and adding $aA + bB + cC$ to each side gives

$$\begin{aligned} 3(aA + bB + cC) &\geqslant aA + aB + aC \\ &\quad + bA + bB + bC \\ &\quad + cA + cB + cC. \\ &= (a + b + c)(A + B + C) \\ &= 180(a + b + c), \end{aligned}$$

since the angles in a triangle sum to 180°. Dividing through by $3(a + b + c)$ gives us

$$\frac{aA + bB + cC}{a + b + c} \geqslant 60.$$

Now we prove the other inequality. We continue to assume that $a \geqslant b \geqslant c$ and consequently that $A \geqslant B \geqslant C$. The triangle inequality states that $a < b + c$, and so

$$aA < (b + c)A = bA + cA.$$

We also know that $bB \leqslant bA$ and $cC \leqslant cA$. Thus

$$aA + bB + cC < aB + aC + bA + cA$$

$$< aB + aC + bA + bC + cA + cB.$$

Thus

$$\begin{aligned} 2(aA + bB + cC) &< aA + aB + aC \\ &\quad + bA + bB + bC \\ &\quad + cA + cB + cC \\ &= (a + b + c)(A + B + C) \\ &= 180(a + b + c). \end{aligned}$$

Dividing through by $2(a + b + c)$ gives us

$$\frac{aA + bB + cC}{a + b + c} < 90$$

as required.

BMO Round 2 – Questions and Solutions

1. Every diagonal of a regular polygon with 2014 sides is coloured in one of n colours. Whenever two diagonals cross in the interior, they are of different colours. What is the minimum value of n for which this is possible?

   (*Proposed by Richard Freeland*)

This problem falls naturally into two parts; proving that at least 1007 colours are required, and exhibiting an example with 1007 colours. We give two solutions to each part.

Solution 1 by Norman Macgregor, Bell Baxter High School: Call a diagonal between directly opposite vertices a primary diagonal. There are 1007 such diagonals, each of which intersects the others at the centre of the polygon, so at least 1007 colours are required.

Now, say that each diagonal leaving a vertex on the clockwise side of its primary diagonal is the same colour as that primary diagonal. No two diagonals of the same colour cross, and this fully describes all diagonals since each non-primary diagonal leaves one vertex on the clockwise side of the primary diagonal and the other vertex on the anticlockwise side.

Hence, 1007 is the minimum value of n.

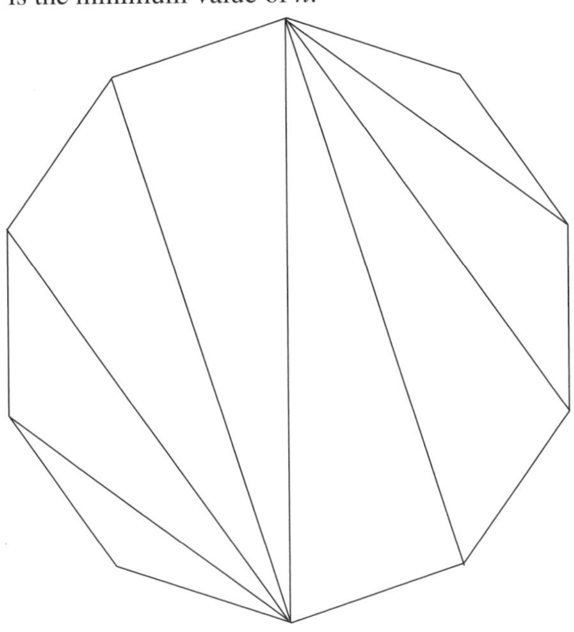

Solution 2 by Ramsay Pyper, Eton College (slightly edited): We prove the first part by induction, and give an alternative construction.

Note that there are $\frac{1}{2}n(n - 3)$ diagonals to colour. Suppose we have $\frac{1}{2}n - 1$ colours. Then, by the pigeonhole principle, we have one colour used to colour $n - 2$ or more diagonals.

We prove by strong induction that this is not possible.

Base case: $n = 3$: There are no diagonals in a triangle, so we cannot colour at least 1.

Base case: $n = 4$: There are only two diagonals in a square, and we cannot colour them both the same colour.

Induction step: Suppose it is true whenever $n \leqslant k$. Consider a $(k + 1)$-gon. Once we draw the first diagonal, we split it into two smaller polygons, with a sides and b sides, where $a + b = k + 3$. Thus, we may draw $a - 3 + b - 3$ further sides, giving a total of $k - 2$, as required.

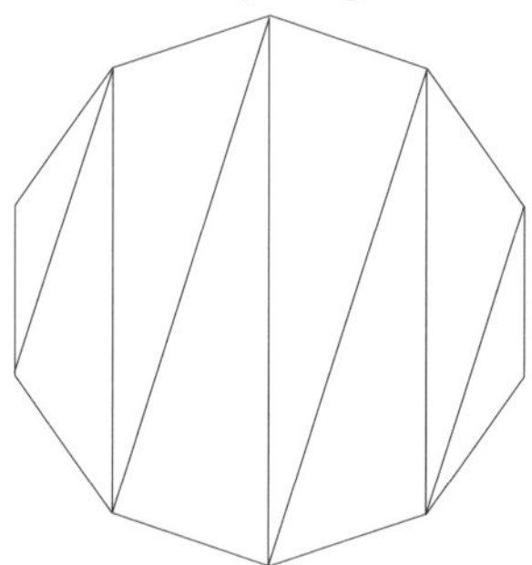

Now, colour the edges as follows:

Label the vertices $0, 1, 2, \ldots, 2n - 1 \bmod 2n$ (where $n = 1007$). To draw the first colour edges, select some a and join $a - i$ to $a + i$ for $i = 1, \ldots, n - 1$ and join $a - i$ to $a + i + 1$ for $i = 1, \ldots, n - 2$. Repeat for $a + 1, a + 2, \ldots, a + 1006$. Since we have drawn $2n - 3$ edges for each colour, we simply need to prove that no edge is coloured twice.

Suppose p to q were drawn twice. If $p - q$ is even, it was drawn when $a = \frac{1}{2}(p + q)$ or $\frac{1}{2}(p + q) + n$. If $p - q$ is odd, it was chosen when $a = \frac{1}{2}(p + q - 1)$ or $\frac{1}{2}(p + q - 1) + n$. This proves the result.

2. Prove that it is impossible to have a cuboid for which the volume, the surface area and the perimeter are numerically equal.
   The perimeter of a cuboid is the sum of the lengths of all its twelve edges.

   (*Proposed by Jeremy King*)

This question proved very popular with candidates, with almost all students submitting serious work. A key to progress was resisting the temptation to substitute for variables without a plan for where the equations were heading. The optimal route was to compare the values of $(\text{Surface Area})^2$ and Perimeter $\times$ Volume directly. A few solutions considered the side lengths as roots of a cubic, then showed that this had only one real root by considering local extrema. It is worth remarking that candidates who explained in words what they were doing generally proved more successful than those who presented unsupported calculations.

Solution 1 by Jongheon Jeon, Winchester College: Let the dimensions of the cuboid be h, w and l.
We have:

$$\text{volume} = hwl,$$

$$\text{surface area} = 2(hw + wl + lh),$$

$$\text{perimeter} = 4(h + w + l).$$

Now, if all three quantities are equal, it means that

$$\text{volume} \times \text{perimeter} = (\text{surface area})^2$$

$$\text{i.e. } 4hwl(h + w + l) = 4(hw + wl + lh)^2$$

$$\text{i.e. } 0 = h^2w^2 + w^2l^2 + l^2h^2 + hwl(h + w + l)$$

which is impossible if none of the dimensions are 0.

Solution 2 by the editors: Let the value for the perimeter, area and volume be $4T$, and the dimensions be h, w and l. As above, we have:

$$4T = hwl$$

$$2T = hw + wl + lh$$

$$T = h + w + l.$$

Hence, h, w and l are the roots of the cubic $f(x) = x^3 - Tx^2 + 2Tx - 4T = 0$.

This is a cubic with a local maximum at

$$u(T) = \frac{T}{3} - \frac{\sqrt{T^2 - 6T}}{3}.$$

For f to have three real roots, we require that $f(u) > 0$.

However, we observe that $T \geqslant 6$, and that $u(T)$ is decreasing (for example by differentiating with respect to T). Hence, we have that $u(T) \leqslant u(6) = 2$, and $u(T) < T$. Hence, $u^3 < Tu^2$ and $2Tu < 4T$, so $f(u) < 0$. Hence, there cannot be three real roots, and so such a cuboid cannot exist.

3. Let $a_0 = 4$ and define a sequence of terms using the formula $a_n = a_{n-1}^2 - a_{n-1}$ for each positive integer n.
   a) Prove that there are infinitely many prime numbers which are factors of at least one term in the sequence.
   b) Are there infinitely many prime numbers which are factors of no term in the sequence?

(Proposed by Jeremy King)

The first part of this question was reasonably well attempted, but the second part was rather harder. In solving the first part, many students did not show that $a_n - 1 \neq 1$. This is a crucial point; if, instead, $a_0 = 2$, then we do not introduce any new prime factors. The vast majority of solutions proceeded in the way shown here.

Solution by the editors:

a) First, note that from the formula $a_{n-1} | a_n$. This means that any prime number which divides one term will divide all subsequent terms.

Now, $a_n = a_{n-1}(a_{n-1} - 1)$. These two factors are coprime, and since the sequence is increasing $(a_{n-1} - 1) > 1$. Hence, there is a prime p which divides $a_{n-1} - 1$, and so divides a_n but not a_{n-1}, and thus not a_m for any $m < n$. There is such a prime for each n, and thus there are infinitely many overall.

b) Notice that if $b_n = a_n - 2$, then $b_n = b_{n-1}(b_{n-1} + 3)$. Also notice that $b_1 = 2$. Since b_1 is not divisible by 3, nor will b_n be divisible by 3 for any n, so the factors $b_{n-1} + 3$ and b_{n-1} will be coprime.

Therefore, the argument above works to show that there are infinitely many primes dividing all but finitely many of the b_i, and these primes (with one exception, $p = 2$) cannot divide any of the a_i.

4. Let ABC be a triangle and P be a point in its interior. Let AP meet the circumcircle of ABC again at A'. The points B' and C' are similarly defined. Let O_A be the circumcentre of BCP. The circumcentres O_B and O_C are similarly defined. Let O'_A be the circumcentre of $B'C'P$. The circumcentres O'_B and O'_C are similarly defined. Prove that the lines $O_AO'_A$, $O_BO'_B$ and $O_CO'_C$ are concurrent.

(*Proposed by Gerry Leversha*)

There were a few solutions, such as the first two, which effectively identified the point of concurrency of the given lines (as the midpoint of OP). The vast majority, however, went down the third route for a quicker solution which did not identify the point of concurrency.

Linden Ralph and Edward Kirkby were the winners of the Christopher Bradley elegance prize for their solutions to this problem.

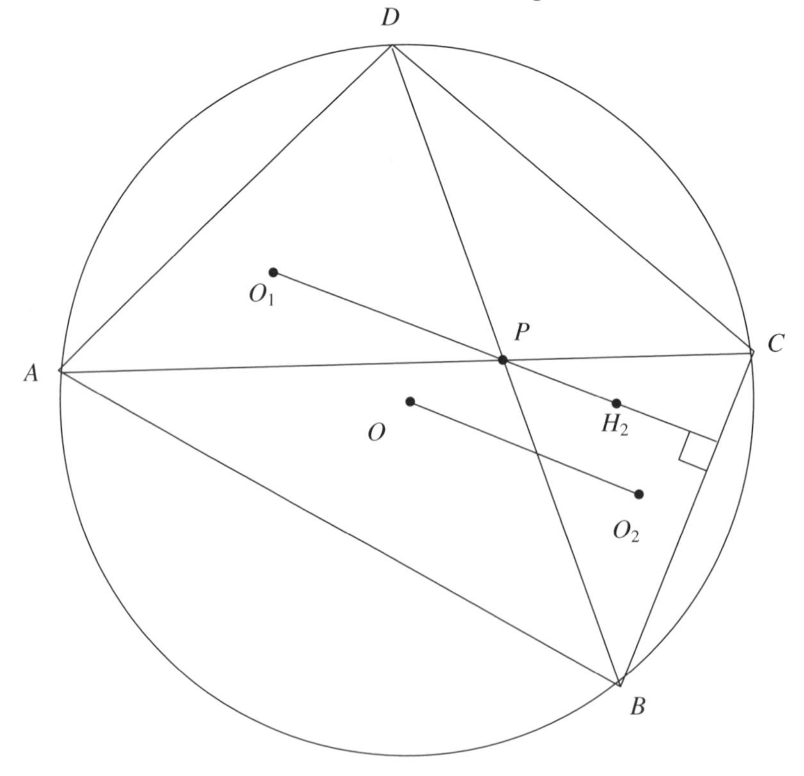

Solution 1 by Linden Ralph, Hills Road VI Form College: Consider a cyclic quadrilateral $ABCD$ with circumcentre O. Let P be the intersection of the diagonals, O_1 and O_2 be centres of circles DAP and BCP respectively, H_1 and H_2 defined similarly for orthocentres. Since $\angle O_1PD = \angle CPO_2$ by similarity, and $\angle CPO_2 = \angle H_2PB$ by the isogonal conjugacy of O_2 and H_2, we find that O_1, P and H_2 are collinear, so O_1P is perpendicular to BC. Similarly, O_2P is perpendicular to AD. Since O and O_2 both lie on the perpendicular bisector of BC, we have that O_2O is parallel to PO_1, and similarly O_1O is parallel to PO_2. Hence, O_1PO_2O is a parallelogram, and so O_1O_2 bisects PO.

We can apply this to the problem, considering cyclic quadrilaterals $BC'B'C$, $CA'C'A$ and $AB'A'B$ in turn. It follows that each of $O_AO'_A$, $O_BO'_B$ and $O_CO'_C$ bisect OP, and thus they concur at the midpoint.

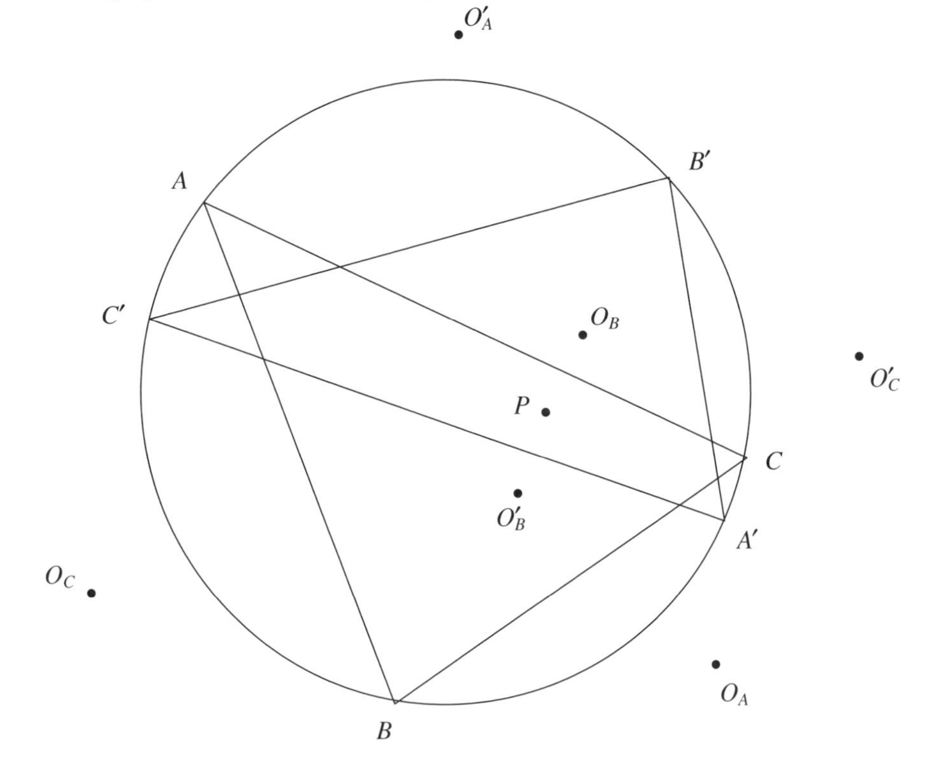

Solution 2 by Edward Kirkby, Alton College: Invert the diagram about P. Circles through P become straight lines, and their centres become the reflections of P in these lines, so, for example, O_A is the reflection of P in BC. Thus, the problem now becomes to prove that the circles $PO_AO'_A$, $PO_BO'_B$ and $PO_CO'_C$ concur somewhere other than P.

The centre of $PO_AO'_A$ must lie on BC, the perpendicular bisector of PO_A, and likewise it must lie on $B'C'$. Hence, it is their intersection, which we will call D. Define E and F similarly. P is a centre of perspective for ABC and $A'B'C'$, so DEF is a straight line by the theorem of Desargues. Hence, the reflection of P in this line lies on all three circles, as required.

Solution 3 by the editors: Note that the lines O_BO_C and $O'_BO'_C$ are perpendicular bisectors of PA and PA', and so are parallel. It follows that triangles $O_AO_BO_C$ and $O'_AO'_BO'_C$ are similar with corresponding sides parallel. Since the corresponding sides are on opposite sides of P, it follows that they are homothetic and the homothecy is inverse. This is enough to guarantee a point of concurrency.

Olympiad Training and Overseas Competitions

Several training camps are held throughout the year to select and prepare students for participation in the UK team at forthcoming International Mathematical Olympiads and other international events.

Oxford Training Camp 2013

The Oxford Training Camp was once again held at Queen's College Oxford. This year 22 students attended the camp which ran from Sunday 25th August until Saturday 31st August. Thanks must go to Peter Neumann who once again organised and directed the camp.

The academic programme was structured and quite intense. There were five 'lecture/tutorial courses' plus some one-off lectures/presentations, all supported by the company acting as tutors going round and helping the students with the problem-solving activities that were a crucial part of the courses. There were two 100-minute sessions each morning Monday to Friday. These were a lecture course on Geometry by Geoff Smith (5 sessions) and Number theory by Vicky Neale (5 sessions). On Monday, Tuesday, Thursday and Friday there were three afternoon sessions, each lasting 60 to 75 minutes: sessions on Problem solving/combinatorics by Jo Harbour (1), Dan Schwarz (3) visiting from Romania, and Dominic Yeo (3), Functional analysis by Alison Zhu (2), Geometric inequalities by Alison Zhu (1), and Combinatorial problems on words as an introduction to the Burnside Problem (2 sessions) designed by Peter Neumann to try to give some insight into mathematical research. On the Tuesday evening Dan Schwarz gave a lecture dissecting in elegant detail a recent IMO problem. On the final Saturday morning the students sat the four-and-a-half-hour Oxford Mathematical Olympiad under IMO conditions and rules of engagement.

Students attending the Oxford Training Camp this year were: Olivia Aaronson (St Paul's Girls School), Jamie Bell (King Edward VI Five Ways School), Joe Benton (St Paul's School), Rosie Cates (Perse School), Jeffrey Chu (Tonbridge School), Esha Dasgupta (Sutton Coldfield Grammar School), Macauley Davy (Wyke Sixth Form College) Madhi Elango (Queen Elizabeth‹s School), Harry Goodburn (Wilson's School), Soomin Jang (Badminton School), Neel Nanda (Latymer School), Marguerite Tong (St Paul's Girls School), Benji Wang (Cantell College), Sam Watt (Monkton Combe School), Alfred Wond (Reading School), Joanna Yass (North London Collegiate School), Danshu Zhang (Blackheath High School).

Hungary Camp

Once again there was a visit to Hungary over the New Year to train with the Hungarian IMO squad. Twenty British students and 20 Hungarian students attended the camp between 27th December 2013 and 4th January 2014. This year a student (Luke Gardiner) from the Republic of Ireland also joined the training camp.

Thanks go to Vesna Kadelburg, Paul Fannon and Fraser Heywood for leading the team this year.

The British students attending were: Olivia Aaronson (St Paul's Girls School), Joseph Benton (St Paul's School), Rosie Cates (The Perse Upper School), Jacob Coxon (Magdalen College School), Tsz hin Fung (Royal Grammar School, Colchester), Gabriel Gendler (Queen Elizabeth's School), Lawrence Hollom (Robert Smyth School), Freddie Illingworth (Magdalen College School), Tomoka Kan (St Paul's Girls School), Andrew Kenyon-Roberts (Aberdeen Grammar School), Warren Li (Fulford School), Akuan Liu (The Cherwell School), Rachel Newhouse (Skipton Girls' High School), Ramsay Pyper (Eton College), Eloise Thuey (Caister Grammar School), Marius Tirlea (Woking College), Adam Weller (Reading School), Harvey Yau (Ysgol Dyffryn Taf), Danshu Zhang (Eltham College).

Romanian Master of Mathematics

The UK has competed as a guest team in the Romanian Master of Mathematics (RMM) competition since 2008. Unfortunately this annual event was this year cancelled by the organisers early in 2014.

Balkan Mathematical Olympiad

The 2014 Balkan Mathematical Olympiad was held in Bulgaria from 2nd May to 7th May 2014. The UK is invited to compete in this event as a guest nation. Students are only invited to join this UK team once, so that it gives many more students the opportunity to experience international competition.

The UK team for 2014 was: Joseph Benton (St. Paul's School), Liam Hughes (Robert Smyth School), Neel Nanda (Latymer School), Linden Ralph (Hills Road 6th Form College), Kasia Warburton (Reigate Grammar School), Harvey Yau (Ysgol Dyffryn Taf).

The team was led by Jack Shotton and the deputy leader was Gerry Leversha.

Trinity College Training Camp

Once again the Easter training and selection camp was held at Trinity College, Cambridge. UKMT are very grateful to Trinity College for its continuing support of this camp.

Twenty three UK students came to Trinity this year. They included all the candidates for this year's IMO team, along with some younger students with potential for future international camps. They were joined by a student from the Republic of Ireland, Luke Gardiner.

UK attending students were: Olivia Aaronson (St Paul's Girls School), Joseph Benton (St Paul's School), James Davies (Fearnhill School), Gabriel Gendler (Queen Elizabeth's School), Ben Grant (Tapton School), Frank Han (Dulwich College), Liam Hughes (Robert Smyth School), Freddie Illingworth (Magdalen College School), Gareth Jones (Clifton College), Andrew Kenyon-Roberts (Aberdeen Grammar School), Samuel Kittle (Simon Langton School), Warren Li (Fulford School), Chen Lu (Eton College), Callum McLean (Harrow School), Harry Metrebian (Winchester College), Neel Nanda (Latymer School), Ramsay Pyper (Eton College), Linden Ralph (Hills Road 6th Form College), Katya Richards (School of St Helen and St Katherine), Eloise Thuey (Caister Grammar School), Kasia Warburton (Reigate Grammar School), Adam Weller (Reading School), Harvey Yau (Ysgol Dyffryn Taf).

We are also very grateful to all the UKMT volunteers who helped at the camp giving sessions and looking after students: James Aaronson, Alex Betts, Robin Bhattacharyya, Richard Freeland, Jo Harbour, Vesna Kadelburg, David Kunszenti-Kovacs, Joshua Lam, Imre Leader, Gerry Leversha, Joseph Myers, Preeyan Parmar, Hannah Roberts, Paul Russell, Jack Shotton, Geoff Smith, Dominic Yeo.

European Girls' Mathematical Olympiad

This year the European Girls' Mathematical Olympiad moved on to Turkey. Since a small beginning in 2012 in Cambridge, when 19 countries participated, the competition in Turkey welcomed 29 countries, including 7 guest countries from outside Europe.

The selection for the UK team was made on performances at BMO1 and BMO2, the two rounds of the British Mathematical Olympiad.

This year's team consisted of: Olivia Aaronson (St Paul's Girls School), Katya Richards (School of St Helen and St Katherine), Eloise Thuey (Caister Grammar School), Kasia Warburton (Reigate Grammar School). The reserve was Alyssa Dayan (Westminster School).

The team leader was Hannah Roberts and deputy leader was Jo Harbour.

A full report of EGMO 2104 can be found at:

http://www.bmoc.maths.org/home/egmo.shtml

Oundle Selection Camp

The final training camp before selection of the team of six for the IMO was once again held at Oundle School at the end of May.

Students participating were: Joseph Benton (St Paul's School), Gabriel Gendler (Queen Elizabeth‹s College), Frank Han (Dulwich College), Liam Hughes (Robert Smyth School), Freddie Illingworth (Magdalen College School), Andrew Kenyon-Roberts (Aberdeen Grammar School), Warren Li (Fulford School), Neel Nanda (Latymer School), Linden Ralph (Hills Road 6th Form College), Harvey Yau (Ysgol Dyffryn Taf).

Staff at the camp were Geoff Smith, Joseph Myers, Dominic Yeo, Jill Parker, and Olga Smith.

The International Mathematical Olympiad

In many ways, a lot of the events and activities described earlier in this book relate to stages that UK IMO team members will go through before they attend an IMO. At this stage, it is worth explaining a little about the structure of the Olympiad, both for its own sake as well as to fit the following report into a wider context.

An IMO is a huge event and takes several years to plan and to execute. In 2014, teams from more than 100 countries went to South Africa to participate. A team consists of six youngsters (although in some cases, a country may send fewer). The focus of an IMO is really the two days on which teams sit the contest papers. The papers are on consecutive days and each lasts $4\frac{1}{2}$ hours. Each paper consists of three problems, and each problem is worth 7 marks. Thus a perfect score for a student is 42/42. The students are ranked according to their personal scores, and the top half receive medals. These are distributed in the ratios gold:silver:bronze = 1:2:3. The host city of the IMO varies from year to year. Detailed contemporary and historical data can be found at

http://www.imo-official.org/

But, whilst these may be the focus, there are other essential stages, in particular the selection of the problems and, in due course, the co-ordination (marking) of scripts and awarding of medals.

As stated, an IMO team is built around the students but they are accompanied by two other very important people: the Team Leader and the Deputy Leader, (many teams also take Observers who assist at the various stages and some of these may turn out to be future Leaders). Some three or four days before the actual IMO examinations, the Team Leaders arrive in the host country to deal with the task of constructing the papers. Countries will have submitted questions for consideration over the preceding months and a short list of questions (and, eventually, solutions) are given to Team Leaders on arrival. The Team Leaders gather as a committee (in IMO parlance, the Jury) to select six of the short-listed questions. This can involve some very vigorous debate and pretty tough talking! But it has to be done. Once agreed, the questions are put into the papers and translations produced into as many languages as necessary, sometimes over 50.

At some stage, the students, accompanied by the Deputy Leader, arrive in the host country. As is obvious, there can be no contact with the Team Leader who, by then, has a good idea of the IMO papers! The Leaders and the students are housed in different locations to prevent any contact, casual or otherwise.

On the day before the first examination, there is an Opening Ceremony. This is attended by all those involved (with due regard to security). Immediately after the second day's paper, the marking can begin. It may seem strange that students' scripts are 'marked' by their own Leader and Deputy. In fact, no actual marks or comments of any kind are put on the scripts themselves. Instead, having looked at scripts and decided what marks they think should be awarded, the Leader and Deputy have to justify their claim to others, called co-ordinators, who are supplied by the host country. Once all the marks have been agreed, sometimes after extremely protracted negotiation, the Jury decides where the medal boundaries should go. Naturally, this is a crucial part of the procedure and results in many tears as well as cheers.

Whilst the co-ordination of marks is going on, the students have time to relax and recover. There are often organised activities and excursions and there is much interaction and getting to know like-minded individuals from all corners of the world.

The grand finale is always the closing ceremony which includes the awarding of medals as well as speeches and numerous items of entertainment – some planned but others accidental.

55th International Mathematical Olympiad, Cape Town, South Africa, 3-13 July 2014, Report by Geoff Smith (UK Team Leader)

The International Mathematical Olympiad was held under an African sky for the first time. The event was held in Cape Town, South Africa, during July 2014 and was a great success. The director, John Webb, is a stalwart of the maths competition circuit, and bringing the event home to Cape Town is the fulfilment of a long cherished ambition. The event was held under the auspices of the South African Mathematics Foundation, but they had help from many sources, including businesses, charities, foundations, government, private individuals and universities.

The IMO is the world championship of secondary school mathematics, and is held each July in a host country somewhere in the world. A modern IMO involves more than 100 countries, representing over 90% of the world's population. The competition was founded in 1959. Each participating country may send up to six team members, who must be under 20 years of age and not have entered university.

The University of Cape Town was the students' site, and it nestles dramatically on the lower slopes of Table Mountain, on land donated by Cecil Rhodes. It was cold at night, but we were well warned in advance, and warm jackets were supplied. The organization was very good indeed, but in an event so large and complex as the IMO, it is impossible to get everything exactly right (unless you are Dutch). Indeed, that is the basis of the more cruel aspects of the UK leader's diary which serve to highlight, dramatise, and if necessary fabricate apparent shortcomings.

The UK Deputy Leader was Dominic Yeo of the University of Oxford, and our Observer C was Jill Parker, formerly of the University of Bath. Here is the UK IMO team of 2014.

Joe Benton	St Paul's School, Barnes, London
Gabriel Gendler	Queen Elizabeth's School, Barnet, London
Frank Zhenyu Han	Dulwich College, London
Freddie Illingworth	Magdalen College School, Oxford
Warren Li	Fulford School, York
Harvey Yau	Ysgol Dy ryn Taf, Carmarthenshire, Wales

First reserve was Neel Nanda of Latymer School, Edmonton, London.

For the second year running, each UK student scored at least 20 points. This has not happened since the run of three similarly successful years during 1994-1996. We look forward to the results of IMO 2015 in Chiang Mai, Thailand with interest. Note that Warren Li has two more years at school, Joe Benton has three, and Harvey Yau has four. The future prospects of the UK IMO side look healthy.

	P1	P2	P3	P4	P5	P6	Σ	Medal
Joe Benton	7	5	1	7	4	0	24	Silver
Gabriel Gendler	7	6	0	7	2	0	22	Silver
Frank Zhenyu Han	7	4	0	7	2	0	20	Bronze
Freddie Illingworth	5	7	0	7	2	0	21	Bronze
Warren Li	7	7	0	7	7	0	28	Silver
Harvey Yau	7	6	0	7	7	0	27	Silver

There are three problems to address on each of two consecutive days. Each exam lasts 4 hours 30 minutes. The cut-offs were 16 for bronze, 22 for silver and 29 for gold.

There were 101 teams at IMO 2014. Warm congratulations to China and the USA for excellent performances. Special celebrations are in order for third placed Taiwan because that is their highest ever ranking, and for Ukraine which equalled its highest ever ranking of sixth. The 13th place for the Netherlands is their best rank position since 1983.

Here are a few of the leading scores. 1 China (201), 2 USA (193), 3 Taiwan (192), 4 Russia (191), 5 Japan (177), 6 Ukraine (175), 7 South Korea (172), 8 Singapore (161), 9 Canada (159), 10 Vietnam (157), 11 Australia (156), 11 Romania (156), 13 Netherlands (155), 14 North Korea (154), 15 Hungary (153), 16 Germany (152), 17 Turkey (147), 18 Hong Kong (143), 18 Israel (143), 20 United Kingdom (142), 21 Iran (131), 21 Thailand (131), 23 Kazakhstan (129), 23 Malaysia (129), 23 Serbia (129), 26 Italy (128), 26 Mexico (128), 26 Poland (128), 29 Croatia (126), 29 Indonesia (126), 29 (Peru) (126).

Anglophone interest in other scores might include 39 India (110), our neighbours and traditional allies 45 France (96), 53 Bangladesh (84), 54 Sri Lanka (82), 60 New Zealand (76), 64 Ireland (67), 64 South Africa (67), 72 Cyprus (53), 75 Pakistan (50), 82 Trinidad and Tobago (32). It was simply excellent to see delegations from Burkina Faso, Gambia, Ghana and Tanzania competing at an IMO for the first time.

Here are the unusual prizewinners for 2014. The first country to have its rank higher than its score was Latvia. The team leader with the most names was from Brazil (5), only one debatable word ahead of the leaders of Bolivia, Cuba, Mexico, Nigeria, Puerto Rico, Vietnam and Uruguay. However, in the leaders' nominal accents competition, Vietnam (four with three different) was a clear winner since no other leader had more than two accents (but Serbia had two accents and a crossed D). Japan was the top constitutional monarchy, and Luxembourg managed to retain the Grand Duchy title. The UK was the 4th Commonwealth country, which actually indicates excellent performances from Singapore, Canada and Australia. Romania topped the European Union and Netherlands the euro area.

The second bullet point of General Regulation 2.8 may or may not apply in 2015, so you might have three IMO teams from the Atlantic Islands next year.

The Papers

Contestants have 4 hours 30 minutes to sit each paper. The three problems on each paper are each marked out of 7. It is intended that the three problems should be in increasing order of difficulty on each day.

Day 1

Problem 1 Let $a_0 < a_1 < a_2 < \ldots$ be an infinite sequence of positive integers. Prove that there is a unique integer $n \geqslant 1$ such that

$$a_n < \frac{a_0 + a_1 + \ldots + a_n}{n} \leqslant a_{n+1}.$$

Problem 2 Let $n \geqslant 2$ be an integer. Consider an $n \times n$ chessboard consisting of n^2 unit squares. A configuration of n rooks on this board is peaceful if every row and every column contains exactly one rook. Find the greatest positive integer k such that, for each peaceful configuration of n rooks, there is a $k \times k$ square which does not contain a rook on any of its k^2 unit squares.

Problem 3 Convex quadrilateral $ABCD$ has $\angle ABC = \angle CDA = 90°$. Point H is the foot of the perpendicular from A to BD. Points S and T lie on the sides AB and AD, respectively, such that H is inside triangle SCT and

$$\angle CHS - \angle CSB = 90°, \qquad \angle THC - \angle DTC = 90°.$$

Prove that line BD is tangent to the circumcircle of triangle TSH.

Day 2

Problem 4 Points P and Q lie on side BC of acute-angled triangle ABC so that $\angle PAB = \angle BCA$ and $\angle CAQ = \angle ABC$. Points M and N lie on lines AP and AQ, respectively, such that P is the midpoint of AM, and Q is the midpoint of AN. Prove that lines BM and CN intersect on the circumcircle of triangle ABC.

Problem 5 For each positive integer n, the Bank of Cape Town issues coins of denomination $\frac{1}{n}$. Given a finite collection of such coins (of not necessarily different denominations) with total value at most $99 + \frac{1}{2}$, prove that it is possible to split the collection into 100 or fewer groups, such that each group has total value at most 1.

Problem 6 A set of lines in the plane is in general position if no two are parallel and no three pass through the same point. A finite set of lines in general position cuts the plane into regions, some of which have finite area; we call these its finite regions. Prove that for all sufficiently large n, in any set of n lines in general position, it is possible to colour at least $\sqrt{n}$ of the lines blue in such a way that none of its finite regions has a completely blue boundary.

Note: Results with $\sqrt{n}$ replaced by $c\sqrt{n}$ will be awarded points depending on the value of the constant c.

Note: (not in the original) the word finite has been inserted as the second word of the second sentence of Problem 6 for reasons of mathematical integrity.

These questions were submitted to the IMO by Austria, Croatia, Iran, Georgia, Luxembourg and Austria respectively. The American juror Po-Shen Loh suggested this modified statement of Problem 6.

Forthcoming International Events

This is a summary of the events which are relevant for the UK. Of course there are many other competitions going on in other parts of the world.

The next few IMOs will be held in Thailand 2015, Hong Kong 2016, Brazil 2017, Romania 2018 and the United Kingdom 2019. Forthcoming editions of the European Girls' Mathematical Olympiad will be in Belarus 2015, Country X in 2016 and Country Y in 2017. In fact matters are far more advanced than this cryptic list suggests, and EGMO is unlikely to need a new host country until 2018. The Balkan Mathematical Olympiad will be held in Greece in 2015, and the Romanian Master of Mathematics will be in business again in 2015, now with the Romanian Mathematical Society deeply involved.

Diary

This diary is a facetious summary of my personal experience at the IMO and is available on:

www.imo-register.org.uk/2014-report.pdf

Team members

Freddie Illingworth burst onto the competitions scene last year with a gold medal in the abnormally late Balkan Mathematical Olympiad in 2013. It is extremely likely that he would have been in the UK team for the Romanian Master of Mathematics in 2014 had it not been cancelled, and this remark applies to some other UK team members of course. Freddie was a reserve for the IMO team of 2013.

Joe Benton's international debut was in the Balkan MO 2014 in Bulgaria where he obtained a bronze medal. Joe will have three more chances to compete in IMOs.

Harvey Yau is our youngest and most Welsh contestant. He made his debut in Bulgaria this year, obtaining a bronze medal. The maths competition community have been aware of Harvey for a long time, and we have been waiting for him to become old enough that we could reasonably take him to an overseas competition without risk of attracting the attention of the social services. He first reached the BMO2, the final round of our national mathematical olympiad, two years ago. He will have four more opportunities to compete in IMOs.

Warren Li is our Yorkshireman. His debut was in the Romanian Master of Mathematics in 2013 where he secured a bronze medal, and he won another bronze in the Balkan Mathematical Olympiad later that year held in Cyprus, and a silver medal in IMO 2013 in Colombia. He won a bronze medal in the Romanian Master of Mathematics in 2013.

Frank Han has the Chinese name Zhenyu. He is being educated at a boarding school in the UK. His debut was also in the Balkan Mathematical Olympiad in Cyprus in 2013 where he won a silver medal. He was a reserve for IMO 2013 in Colombia.

Gabriel Gendler won a bronze medal in the Balkan Mathematical Olympiad of 2012 in Turkey. He was a reserve for IMO 2012 in Argentina, and secured an Honourable Mention at the Romanian Master of Mathematics in 2013. He won a silver medal at IMO 2013 in Colombia.

Girls

The UKMT effort to promote interest in maths competitions amongst girls continues. It is pleasing to observe that many female IMO 2014 medallists, including the unique girl to win a gold medal, Michelle Sweering of the Netherlands, were former EGMO medallists. Two medal winners in the Ukrainian IMO team were members of their triumphant EGMO 2014 team in Antalya, Turkey.

We now have a dedicated girls' summer camp in Oxford to supplement our other camps, and a talent search exam, the UK Mathematical Olympiad for Girls to try to locate promising female students. I urge other nations to develop their own structures with a similar purpose.

Acknowledgements

There is a vast range of competitions, mentoring, camps and publications apparatus which underpins the IMO team. Almost all young mathematicians in our country make contact with UKMT via the excellent Mathematics Challenges which form the heart of our national effort. These Challenges are the foundation of a structure which tries to stimulate, develop and encourage enthusiastic young mathematicians, both inside and outside the classroom. I pay tribute to everyone involved in helping to make this possible: the hundreds of UKMT volunteers, the small band of professional UKMT administrators, and the families whose lives we disrupt with our camps and competitions.

Dominic Yeo was a brilliant deputy leader, and our observer Jill Parker managed our crises with discretion and calm aplomb. Many thanks to them both. It was also a pleasure to have Joseph Myers around, though he was not part of the UK delegation.

The team acquitted themselves perfectly throughout, both mathematically and in terms of behaviour, and it has been a pleasure to work with them. The reserves were all splendid.

I must specifically thank Oxford Asset Management for their generous sponsorship of the UK IMO team, and the other donors, both individual and corporate, who give so generously. Why not join in?

http://www.ukmt.org.uk/about-us/

UKMT Mentoring Schemes (Administered by BMOS)

After a year in the hands of Vicky Neale, the UKMT Mentoring Schemes passed to me. Many thanks are due to Vicky for her hard work!

The Schemes have had a steady and successful year. The materials are used in over 850 schools, and by about 200 individual students working with external mentors. These resources have been free since their early days, fifteen years ago, and the UKMT will continue to keep them free. We hope that they will be used by any British school or teacher with an interest in materials which can be used to challenge their stronger students.

The schemes are designed for pupils ranging from Years 7 to 13 in England and Wales, Years 8 to 14 in Northern Ireland, and Years S1 to S6 in Scotland.

There are four schemes: Junior, Intermediate, Senior and Advanced. The idea is that a student receives a monthly sheet of problems through the months October to May. They are intended to work on the problems with the help and encouragement of a mentor.

At the Junior and Intermediate levels, we encourage teachers to mentor their own pupils: regular contact with someone they know personally is ordinarily very valuable for younger students.

At the Senior and Advanced levels, we assign an expert mentor: typically, an undergraduate or postgraduate student or teacher with familiarity with problem-solving techniques. They will communicate with a small number of students by post and by email. In exceptional circumstances, we are willing to provide external mentors for students on the Intermediate scheme.

Anyone who is interested in participating (either as a mentee or a mentor) should email us at mentoring@ukmt.org.uk to register with Beverley Detoeuf in the UKMT office. Teachers registering in this way will then receive the problems and solutions monthly, which they can use however they wish.

There now follows a brief description of each scheme:

Junior scheme: Currently run by John Slater and Julian Gilbey, this is used by more than 750 schools. This scheme is suggested for strong students aged 11-14, who have perhaps had success in the Junior Mathematical Olympiad or similar. However, there are no rules on on how the material is used, and it is known that some teachers use the questions to provide unusual exercises for older students. All students are mentored in school by teachers on this scheme.

Here is a question from the first sheet of the year 2013-2014:

Which of these numbers are the same as $\sqrt{2000^{2000}}$?

(a) 2000^{1000} (b) 1000^{2000} (c) $(20\sqrt{5})^{2000}$ (d) $2000^{20\sqrt{5}}$

Intermediate scheme: This is used by more than 700 schools. James Cranch is currently overseeing it, though the sheets are recycled from several years ago. This scheme is mostly appropriate for students aged 14-16 who have succeeded in the Intermediate Mathematical Olympiad or some similar pursuit.

While it is mostly used in-school, we currently have a team of thirteen external mentors, who work with thirty-two students.

Here is a question from last year's first sheet:

The number 12 has 6 factors: 1, 2, 3, 4, 6, 12. Find a criterion for a number to have an odd number of factors. (That is, find some simple property that is held by all numbers with an odd number of factors, but is not held by any number with an even number of factors.)

Senior scheme: The Senior sheets are used by more than 350 schools. In addition, we have seventy mentors working with 190 students. Students are usually appropriate who are aged 16-18 and who have had success in the BMO or suchlike. The sheets are currently set by André Rzym.

Here is a sample question from the first sheet of last year:

Alison and Josh are standing at the top of a flight of ten stairs. Alison can jump down one or two stairs at a time (for example, she could get to the bottom by taking five jumps of two stairs at a time). In how many distinct ways can Alison get from the top of the stairs to the bottom?
Josh can jump up to ten stairs in one go. In how many distinct ways can Josh get from the top of the stairs to the bottom?

Advanced scheme: Unlike the other schemes, access to the Advanced scheme is available only by invitation. It is explicitly intended for students who have had considerable success in national mathematics competitions and who wish to compete in international competitions for the UK. The sheets are set by a group of undergraduate students at Trinity College, Cambridge, headed by Richard Freeland.

Over the last year, there were twenty-one students working with ten expert mentors.

A mentoring conference and dinner was held on November 23rd, 2013 at Murray Edwards College, Cambridge, in order to train mentors and exchange advice. We are grateful to Vicky Neale for supplying the venue, and to Imre Leader and Paul Russell for giving sessions.

James Cranch, Director of Mentoring

UKMT Team Maths Challenge 2014

Overview

The Team Maths Challenge (TMC) is a national mathematics competition which gives pupils the opportunity to participate in a wide range of mathematical activities and compete against other pupils from schools in their region. The TMC promotes team working and, unlike the Junior, Intermediate and Senior Challenges, students work in groups and are given practical tasks as well as theoretical problems to add another dimension to mathematics.

The TMC is designed for teams of four pupils in:

- Y8 & Y9 (England and Wales)
- S1 & S2 (Scotland)
- Y9 & Y10 (Northern Ireland)

with no more than two pupils from the older year group.

Sample TMC material is available to download from the TMC section of the UKMT website (www.tmc.ukmt.org.uk) for use in school and to help teachers to select a team to represent their school at the Regional Finals.

Report on the 2014 TMC

The twelfth year of the competition saw yet another record number of participating schools. Entries were received from 1730 teams, of which 1593 turned up to take part at one of 68 Regional Finals, including the first ever TMC in North Wales.

As usual, competition details and entry forms were sent to schools in early October and made available on the UKMT website, which also provided up-to-date information on Regional Final venues and availability of places, as well as past materials for the use of schools in selecting and preparing their team of four. Schools also received a copy of the winning poster from the 2013 National Final, originally created by The Perse School (Cambridge) and professionally reproduced by Arbelos.

Each team signed up to participate in one of the 68 Regional Finals, held between late February and the end of April at a widely-spread set of venues. Each Regional Final comprised four rounds which encouraged the teams to think mathematically in a variety of ways. The Group Round is the only round in which the whole team work together, tackling a set of ten challenging questions. In the Crossnumber the team splits into two pairs; one pair gets the across clues and the other pair gets the down clues. The two pairs then work independently to complete the Crossnumber using logic and deduction. For the Shuttle, teams compete against the clock to answer a series of questions, with each pair working on different questions and the solution of each question dependent on the previous answer. The final round of the day, the Relay, is a fast and furious race involving much movement to answer a series of questions in pairs. Each Regional Final was run by a regional lead coordinator with support from an assistant coordinator and, at some venues, other local helpers. The teachers who accompanied the teams were fully occupied too – they were involved in the delivery and marking of all of the rounds.

TMC National Final

Eighty teams (the winners from each Regional Final plus a few runners-up) were invited to the National Final on 23rd June, which was again held at the Lindley Hall, part of the prestigious Royal Horticultural Halls, in Westminster, London. As usual, the four rounds from the Regional Finals also featured at the National Final except that the Group Round became the Group Circus: a similar round but with the inclusion of practical materials for use in solving the questions. In addition, the day began with the Poster Competition, which is judged and scored separately from the main event. The Poster theme for 2014 was 'Mathematical Billiards' and the entries were exhibited down the side of the hall throughout the day for the perusal of the participants as well as the judges.

The following schools (slightly more state than independent), coming from as far north as Aberdeen and as far south as Jersey, participated at the National Final:

Abingdon School, Oxfordshire
Altrincham Grammar School for Boys, Cheshire
Bablake School, Coventry
Backwell School, North Somerset
Bancroft's School, Essex
Beechwood Park School, Hertfordshire
Belfast Royal Academy
Birkenhead School, Merseyside
Bishop Bell C of E School, East Sussex
Bridgewater High School, Warrington
Bristol Grammar School
Caistor Grammar School, Lincolnshire
Cardiff High School
Cargilfield Preparatory, Edinburgh
Christ's Hospital, West Sussex
City of London School
Cockermouth School, Cumbria
Colchester Royal Grammar School, Essex
Comberton Village College, Cambridge
Dame Alice Owen's School, Hertfordshire
Dean Close Senior School, Gloucestershire
Debenham High School, Suffolk
Devonport High School for Girls, Devon
Dragon School, Oxford
Durham Johnston School
Eltham College, London
Ermysted's Grammar School, North Yorkshire
Forest School, London
Fulford School, York
Glasgow Academy
Gosforth East Middle Sch., Newcastle upon Tyne
Henry Beaufort School, Hampshire
Horris Hill School, Berkshire
King Edward VI School, Southampton
King Edward VII School, Sheffield
King Edward's School, Bath
King Edward's School, Birmingham
King's College School, London

Lancaster Girls' Grammar School
Liverpool Blue Coat School, Merseyside
Loretto School, Midlothian
Loughborough High School, Leicestershire
Macmillan Academy, Middlesbrough
Manchester Grammar School
Merchant Taylors' School, Middlesex
Monmouth School, Monmouthshire
Moreton Hall School, Shropshire
Netherhall School, Cambridge
Norton Hill School, Bath
Norwich School, Norfolk
Oundle School, Peterborough
Penair School, Cornwall
Pocklington School, York
Poole Grammar School, Dorset
Queen Elizabeth's Grammar School, Lincolnshire
Queen Mary's Grammar School, West Midlands
Reading School, Berkshire
Reigate Grammar School, Surrey
Robert Gordon's College, Aberdeen
Royal Wootton Bassett Academy, Wiltshire
Ryde School with Upper Chine, Isle of Wight
Sevenoaks School, Kent
Simon Langton Boys' Grammar School, Kent
Solihull School, West Midlands
St Nicholas High School, Cheshire
St Paul's Girls' School, London
St Paul's School, London
St Robert of Newminster School, Tyne & Wear
Stockport Grammar School, Cheshire
Tapton School, Sheffield
The De Ferrers Academy, Staffordshire
The Grammar School at Leeds, West Yorkshire
The Royal Grammar School, Buckinghamshire
The Royal Latin School, Buckingham
Tonbridge Grammar School, Kent
Torquay Boys' Grammar School, Devon
Ulverston Victoria High School, Cumbria
Victoria College, Jersey
Wilson's School, Surrey
Wolverhampton Girls' High Sch., West Midlands

We were delighted to have in attendance David Wells, author of books on popular mathematics, puzzles and recreations such as *The Penguin Dictionary of Curious and Interesting Numbers* and *Games and Mathematics: Subtle Connections*, who addressed the teams and awarded the prizes at the end. We are also grateful to Arbelos and Hewlett-Packard for providing additional prizes for the event and to UKMT volunteer Andrew Bell for capturing the day's excitement in his additional role as official photographer. Congratulations go to the 2014 Team Maths Challenge champions City of London School (who retained their 2013 title) and to the winners of the Poster Competition: Tonbridge Grammar School.

As usual, thanks are due to a great number of people for ensuring another successful year of the TMC: the team of volunteers (listed at the back of this book) who generously give up their time to write, check and refine materials, run Regional Finals (with a helping hand from family members in a few cases!) and readily carry out countless other jobs behind the scenes; the staff in the UKMT office in Leeds for the way in which the competition is administered (particularly Nicky Bray who has responsibility for the central coordination of the competition, assisted by Shona Raffle with additional support from Jo Williams) and the team of packers for their efficient and precise preparation and packing of materials; the teachers who continue to support the competition and take part so willingly, some of whom also undertake the significant task of organising and hosting a Regional Final at their own school and, of course, the pupils who participate so enthusiastically in the competition at all levels. Our thanks also go to additional contacts at schools and other host venues responsible for organising and helping with Regional Finals (listed at the back of this book).

TMC Regional Finals Material

Each of the 68 Regional Finals held across the UK involved four rounds:

1. Group Round
2. Crossnumber
3. Shuttle
4. Relay Race

Group Round

Teams are given a set of 10 questions, which they should divide up among themselves so that they can answer, individually or in pairs, as many as possible in the allotted time.

Question 1

A bag contains £20.14 consisting of 50p, 20p, 10p, 5p, 2p and 1p coins only. If there are at least 14 of each of these coins in the bag, what is the least possible number of coins in the bag?

Question 2

Points A, B and C lie in that order on a straight line.

A point D, not on the line, is placed such that $AD = AB$, $BD = BC$ and $\angle BDC = 25°$.

What is the value of $\angle DAB$?

Question 3

On a certain Monday, whilst Jo and Nicky tweeted, Steve had his face in a book.

The next day, whilst Jo and Steve tweeted, Nicky had her face in a book. A day later, whilst Nicky and Steve tweeted, Jo had her face in a book. This pattern repeated every three days until once again on a Monday, Jo and Nicky tweeted whilst Steve had his face in a book.

On how many days did Steve tweet over this period?

Question 4

Every day Keith has a breakfast, a lunch and a dinner.

The options for each meal are:

Breakfast: Cereal and/or Fruit
Lunch: Soup and/or a Sandwich
Dinner: Pasta and/or Curry

One day Keith eats four items. In how many different ways can he do this?

Question 5

Pam was born on Saturday 2nd February 2002. From then on Pam's grandparents saved £1 every Sunday until her 6th birthday.

How much money did they save?

Question 6

In a junior league each team plays each of the other teams twice during the season – once at home and once away. There are 56 matches in total during the season.

How many teams are there in the league?

Question 7

A cube is placed on a horizontal table. The vertices around the top face are labelled A, B, C and D in that order, going clockwise. The corresponding vertices around the base of the cube are labelled E, F, G and H. This means that vertex E is directly below vertex A, F is directly below B and so on.

Find the size of the angle made at C by the lines AC and CH.

Question 8

The length of a rectangle is five times its width. The rectangle is divided into three smaller sections by two vertical lines. The areas of the three smaller sections are in the ratio 3 : 7 : 15. The area of the middle section is 35 cm^2.

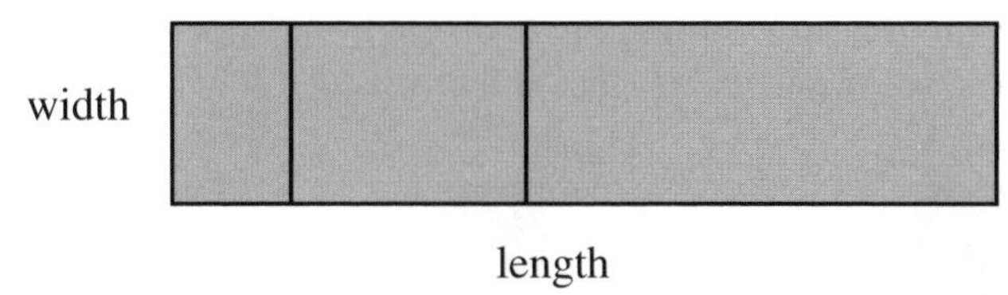

What is the base length of the original rectangle?

Question 9

In a list of seven consecutive numbers, a quarter of the smallest number is five less than a third of the largest number.

What is the value of the smallest number in the list?

Question 10

Six of the prime numbers less than 20 are separated into three pairs. Each pair has the same sum.

What is the value of this sum?

Crossnumber

Teams are divided into pairs, with one pair given the across clues and one pair given the down clues. Each pair answers as many questions as possible on the grid, showing their answers to the supervising teacher who either confirms or corrects them. The correct version is then shown to both pairs. Pairs only communicate through the supervisor, but they may make a request for particular clues to be solved.

■	1		2	■	3		4	
5		■	6			■		■
■	7	8		■	■	9		10
11	■		■	12	13		■	
14		■	15	■		■	16	
	■	17			■	18	■	
19	20		■	■	21		22	■
■		■	23			■	24	
25				■	26			■

Across:

1. 75% of 4 Down (3)
3. A seventh power (4)
5. An angle of an isosceles triangle that has 68° as one of its angles (2)
6. A multiple of the sum of its digits (3)
7. A square number multiplied by 24 Across (3)
9. The largest three-digit Fibonacci number (3)
12. The sum of its digits is 15 Down (3)
14. The product of an even square and a prime (2)
16. Twenty less than 5 Across (2)

17. A multiple of 15 Down (3)
19. The product of 28 and the previous triangular number (3)
21. A square number (3)
23. Its digits sum to ten (3)
24. Half of 9 Down (2)
25. The number of minutes in four days (4)
26. The mean of 1 Down and 9 Across (3)

Down:

1. The product of all the primes in the twenties (3)
2. Six more than 1 Across (3)
3. A factor of 3 Across (2)
4. The product of an even cube and a prime (3)
8. The next prime after 24 Across (2)
9. Twice a prime number (2)
10. 11 Down minus 3 Across (4)
11. The product of two consecutive triangular numbers (4)
13. The sum of all the factors of 28 (2)
15. The sum of the fourth powers of two different numbers (2)
17. Half of 5 Across (2)
18. A square number that is also a triangular number (2)
20. The remainder when 11 Down is divided by 3 Across (3)
21. A power of two (3)
22. 9 Across minus 40 (3)
23. 13 Down minus 16 Across (2)

Shuttle

Teams are divided into pairs, with one pair given Questions 1 and 3 (along with the record sheet on which to record their answers) and the other pair given Questions 2 and 4. The first pair works on Question 1 and then passes the answer to the students in the other pair who use it to help them answer Question 2, for which they can first carry out some preparatory work. This continues with the second pair passing the answer to Question 2 back to the first pair and so on until a full set of answers is presented for marking. Bonus points are awarded to all teams which present a correct set of answers before the 6-minute whistle, then the other teams have a further 2 minutes in which to finish. Four of these shuttles are attempted in the time given.

A1

$A =$ the 5th triangular number
+ the 4th prime number
– the 3rd square number
– the 2nd cube number

Pass on the value of A.

A2 *T is the number that you will receive.*

Pass on the value of x that solves the equation

$$x + T = 2(2T - x) + 6.$$

A3 *T is the number that you will receive.*

To celebrate the New Year, three bells in Mathstown ring at constant intervals of 8 seconds, 10 seconds and $3T$ seconds respectively.

They all ring together at midnight and continue ringing at their particular intervals for a whole hour.

The next time at which the three chime together is K minutes past midnight.

Pass on the value of K.

A4 *T is the number that you will receive.*

T years ago, Hannah was five times as old as Claire.
In $\frac{1}{2}T$ years' time, Hannah will be twice as old as Claire.
Write down Claire's current age.

B1 There are N whole numbers between 1 and 100 that contain the digit 5.
Pass on the value of N.

B2 *T is the number that you will receive.*

The prime factors of 2014 are T, a and b.
Pass on the value of $a + b$.

B3 *T is the number that you will receive.*

The mean of 5 numbers is T.
The mean of 10 other numbers is $T + 30$.
The mean of all 15 numbers is M.

Pass on the value of M.

B4 *T is the number that you will receive.*

A linear sequence starts 8, 17, 26, 35, . . .
Write down the numerical value of the $\left(\frac{T}{3}\right)$th term.

C1 Pass on the value of $3^2 + 3^4 + 3^5$.

C2 *T is the number that you will receive.*

The parallelogram below has perimeter P cm and area A cm^2.

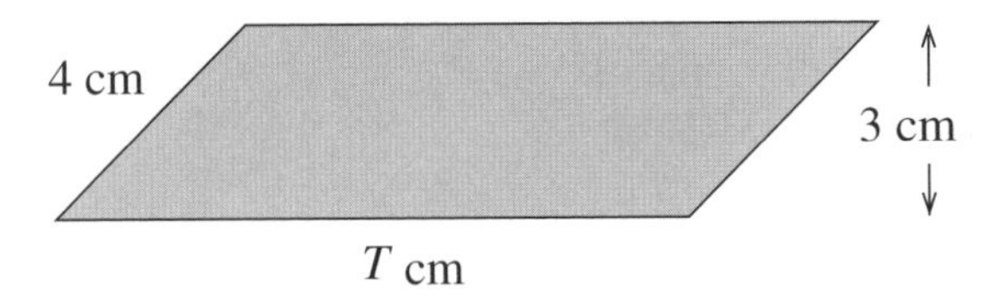

Pass on the value of the whole number $\frac{A - P}{13}$.

C3 *T is the number that you will receive.*

$$\frac{K}{3} = \frac{T}{3} + \frac{4}{5} + \frac{13}{15}$$

Pass on the value of K.

C4 *T is the number that you will receive.*

At T minutes past midday, the obtuse angle between the hands on a clock is exactly $C°$.
Write down the value of C.

D1

$$K = (98 - 76 - 5 \times 4 + 3) \div 2 - 1$$

Pass on the value of K.

D2 *T is the number that you will receive.*

The shape below has perimeter P cm and area A cm^2.

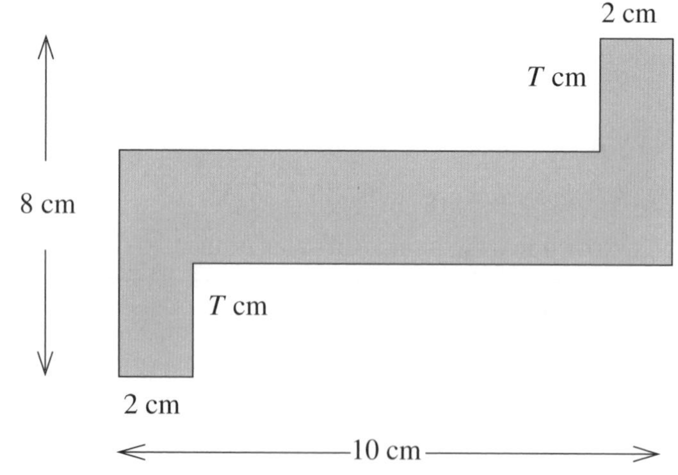

Pass on the value of $A - P$.

D3 *T is the number that you will receive.*

H is the highest common factor of $24T$ and $42T$.
Pass on the value of H.

D4 *T is the number that you will receive.*

Speedy Steve travels the first 100 km of his journey at T km/h, and the next 100 km of his journey at $\frac{2}{3}T$ km/h.

His average speed over the whole journey is S km/h.

Write down the value of S.

Relay

The aim here is to have a speed competition with students working in pairs to answer alternate questions. Each team is divided into two pairs, with each pair seated at a different desk away from the other pair and their supervising teacher.

One member of Pair A from a team collects question A1 from the supervising teacher and returns to his/her partner to answer the question together. When the pair is certain that they have answered the question, the runner returns to the front and submits their answer. If it is correct, the runner is given question B1 to give to the other pair (Pair B) from their team. If it is incorrect, Pair A then has another go at answering the question, then the runner returns to the front to receive question B1 to deliver to pair B. (Pair A can only have one extra attempt.) The runner then returns, empty handed, to his/her partner. Pair B answers question B1 and a runner from this pair brings the answer to the front, as above, then takes question A2 to Pair A. Pair A answers question A2, their runner returns it to the front and collects question B2 for the other pair, and so on until all questions are answered or time runs out. Thus the A pairs answer only A questions and the B pairs answer only B questions. Only one pair from a team should be working on a question at any time and each pair must work independently of the other.

A1 Using only the numbers between 122 and 128 inclusive, find the difference between the number that is one more than a multiple of four and the number that is a multiple of seven.

A2 The mean of five numbers is 8. The mode is 9 and the range is 4. What are the numbers?

A3 Ann thinks of a number. When she multiplies it by 10 and subtracts 4, she obtains the same number as if she had multiplied by 7 and added 2.

What is Ann's starting number?

A4 What is the sum of the different prime numbers that divide exactly into 3528?

A5 There are 14 pounds (lb) in a stone (st).
Three children weigh 4 st 5 lb, 5 st 2 lb and 5 st 4 lb.
What is their mean weight in stones and pounds?

A6 The paint department has to paint a batch of widgets. On Monday they paint one third of the batch, and on Tuesday 45% of what is left. On Wednesday they find they have 99 widgets left to paint.
How many widgets are in the batch?

A7 Lawn feed is sold to the horticultural society in 3.5 kg tubs and they then repackage it into 400 g packets for their members.
How many full packets can they make from six tubs?

A8 The coordinates of two of the vertices of a trapezium are (3, 5) and (2, 7). It has a line of symmetry $x = 4$.
What are the coordinates of the other two vertices?

A9 Each term in a sequence of numbers is formed by doubling the previous number and then adding one. The third number is 31.
What is the first number of this sequence?

A10 Last year, at the TMC National Final on 18th June 2013, I calculated that my next birthday would be in 3 months, 3 weeks and 3 days.
On what date is my birthday?

A11 A mathematics teacher has a 45-minute lunch break. She spends 15 minutes eating her lunch, 10 minutes helping a student, 12 minutes marking and the rest of the time talking to a colleague.
When this information is drawn on a pie chart, what is the angle for ‘talking to a colleague’?

A12 Twenty people take apple pie or ice cream or both from the buffet. 65% have apple pie and 95% have ice cream.
How many have only one?

A13 Trevor makes a rectangular lawn 7.5 metres by 3.2 metres.
Turf costs £5 per square metre.
What will it cost to turf the area completely?

A14 The figure shows a partially completed magic square.

	(shaded)	2.6
	2.5	3.1
2.4		

What number goes in the shaded cell?

A15 To the nearest thousand minutes, how many minutes are there in the year 2014?

B1 A bucket contains 7.5 litres of weed killer.
The instructions say “use 50 ml per square metre”.
What area can be treated with this bucket?

B2 Each term in a sequence of numbers is formed by halving the previous number and then subtracting four. The third number is 6.
What is the first number in this sequence?

B3 New Year's Day 2020 will be a Wednesday.
What day of the week is 1st June 2020?

B4 Using only the numbers between 160 and 167 inclusive, find the difference between the number that is one less than a multiple of six and the number that is a multiple of eleven.

B5 Bill is on a ten-day cycling holiday. In the first five days his mean daily distance is 5.2 km.
In the next five days Bill cycles a total of 50.5 km.
What is his overall mean daily distance?

B6 Sue thinks of a number. When she multiplies it by 7 and adds 3 she obtains the same number as if she had multiplied by 2 and added 18.
What is Sue's starting number?

B7 There are 12 inches (in) in 1 foot (ft).
Three children are measured and their heights are 4 ft 4 in, 4 ft 6 in and 5 ft 2 in.
What is their mean height in feet and inches?

B8 What is the sum of the different prime numbers that divide exactly into 13068?

B9 A mathematical grandmother bakes a huge batch of biscuits for her grandchildren. On Saturday they eat $\frac{2}{5}$ of the biscuits, on Sunday they eat 85% of the rest, and then just 9 biscuits remain.

How many biscuits were in the batch?

B10 A renard is a Thai musical instrument made from nine wooden bars. The shortest bar is 20 cm long. The length of each bar is 1 cm longer than the previous one. The bars are cut from strips of wood that are 30 cm in length.

What total length of wood is wasted?

B11 The figure shows a partially completed magic square.

	(shaded)	3.6
	3.0	4.2
2.4		

What number goes in the shaded cell?

B12 Two of the angles of a kite are 75° and 85°.

What is the largest possible remaining angle?

B13 Sixty students are studying French or German or both languages. 80% study French and 75% German.

How many students study both languages?

B14 A student in the 45-minute group round of a Regional Final spent 12 minutes talking, 20 minutes writing, 8 minutes checking and the rest staring into space.

When this information is drawn on a pie chart, what is the angle for “staring into space”?

B15 The coordinates of two of the vertices of a rhombus are (2, 3) and (6, 1). One of the diagonals has the equation $x + y = 7$.

What are the coordinates of the other two points?

TMC National Final Material

At the National Final, the Group Round is replaced by the Group Circus.

Group Circus

Teams move around a number of stations (eight at the 2014 National Final) to tackle a variety of activities, some of which involve practical materials.

Station 1

A regular hexagon has vertices A, B, C, D, E and F.

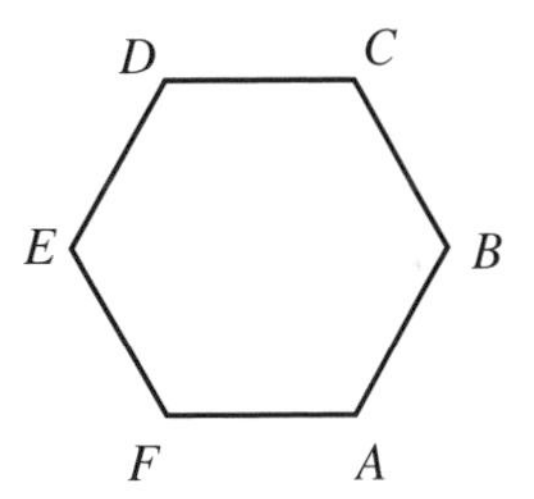

How many non-congruent polygons can be drawn by joining 3, 4 or 5 vertices from this regular hexagon?

Two polygons are congruent if they have both the same shape and the same size.

Station 2

In the 4×2 grid, the squares B1 and D2 are shaded, as shown.

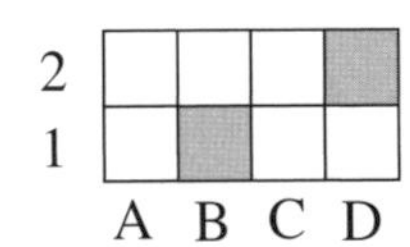

Megan and Julie take turns shading some of the unshaded squares. At each turn the unshaded squares that they shade must be in the shape of a square or a rectangle.

The person who has no squares left to shade loses the game.

Megan starts first and shades just one square.

Which square should Megan shade in order that she can force a win?

Station 3

Place the number cards provided (1 - 8) on the grid below, one in each blank space, so that *all* the following are true.

(a) Each pair of *adjacent* numbers differs by more than 1.

(b) Each of the four pairs of *directly opposite* numbers differs by more than 1.

(c) Each of the four pairs of *directly opposite* numbers add up to a prime number.

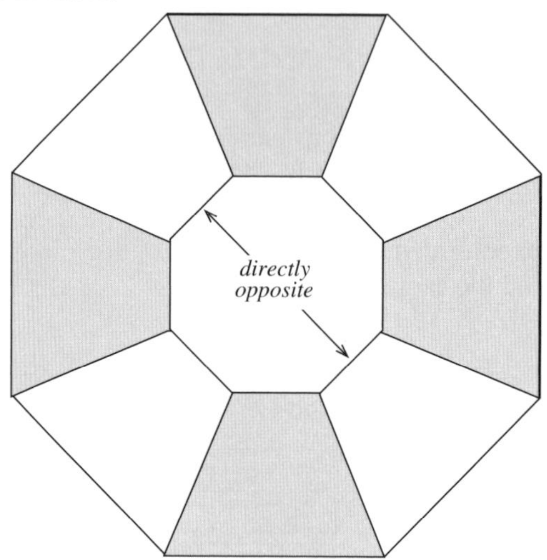

Station 4

The triangle ABC is isosceles with $AC = BC$, as shown.

The point D lies on the line BC such that the triangle ABD is isosceles with $AB = BD$, as shown.

Given that $\angle BAC = 2\angle BCA$, what is the value of $\angle ADC$?

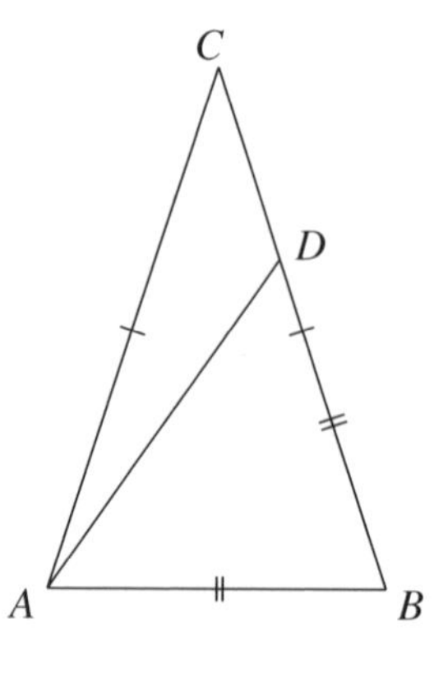

Station 5

In a quiz, the Smith family scored twelve points fewer than the winning team.

If they had scored 10% more than they actually did, they would have beaten the winning team by six points.

What was the winning team's score?

Station 6

You are provided with four pieces of red card cut into different shapes and four identical pieces of blue card.

(a) Arrange the four pieces of red card into a rectangle which is not a square.

(b) Arrange the four pieces of blue card into a square.

In each case, the pieces of card should not overlap, and there should be no gaps between them.

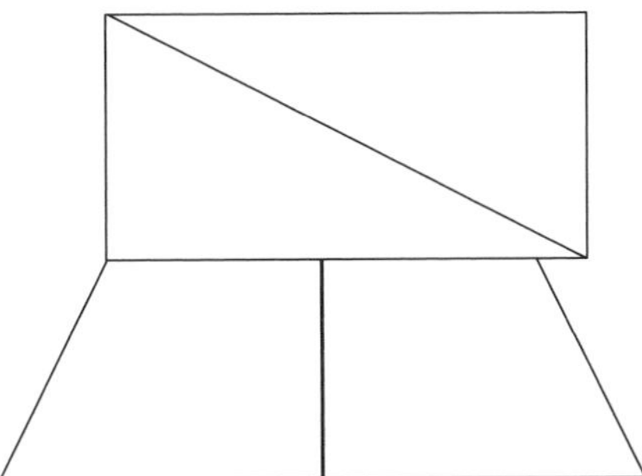

Station 7

Place *exactly* three common mathematical operations (which need not all be different) between the digits below so that the result equals 100.

You are not allowed to rearrange the order of the digits.

$$1 \quad 2 \quad 3 \quad 4 \quad 5 \quad 6 \quad 7 \quad 8 \quad 9$$

For example,

$$1234 \times 5 - 67 \times 89.$$

We know this example is wrong because the result is 207.

Station 8

Each of the letters J, K, L, M and N is used to represent a single digit in the two statements below.

The same letter always stands for the same digit.

In the second statement, 'NJ' stands for the two-digit number formed by replacing each of N and J by a single digit.

Find the value of $K + M$.

$$J + K = L$$

$$L + M = NJ$$

Crossnumber

1		2	■	3		4		5
	■	6			■		■	
7	8		■	■	9		10	
■		■	11			■		■
12		■		■		■	13	
■		■	14			■		■
15		16		■	■	17		18
	■		■	19			■	
20					■	21		

Across:

1. Nine less than 4 Down (3)
3. 15 Across plus 20 Across plus 2 Down (5)
6. A Fibonacci number (3)
7. A multiple of seven (3)
9. 1 Across multiplied by ten plus a square number (4)
11. The product of 19 Down and the square root of 6 Across (3)
12. The sum of the digits in the first column (2)
13. 18 Down minus seventeen (2)
14. The sum of the cubes of its digits (3)
15. 88 squared (4)
17. 19 Across minus 13 Across (3)
19. The product ab where a and b are integer solutions of $5a + 7b = 223$ (3)

20. $(3^3 + 4^4 + 3^3 + 5^5) \times 10$ (5)

21. 6 Across plus the square of 19 Down (3)

Down:

1. The mean of 4 Down and 11 Across (3)
2. A multiple of nine (3)
3. A multiple of eleven (2)
4. The product of the first four prime numbers (3)
5. 6 Across minus twice 19 Down (3)
8. $2^{2^4} + 1$ (the 5th Fermat number) (5)
9. The product of three primes (not all different) that have the same units digit (4)
10. Multiply this number by nine and you will have reversed it! (5)
11. The mean of 9 Across and 11 Down (4)
15. 840 minus 13 Across (3)
16. 17 Down plus 19 Across (3)
17. The product of its digits is 40 (3)
18. Seventeen more than a prime (3)
19. Five more than the square root of 1 Down (2)

Shuttle

A1 The four members of the *Mean Girls* pop group have mean height 149 cm.

Nicky joins the group, and is N cm taller than the previous mean. This increases the mean height of the *Mean Girls* to 152 cm.

Pass on the value of $N - 1$.

A2 *T is the number that you will receive.*

This year, 2014, contains 365 days.

365 can be written as the sum of two squares in the form

$$365 = A^2 + T^2.$$

Pass on the positive value of A.

A3 *T is the number that you will receive.*

R is the remainder when $(T^2 + 17^2)$ is divided by 7.

Pass on the value of R.

A4 *T is the number that you will receive.*

Timmy has made a wooden bowl, starting with a hemisphere of wood of radius 10 cm and cutting a hemisphere of radius 8 cm out from the centre of it.

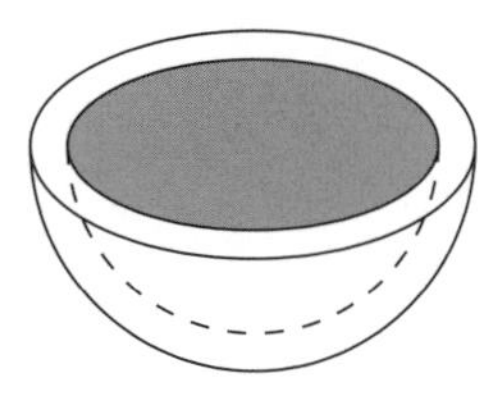

He wishes to varnish the whole of it, and he finds that he needs T ml of varnish per 4π cm^2 of surface area.

Write down the number of ml of varnish Timmy needs.

[*The surface area of a sphere of radius r is $4\pi r^2$.*]

B1 The value of

$$\frac{1}{2} \div \frac{3}{4} \times \left(\frac{5}{6} + \frac{7}{8}\right) \times \frac{9}{10}$$

can be written as an improper fraction $\frac{a}{b}$, which is in its lowest terms.

Pass on the value of $a - b$.

B2 *T is the number that you will receive.*

The angles in an irregular quadrilateral form a sequence in which each term is $8T°$ larger than the previous one.

The smallest angle is $A°$.

Pass on the value of A.

B3 *T is the number that you will receive.*

The difference between the squares of two consecutive numbers is $T + 1$.

Pass on the value of the smaller of these two numbers.

B4 *T is the number that you will receive.*

The rectangle and the right-angled triangle in the diagram have the same area.

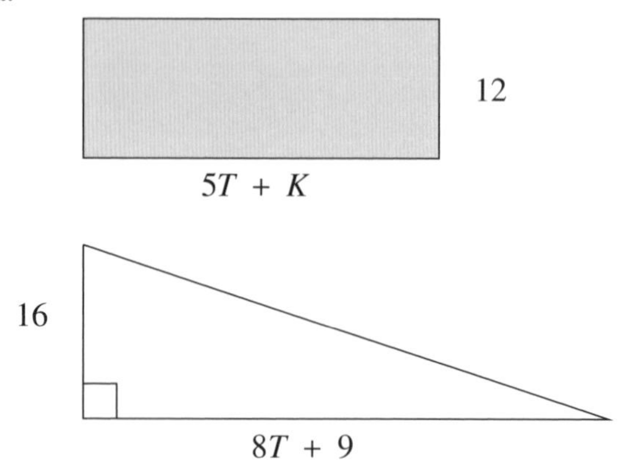

Write down the value of K.

C1 Every week, Jo buys apples, bananas, pears and oranges to feed her pet monkeys. Last week she bought J pieces of fruit, where $J < 150$.

She noticed that the ratio of apples to bananas was 3 : 2, the ratio of bananas to pears was 5 : 4 and the ratio of pears to oranges was 3 : 1.

Pass on the value of J.

C2 *T is the number that you will receive.*

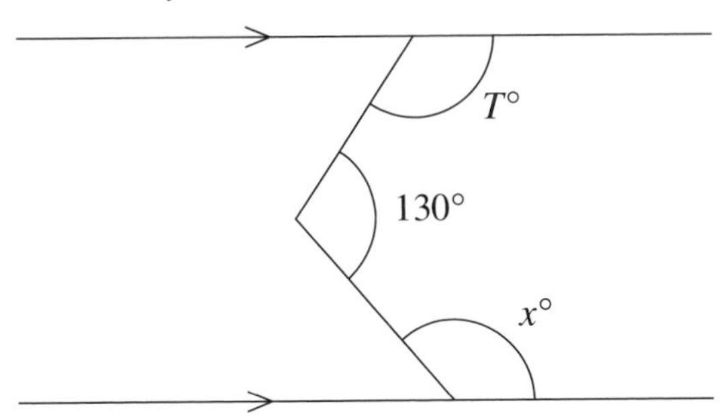

Pass on the value of x.

C3 *T is the number that you will receive.*

In the graph below, the area of the shaded triangle is $T + 5$.

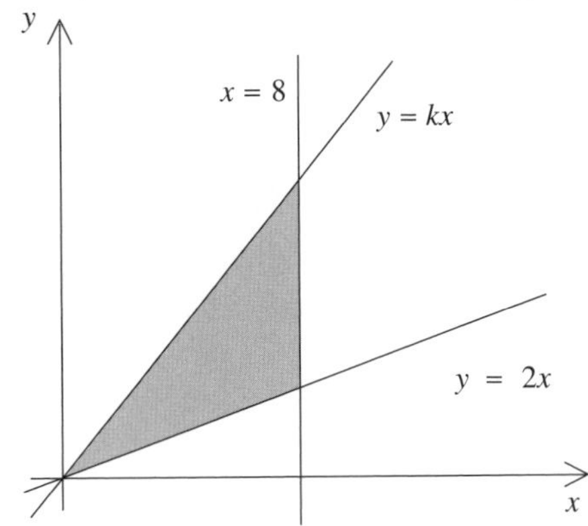

Pass on the value of k.

C4 *T is the number that you will receive.*

When Niall's class were surveyed to find out how many pet dogs each person had at home, the results were:

Number of dogs	0	1	2	3
Frequency	$T + 2$	9	2	1

Let K = mean + mode + range.
Write down the value of $10K$.

D1 In a class survey of 20 people about crisp flavours:

12 like Cheese & Onion
15 like Salt & Vinegar
2 like neither flavour

Pass on the number of people who like both flavours.

D2 *T is the number that you will receive.*

In this question, the diamond symbol $\diamond$ means "the difference between the squares of the numbers on either side".
For example, $6 \diamond 8 = 8^2 - 6^2 = 28$.
You are told that D is a positive integer and $(2 \diamond 3) \diamond D = T$.
Pass on the value of $D - 1$.

D3 *T is the number that you will receive.*

The diagram shows five right-angled triangles, with lengths as shown.

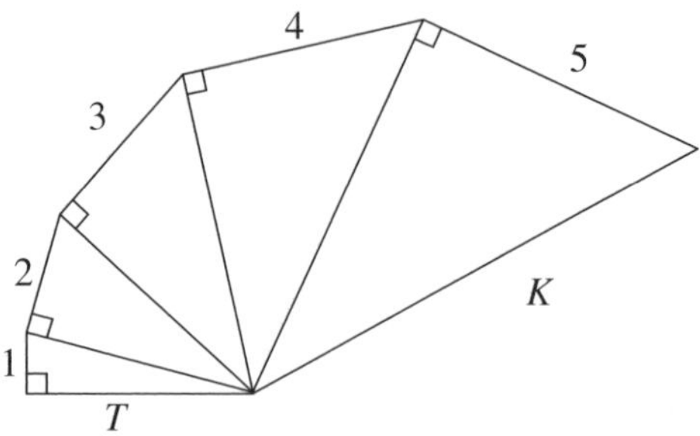

Pass on the value of K.

D4 *T is the number that you will receive.*

A fair die marked

$$1, \ 2, \ 3, \ 4, \ 5, \ 6$$

and a fair die marked

$$2, \ 4, \ 7, \ (T - 1), \ (T + 1), \ 15$$

are rolled together.

Write down, as a fraction, the probability that the sum of the scores is a prime number.

Relay

A1 Calculate the value of $1^1 \times 2^2 \times 3^3$.

A2 One machine made 70 bricks per hour and then its rate was increased by 5%.

Another machine made 80 per hour and then its rate was decreased by 5%.

What is the new mean rate of the two machines?

A3 Nicky walks at 4 km/h towards a café 6 km away.

Her cyclist friend, Rachel, who rides at 10 km/h sets off an hour later.

How long does Nicky have to wait for Rachel to arrive at the café?

A4 A set of six solid shapes contains various prisms and pyramids.

There is one of each with a triangular base, a square base and a hexagonal base.

How many triangular faces do these solids have between them?

A5 A recent study of animals' sleeping habits showed that the ant had 253 naps a day, with an average time of 1.1 minutes for each nap.

To the nearest hour, how long is the ant awake in a 24 hour period?

A6 The coordinates of the vertices of a square are $A(2,3)$, $B(5,4)$, $C(6,1)$ and $D(3,0)$.

The square is rotated 180° about B.

What are the coordinates of the image of C?

A7 The bridge over the River Pi lifts up to let yachts out of the marina.

Jack recorded the number of yachts leaving at each lift.

He made a mistake in the seventh value; he should have recorded another 2 yachts.

What is the mean number of yachts per lift?

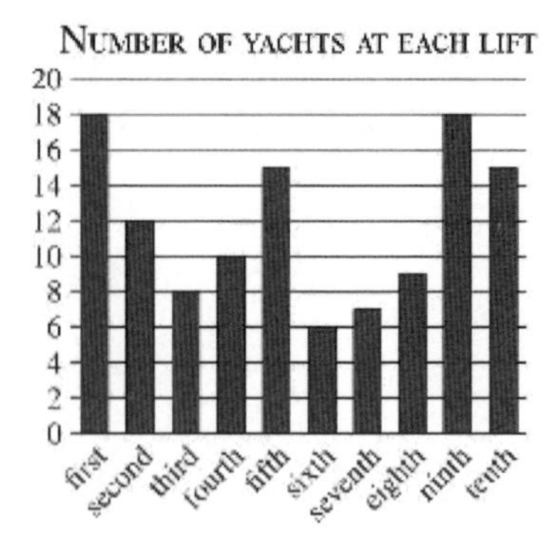

A8 Every Christmas Harry and Martha share a tin of 24 sweets in the ratio of their ages. Last year they were 4 and 2 years old respectively.

What is the difference between Harry's number of sweets last year and this year?

A9 Find a four-digit number divisible by 7, 11 and 13 with a digit sum of 12.

A10 Find the sum of M and N in this magic square.

M	− 4		−5
	N	− 2	5
− 6		− 3	6
	− 1		−8

A11 My friend and I calculate the petrol consumption of a journey which he says uses 8 litres for 100 km.

What should I say (to the nearest mile) in miles per gallon?

[*Use* 8 km ≈ 5 miles *and* 1 gallon ≈ 4.5 litres.]

A12 A set of axes is drawn on paper with centimetre squares.

What is the area of the triangle whose vertices have coordinates (3,2), (5,7) and (4,2)?

A13 I save 48p by buying a £6 bag of 24 oranges instead of 24 individual oranges.

What is the cost of one orange if bought on its own?

A14 Nicky, Steve and Rachel share 45 sweets.

Rachel has seven fewer than Nicky, but one more than Steve.

What fraction of the sweets are Nicky's?

A15 Nicole Kidman was born on 20th June 1967 in Hawaii.

How many full weeks has she been alive?

B1 Syd buys bags of crisps at ten bags for £1 and sells them at six for £1.

How many bags of crisps must he sell to make a profit of £10?

B2 When these points are plotted on a graph, which one is not on the same straight line as the others?

(2,5) (4,9) (0,3) (3,7)

B3 Calculate the value of $2^0 \times 3^1 \times 4^2$.

B4 A boat is motoring upstream, moving at 20 km/h through the water.

The river is flowing downstream at 5 km/h.

How long does the boat take to travel between two bridges 3 km apart?

B5 In Becky's computer game she gets five points for hitting a target, but loses seven points if she misses.

After 50 shots her score is 70.

How many targets did she hit?

B6 A set of six solid shapes contains various prisms and pyramids.

There is one of each with a triangular base, a square base and a hexagonal base.

How many quadrilateral faces do these solids have between them?

B7 A mathematical grandmother has coins of five different denominations in her purse and gives them all to her grandchildren.

Each child gets the same number of coins of each denomination.

She has £4.15 in her purse.

How many grandchildren does she have?

B8 The coordinates of the vertices of a triangle are $A(2,3)$, $B(5,4)$ and $C(6,1)$.

The triangle is translated so that the image of A is at B.

What are the coordinates of the image of C?

B9 The teacher has recorded Fred and Jane's test results for one week, on a chart, rounding the results to the nearest five. All the original marks were integers.

All of Fred's results were rounded up while all of Jane's were rounded down, both by the maximum possible number of marks.

What is the difference in their real totals for the week?

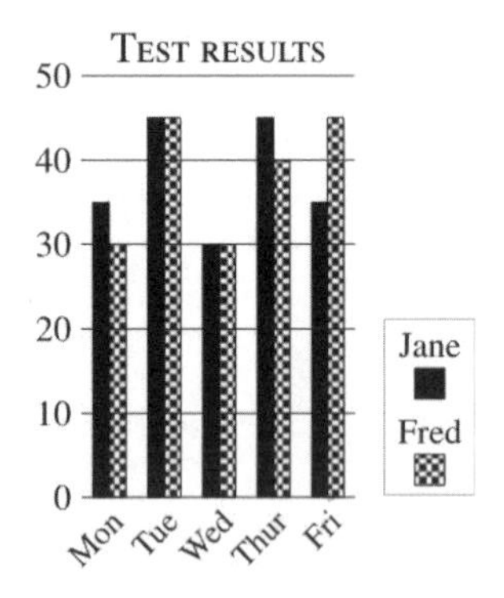

B10 While cycling, Bradley had a flat tyre after he had completed $\frac{2}{3}$ of the distance.

He walked the rest of the way, spending twice as long walking as he did riding.

What is the ratio of cycling speed to walking speed?

B11 Bananas cost 12p each in the café, but I can buy a box of 18 and save 16 pence.

How much will 5 boxes cost?

B12 Angle A is 90° and $CD = CE$.
Angle B is 57°.
Find $\angle DEC$.

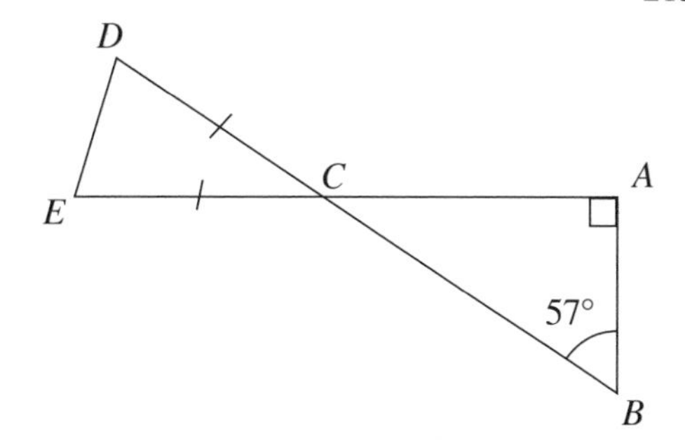

B13 The volume of a square-based cuboid is 8.45 cm^3, and its height is 5 cm.
What is the length of one side of the square base?

B14 Find the sum of P and Q in this magic square.

2	12	13	−1
	5	4	
3	P		6
Q		7	

B15 An early mathematician, Bhaskhara II, was born in 1114.
This is a simplified version of one of his problems.
What is the smallest positive integer which, when it is multiplied by 13 and 3 is added to the product, gives an answer that is a multiple of 17?

Solutions from the Regional Finals

Group Round Answers

1.	102	6.	8
2.	80°	7.	60°
3.	14	8.	25 cm
4.	12	9.	36
5.	£313	10.	24

Crossnumber

	[1] 6	0	[2] 6		[3] 2	1	[4] 8	7
[5] 5	6		[6] 1	1	7		0	
	[7] 7	[8] 5	2			[9] 9	8	[10] 7
[11] 9		3		[12] 8	[13] 5	4		3
[14] 5	2		[15] 1		6		[16] 3	6
5		[17] 2	7	2		[18] 3		8
[19] 5	[20] 8	8			[21] 1	6	[22] 9	
	0		[23] 2	6	2		[24] 4	7
[25] 5	7	6	0		[26] 8	2	7	

Shuttle

A1	5
A2	7
A3	14
A4	21

B1	19
B2	55
B3	75
B4	224

C1	333
C2	25
C3	30
C4	165

D1	1.5 or $\frac{3}{2}$ or $1\frac{1}{2}$
D2	20
D3	120
D4	96

Relay

A1	1	B1	150 m^2
A2	5, 8, 9, 9, 9	B2	48
A3	2	B3	Monday
A4	12	B4	4
A5	4 st 13 lb	B5	7.65 km
A6	270	B6	3
A7	52	B7	4 ft 8 in
A8	(5, 5), (6, 7)	B8	16
A9	7	B9	100
A10	12th October	B10	54 cm
A11	64°	B11	0.6
A12	8	B12	125°
A13	£120	B13	33
A14	1.7	B14	40°
A15	526 000	B15	(0, 7), (4, 5)

Solutions from the National Final

Group Circus

1. 7
2. A2
3.

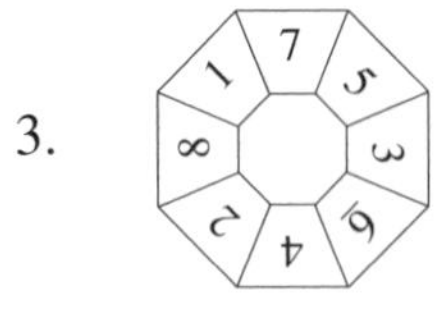

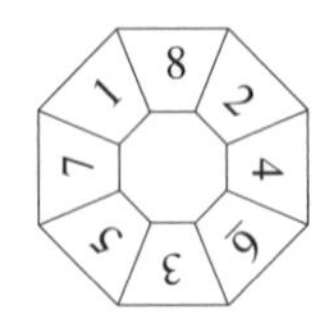

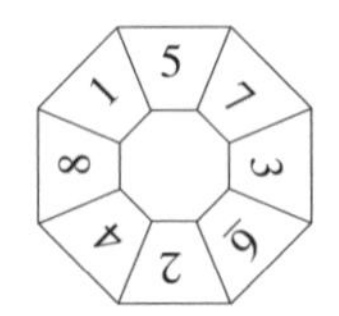

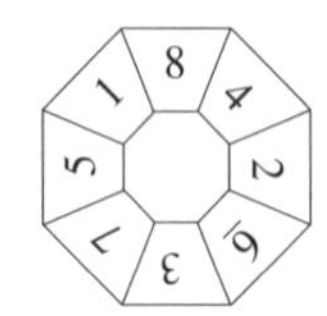

4. 126
5. 192
6.

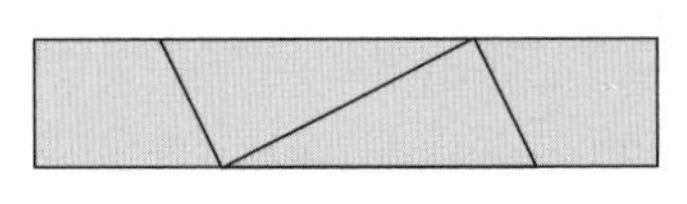

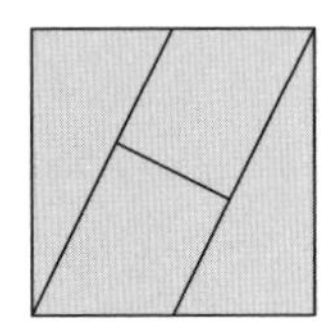

7. 123 − 45 − 67 + 89
8. 10

Crossnumber

[1]2	0	[2]1		[3]4	2	[4]2	1	[5]1
2		[6]1	4	4		1		0
[7]5	[8]6	7			[9]2	0	[10]1	4
	5		[11]2	4	0		0	
[12]2	5		0		2		[13]9	7
	3		[14]1	5	3		8	
[15]7	7	[16]4	4			[17]1	9	[18]1
4		7		[19]2	8	8		1
[20]3	4	3	5	0		[21]5	4	4

Shuttle

A1	14
A2	13
A3	3
A4	273

B1	1
B2	78
B3	39
B4	19

C1	107
C2	123
C3	6
C4	48

D1	9
D2	3
D3	8
D4	13/36

Relay

A1 108

A2 74.75 or $74\frac{3}{4}$

A3 6

A4 16

A5 19

A6 (4, 7)

A7 12

A8 1

A9 6006

A10 9

A11 35

A12 2.5 or $2\frac{1}{2}$

A13 27

A14 $\frac{4}{9}$

A15 2452

B1 150

B2 (0, 3)

B3 48

B4 12

B5 35

B6 16

B7 5

B8 (9, 2)

B9 20

B10 4 : 1

B11 10

B12 73.5 or $73\frac{1}{2}$

B13 1.3

B14 23

B15 5

UKMT and Further Maths Support Programme Senior Team Maths Challenge 2014

The Senior Team Maths Challenge is now entering into its 8th year and continues to grow in size and popularity. The 2013-14 competition comprised of over 1140 schools competing in 55 Regional Finals held across the United Kingdom; a higher number of competing teams than ever before.

Each team was made up of four students from years 11, 12 and 13 (at most two year 13 students per team) and the Regional Competition consisted of 3 Rounds; The Group Round, the Crossnumber and the Mini-Relay. For the Group Round, 10 questions were to be answered by each team in 40 minutes, while the Crossnumber involved each team solving a mathematical version of a crossword by splitting in two to work on the 'Across' and the 'Down' clues. The competition finished with the Mini-Relay round, which consisted of sets of four linked questions, answered in pairs against a timer.

National Final

The culmination of the competition was held at the National Final in February, where the top 60 teams were invited to the Camden Centre in Central London to compete for the title of 'National Champions'. It was a wonderful finale, at which the high level of energy and enthusiasm throughout the day created a wonderful celebration of mathematics.

Congratulations to all the schools who took part in the STMC National Final. These schools were:

Alton College;
Badminton School;
Bancrofts School;
Bilborough VI Form College;
Blundell's School;
Brentwood School;
Cheltenham Ladies College;
City of London School;
Clitheroe Royal Grammar School;
Cockermouth School;
Colchester Royal Grammar School;
College of Richard Collyer;
Devonport High School for Boys;
Norwich School;
Nottingham High School;
Oundle School;
Pocklington School;
Portadown College;
Queen Elizabeth High School (Gainsborough);
Queen Elizabeth Sixth Form College (Darlington);
Queen Elizabeth's Academy (Devon);
Queen Elizabeth's Grammar School (Derbyshire);
Queen Elizabeth's School (Barnet);
Queen Mary's Grammar School;
Rainham Mark Grammar School;
Robert Gordon's College;

Dr Challoner's Grammar School;
Eltham College;
Eton College;
Glasgow Academy;
Guernsey Grammar School;
Hampton School;
Harrogate Grammar School;
Harrow School;
High School of Dundee;
King Edward VI Camp Hill Boys' Sch.;
King Edward VI School;
King Edwards School, Birmingham;
Lancing College;
Leicester Grammar School;
Liverpool Blue Coat School;
Manchester Grammar School;
New College;
Robert Smyth Academy;
Royal Grammar School, Newcastle;
Ruthin School;
Shrewsbury School;
Sir Roger Manwood's School;
St Dunstan's College;
St Paul's School;
Strathallan School;
Tapton School;
The Cherwell School;
The Grammar School at Leeds;
The King's School Worcester;
Uppingham School;
Wellingborough School;
Wolverhampton Girls' High School;
Ysgol Dyffryn Taf.

The overall winners for 2013-14 were Hampton School and the Poster Competition winners were The Grammar School at Leeds.

The National Final consisted of the Group Round, the Crossnumber and the Mini-Relay with the addition of a Poster Competition at the start of the day. Teams were required to answer questions on 'Ruled Surfaces' and set these in the form of an attractive poster. Thanks to Peter Neumann, Matthew Baker, Colin Campbell, Alexandra Hewitt, Andrew Jobbings and Richard Lissaman for their hard work in preparing the materials and judging the posters once again. The Poster Competition did not contribute to the overall result of the National Final but a poster based on the work of the winning team has been professionally produced and printed. This will be sent to all of the schools that took part in the competition.

Thanks

As with all UKMT competitions, thanks must be given to all of the volunteers who wrote questions, acted as checkers for the materials produced, ran Regional Finals alongside FMSP coordinators and who helped on the day at the National Final.

The checkers of the questions were: John Silvester, Jenny Ramsden and Martin Perkins.

The 4 Round Rulers, who oversaw the materials for each round, were:

Karen Fogden (Group round), Peter Hall (Crossnumber), Mark Harwood (Mini-Relay) and James Cranch (Starter questions).

The writers of the questions were: Kerry Burnham, Tony Cheslett, Anthony Collieu, David Crawford, Andrew Ginty, James Munro, Charlie Oakley, Dennis Pinshon, Alexandra Randolph and Katie Ray.

As ever, many thanks to everyone involved for making 2013-14 another successful year.

The following pages contain much of the material which was used in both the Regional Finals and the National Final.

Regional Group Round

1

1	2	3	4					…			100

$\longrightarrow$

Lucy has a long straight path in her garden that is made from 100 paving slabs. Standing on slab 1 and whilst always facing forwards, she repeatedly takes two steps forwards and then one step back. Each step takes her from the slab on which she is standing to the next slab, either in front or behind. So her first three steps are from slab 1 to slab 2, from slab 2 to slab 3 and then from slab 3 back to slab 2.

Following this pattern, how many steps has Lucy taken when she steps onto slab 100 for the first time?

2 The recurrence relation connecting terms of a sequence $a_0, a_1, a_2, \ldots$ is $a_{n+1} = a_n + a_{n-1}, n \geqslant 1$.
Also, $a_0 = 5$ and $a_{10} = a_0$.

What is the value of a_1?

3 The sum of the squares of five consecutive positive integers is 9255. What is the value of the square of the next integer?

4

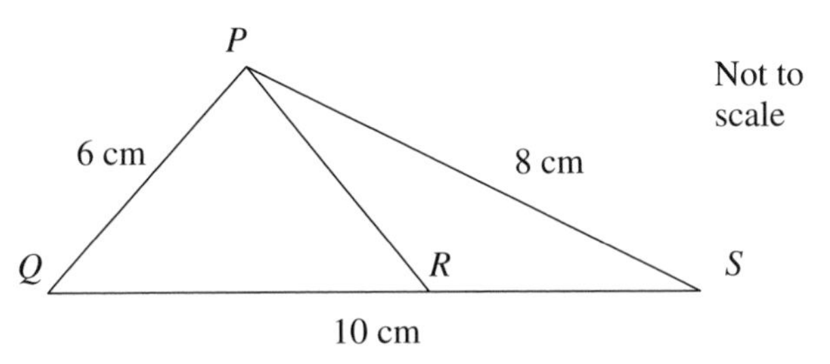

In triangle PQS, $PQ = 6$ cm, $PS = 8$ cm and $QS = 10$ cm.

An additional straight line is drawn from P to the point R on QS, such that the area of triangle PRS is 8 cm^2.

What is the length of RS ?

5 When Charlie took his car for a service last week he noticed that his odometer, which displays the cumulative mileage of the car, showed 54321 miles. A year ago his odometer read 43125.

Excluding 43125 and 54321, how many different permutations of the digits 1, 2, 3, 4 and 5 (each digit appearing exactly once in a 5-digit number) have occurred on Charlie's odometer during the intervening year?

6

n! (read as 'n factorial'), where n is a positive integer, is the product of all the positive integers less than or equal to n. For example, $5! = 5 \times 4 \times 3 \times 2 \times 1$.

The quantity

$$\frac{7!}{9! - 8!} \times \frac{5!}{7! - 6!} \times \frac{3!}{5! - 4!} \times \frac{1!}{3! - 2!}$$

may be written in the form $2^a \times 3^b$.

What is the value of $a + b$?

7

×	1	2	3	4	5	…	2013
1	1	2	3	4	5		
2	2	4	6	8	10		
3	3	6	9	12	15		
4	4	8	12	16	20		
5	5	10	15	20	25		
⋮							
2013							4052169

This is a multiplication grid with 2013 rows and 2013 columns inside it. How many times does the number 2013 appear as a product inside the grid?

8

Robert Wallace (1796-1858) was a scientist and mathematician. He was well ahead of his time in expounding the virtues of the use of demonstration to explain the principles of applied mathematics. Below is a question taken from his book 'Elements of Algebra or the Science of Quantity', published in 1853 and intended for use by self-taught students.

Two positive real numbers x and y are such that

$$x \neq y, \qquad xy = \frac{56}{x - y} \qquad \text{and} \qquad x^2 + y^2 = \frac{113}{x - y}.$$

What is the value of $x + y$?

9

The 26 pupils in a class are labelled A, B, C, …, Z. They sit in order in a circle and, starting with pupil A, count from 1 to 156, each pupil saying the number that is one more than the previous pupil's number.

As well as saying their number, pupils must follow these rules:

For each factor of 3 in a pupil's number, they say 'fizz'.

For each factor of 5 in a pupil's number, they say 'buzz'.

Each time a digit 3 appears in a pupil's number, they say 'dizz'.

Each time a digit 5 appears in a pupil's number, they say ‘fuzz’.

e.g. Pupil W says ‘153 fizz, fizz, dizz, fuzz’ as $153 = 3 \times 3 \times 17$.

Which pupil will say the number that generates the most ‘zz’s ?

10

A stack of 10 identical cones is placed on a horizontal table. The material from which the cones are made has a constant thickness of $\frac{\sqrt{3}}{4}$ cm.

The vertical cross section through the vertex of the lowest cone is the hexagon *ABCDEF*.

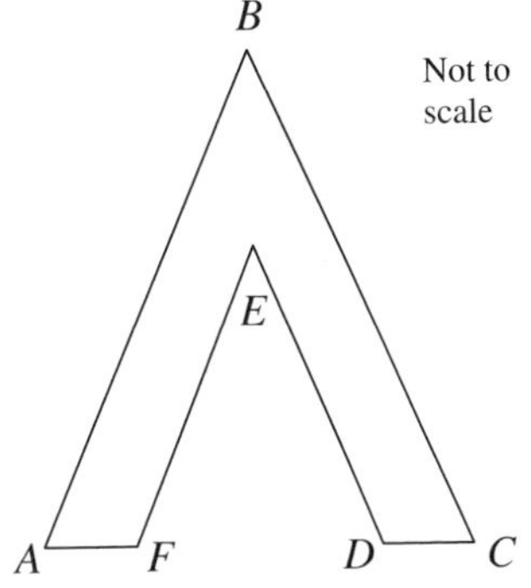

AF and *DC* rest on the table.

A line of symmetry passes through *B* and *E*.

Angle $DEF = 60°$.

$AC = 5$ cm.

What is the height of the stack of cones?

Regional Final Crossnumber

1		2	■	■	■	■	3		4
	■	5			6			■	
7	8		■	■		■	9	10	
■		■	11			12	■		■
■	13			■	■		■		■
■		■		■	■	14			■
■		■	15	16			■		■
17		18	■		■	■	19		20
	■	21						■	
22			■	■	■	■	23		

Across

1 A square number with digits in descending order and whose digit sum is prime [3]

3 The larger x-coordinate of the two points where $x + y = 455$ meets $(x - 80)^2 + (y - 80)^2 = 55525$ [3]

5 The sum of 8 Down and 24 times 15 Across [6]

7 The interior angle of a regular polygon [3]

9 The value of $n(4n + 1)$ where n is an integer [3]

11 $1.0\dot{4}\dot{2} = \dfrac{(11 \text{ across})}{990}$ [4]

13 The mean of 19 Down and 13 Across [3]

14 The interior angle of a regular polygon; also the product of two consecutive integers [3]

15 The value of $66x$ when $(2 \text{ down})x + (3 \text{ across})y = 18200$ and $(3 \text{ across})x + (2 \text{ down})y = 32305$ [4]

17 The product of 6 and one of the factors of 899 [3]

19 One tenth of the number of distinct rearrangements of the word 'COMPASS' [3]
21 n^n where n is an integer [6]
22 Product of two primes differing by two [3]
23 A power of eight [3]

Down

1 One less than twice a square number [3]
2 The smaller x-coordinate of the two points where $x + y = 455$ meets $(x - 80)^2 + (y - 80)^2 = 55525$ [3]
3 The product of two primes differing by two [3]
4 The difference between 1 Down and 1 Across, subtracted from 16 Down [3]
6 A multiple of 13 [3]
8 The difference between 10 Down and 21 Across [6]
10 The value of $n^{2(n-1)}$ where n is an integer [6]
11 One more than a multiple of 3 Across [4]
12 A square which is 91 more than another square [4]
16 The sum of one hundred and the product of three and the interior angle of a regular polygon [3]
17 The value of x when $(2 \text{ down})x + (3 \text{ across})y = 18200$ and $(3 \text{ across})x + (2 \text{ down})y = 32305$ [3]
18 One hundred more than a multiple of 11 [3]
19 The mean of 13 Across and 19 Down [3]
20 A quarter of the sum of seven and 1 Across [3]

A1 Bill writes down a list of five different integers, all of which are greater than 1.

Adam spots that the first is a prime number,
the second is a triangular number,
the third is a square,
the fourth is a Fibonacci number
and the fifth is a cube.

Pass on the smallest possible total of the five numbers.

A2 *T is the number that you will receive.*

Pass on the number of primes that lie between

$$48 + T \text{ and } 69 + \frac{T}{2}.$$

A3 *T is the number that you will receive.*

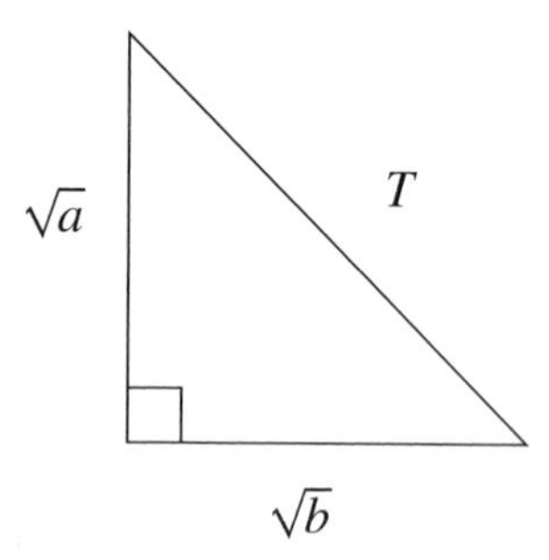

a and b are integers such that $a - b = 5$, and $\sqrt{a}$, $\sqrt{b}$ are the lengths of the shorter sides of a right triangle with hypotenuse of length T, as shown.

Pass on the value of $a^2 - b^2$.

A4 *T is the number that you will receive.*

Let $x * y = xy - 2x - 2y + 4$ for all x and y.

Write down the value of $(4 * T) * 3$.

B1 The mid-point of the line joining $A(4, 7)$ to $B(12, 5)$ is at C.
The mid-point of the line joining $D(-4, 18)$ to $E(8, 30)$ is at F.
The co-ordinates of the mid-point of the line joining C to F are (p, q).

Pass on the value of $p + q$.

B2 *T is the number that you will receive.*

In triangle ABC, $\angle ABC = 54°$ and $\angle CAB = 2T°$.
The point D is placed on AB so that $\angle CDB = 2 \times \angle DCB$.
$\angle ACD = x°$.

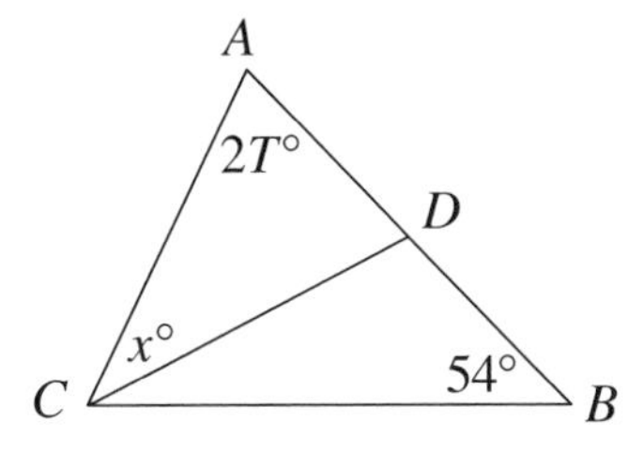

Pass on the value of x.

B3 *T is the number that you will receive.*

The ratio of red sweets to green sweets in a large jar of sweets is $(T - 4) : 25$.
The ratio of green sweets to blue sweets in the same jar is $(T + 1) : 36$.
The ratio of blue sweets to yellow sweets in the same jar is $20 : 9$.
The ratio of red sweets to yellow sweets in the same jar is $a : b$, where a and b are positive integers with no common factor greater than 1.

Pass on the sum of the digits of the number $a + b$.

B4 *T is the number that you will receive.*

The simultaneous equations

$$x^2 + xy + y^2 = T$$

$$2x + y = 7$$

have two pairs of solutions (a, b) and (c, d).

Write down the value of $a + b + c + d$.

C1 Two vases are similar.

The volume of the smaller vase is 27 cm^3 and it has a height of 2.5 cm.

The volume of the larger vase is 216 cm^3 and it has a height of h cm.

Pass on the value of h.

C2 *T is the number that you will receive.*

On the network below, distances between points are shown.

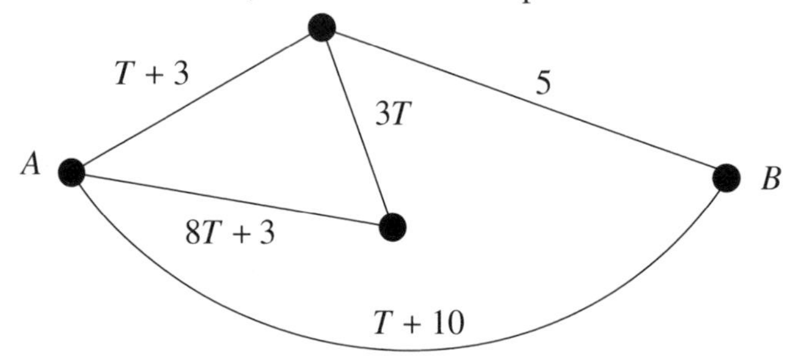

Calculate the length of the shortest route from A to B.

Pass on one thirteenth of the answer.

C3 *T is the number that you will receive.*

Solve the following equation

$$\frac{3T^2 + 10T + 3}{9T^2 - 1} = \frac{a}{b}$$

where a and b are positive integers having no common factor greater than 1.

Pass on the value of $2(a + b)$.

C4 *T is the number that you will receive.*

A circular disc has a circumference of 56π cm.

A sector of angle $30T°$ is removed.

The remaining area is $k\pi$ cm^2. Write down the value of k.

D1 Evaluate the following:

$$\sqrt{75} \times \sqrt{32} \times \sqrt{150}.$$

Pass on one sixtieth of your answer.

D2 *T is the number that you will receive.*

The diagram below shows a large right-angled isosceles triangle with hypotenuse $3T$ cm.
Three right-angled isosceles triangles are set within the large triangle each having a hypotenuse of T cm.

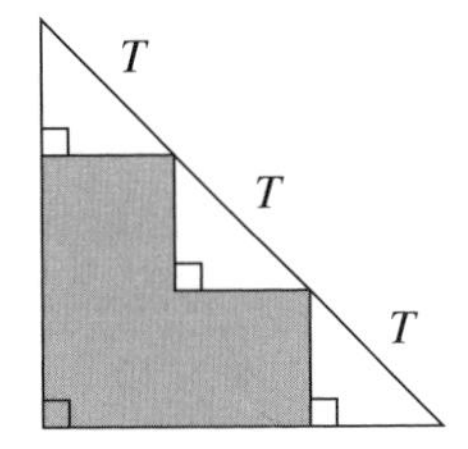

Pass on one tenth of the area in cm^2 of the shaded region.

D3 *T is the number that you will receive.*

Given that

$$n! = n \times (n - 1) \times (n - 2) \times \ldots \times 3 \times 2 \times 1,$$

calculate the value of

$$\frac{16!}{(T - 1)!}.$$

Pass on one eighth of your answer.

D4 *T is the number that you will receive.*

The mean of the distribution given in the first table is $\frac{1}{5}T - 4$ less than the mean of the distribution given in the second table.

Table 1

Value	4	5	6	8	10
Frequency	9	2	5	3	1

Table 2

Value	4	6	8	9	10
Frequency	3	5	$\frac{1}{6}T$	x	$\frac{1}{6}T$

Write down the value of x.

Group Round answers

1.	Number of steps	293
2.	Value of a_1	-3
3.	Next square	2116
4.	Length of RS	$\frac{10}{3}$ cm
5.	Number of permutations	34
6.	Value of $a + b$	-16
7.	Number of appearances of 2013	8
8.	Value of $x + y$	15
9.	Pupil's letter	E
10.	Height of the stack of cones	$7\sqrt{3}$ cm

Crossnumber: Completed grid

[1] 8	4	[2] 1	■	■	■	■	[3] 3	0	[4] 5
8	■	[5] 5	9	2	[6] 9	0	2	■	7
[7] 1	[8] 4	0	■	■	2	■	[9] 3	[10] 3	3
■	3	■	[11] 1	0	3	[12] 2	■	9	■
■	[13] 2	3	5	■	■	1	■	0	■
■	9	■	2	■	■	[14] 1	5	6	■
■	1	■	[15] 6	[16] 6	6	6	■	2	■
[17] 1	8	[18] 6	■	1	■	■	[19] 2	5	[20] 2
0	■	[21] 8	2	3	5	4	3	■	1
[22] 1	4	3	■	■	■	■	[23] 5	1	2

Mini-Relay answers

	1	2	3	4
A	22	3	45	84
B	20	44	13	7
C	5	1	6	392
D	10	15	30	2

National Final Group Round

1 Amal wants to write the number 1000 as the sum of different powers of 3. How many powers does he require?

2 What is the value of x that makes all of these fractions equal?

$$\frac{5 + x}{15}, \qquad \frac{x + 13}{x + 18} \qquad \text{and} \qquad \frac{4}{9 + x}.$$

3 Starting with the number 1, consecutive integers are used to fill the grid as shown. The number 18 is at position (4 , 3).

…						
21	…					
11	20	…				
10	12	19	…			
4	9	13	18	…		
3	5	8	14	17	…	
1	2	6	7	15	16	…

What is the position of the number 2014?

4 $ACEG$ is a square which is white on the front and black on the reverse.

The point B divides the edge AC in the ratio $1 : m$.
The point D divides the edge CE in the ratio $1 : m$.
The point F divides the edge EG in the ratio $1 : m$.
The point H divides the edge GA in the ratio $1 : m$.
The square is folded towards you, along each of BD, DF, FH and HB so that the resulting shape continues to have rotational symmetry of order 4.
The visible white area is now $\frac{1}{3}$ of the area of $ACEG$.
Given that $m < 1$, what is the exact value of m?

5 The first term of a sequence is a positive three digit integer.
Subsequent terms are created as follows:

If the previous term is even, halve it.

If the previous term is odd, add 1.

The sequence ends at the first occurrence of the number 1.

What is the value of the first term which gives rise to the sequence with the greatest number of terms?

6 A regular octahedron has surface area $24\sqrt{3}$ cm^2.

Jo draws the shortest, continuous, non-intersecting path on the surface of the octahedron which passes through the centre of each face and returns to its starting point.

What is the length of her path in cm?

7 The radius of the circle at the top of a frustum of a right circular cone is half the radius of the circle at its base. This frustum has the same volume as a hemisphere whose radius is equal to that of the circle at the frustum's base.

What is the ratio of the height of the frustum to the radius of its base?

8

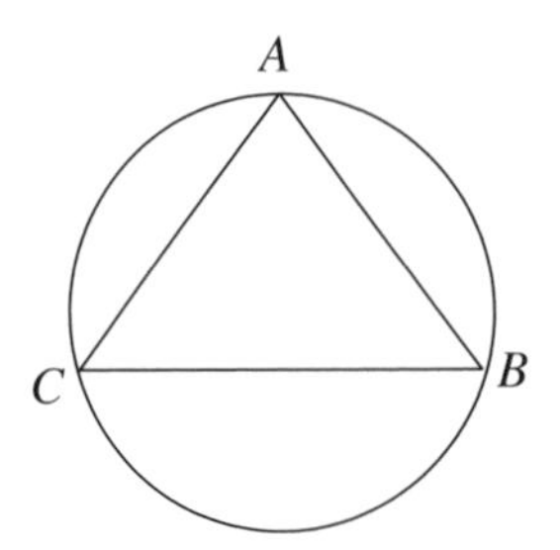

An isosceles triangle ABC is inscribed in a circle of radius R.

$AB = AC = 10$ cm

$BC = 12$ cm

What is the value of R?

9 Given that $x = \sqrt{1 + \sqrt{1 + \sqrt{1 + \sqrt{1 + \sqrt{1 + \ldots}}}}}$, write down an expression for x^2, and hence find the exact value for x.

10 An octagon $ABCDEFGH$ has the following properties:

$AB = 1$ cm, $BC = 2$ cm, $CD = 3$ cm, $DE = 4$ cm,
$EF = 5$ cm, $FG = 6$ cm, $GH = 7$ cm, $HA = 8$ cm.

Also, any two adjoining edges meet at 90°.

What is the area of the octagon in cm^2 ?

National Final Crossnumber

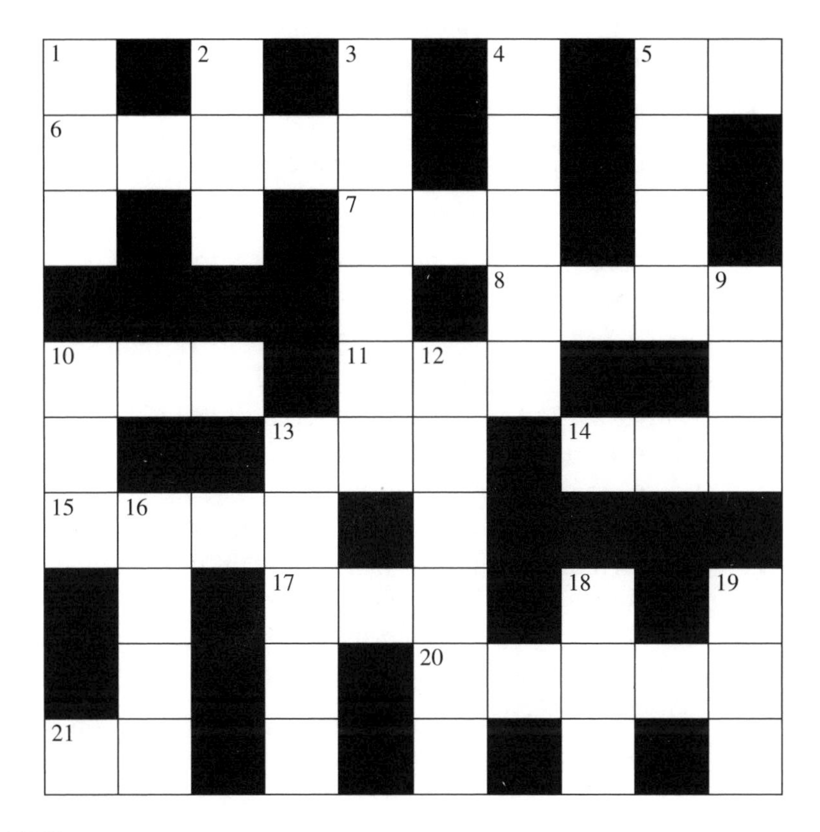

Across

5. The value of x given by the simultaneous equations

$$(14\text{ Across})x - (18\text{ Down})y = -2124$$

$$3(14\text{ Across})x - 2(18\text{ Down})y = 1128 \qquad (2)$$

6. Half of the sum of 8!, 6!, 4! and 2! (5)
7. The square of the distance from the origin to the image of the point $\left(\frac{2\text{ Down}}{50}, \frac{1\text{ Down}}{16}\right)$ under a 90° anticlockwise rotation about the point (0, 2) (3)
8. 13 Down divided by 3 (4)
10. The value of $10b$ where $\sqrt{a} + \sqrt{b} = \sqrt{45 + 10\sqrt{14}}$ (3)
11. A multiple of 9 (3)
13. One less than the sum of the smallest perfect number and 14 Across (3)

14. A power of 4 (3)
15. The product of 17 Across and 17 (4)
17. The difference between 18 Down and 2 Down (3)
20. The first five decimal places of $\frac{101}{900}$ (5)
21. The value of y given by the simultaneous equations

$$(14\text{ Across})x - (18\text{ Down})y = -2124$$

$$3(14\text{ Across})x - 2(18\text{ Down})y = 1128$$

(2)

Down

1. The positive value of c such that the equation $x^2 + cx + 16 \times (14\text{ Across}) = 0$ has repeated roots (3)
2. The value of $10a$ where $\sqrt{a} + \sqrt{b} = \sqrt{45 + 10\sqrt{14}}$ (3)
3. The value of $a(2c - b)$ where a is 20 Across, b is 7 Across and c is 10 Across (6)
4. The smallest five-digit number with no two digits the same and no digits in common with 2 Down or 19 Down (5)
5. Three more than the product of ten and (13 Across) (4)
9. The square of the distance from $(-23, 0)$ to the image of the point $\left(\frac{10\text{ Across}}{20}, \frac{14\text{ Across}}{8}\right)$ under a 90° anticlockwise rotation about the point (0, 9) (3)
10. One fifth of 6! (3)
12. A palindromic number (6)
13. The difference between ten times 8 Across and 59 017 (5)
16. One third of a power of 21 Across (4)
18. A power of 25 (3)
19. The average of the first twenty-five square numbers (3)

National Final Mini-Relay

A1 A proper factor of a number is any factor of that number apart from the number itself, so for example 6 has three proper factors, 1, 2 and 3.

Pass on the number of proper factors of 600.

A2 *T is the number that you will receive.*

In the diagram below, triangles *ABC* and *PQR* are similar.

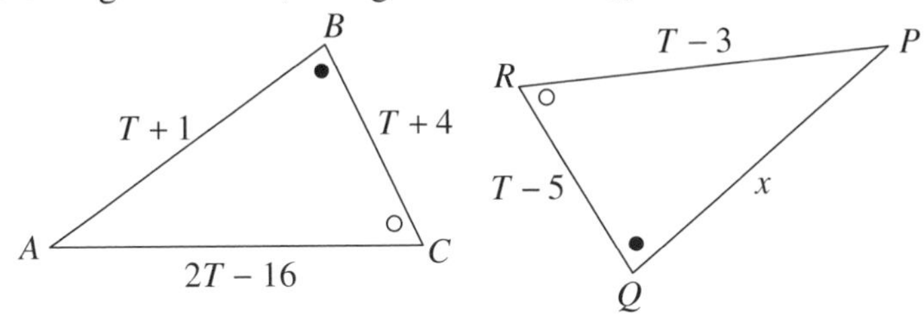

Pass on the value of x.

A3 *T is the number that you will receive.*

Evaluate

$$x = \sqrt{(T^2 - 14^2)(T^2 - 6^2)(17^2 - T^2)}.$$

Pass on the value of $\frac{x}{10}$.

A4 *T is the number that you will receive.*

In the diagram, $AD = DC$ and $\angle ABC = T°$.

Write down the value of x.

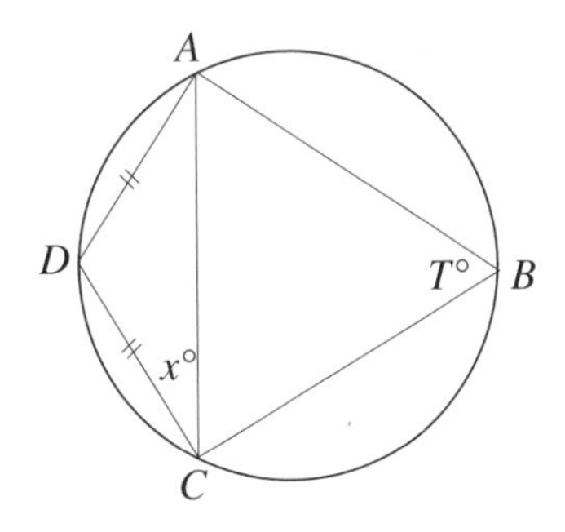

B1 Solve the equation

$$27^{4(x+1)} = 9^{2(9+2x)}.$$

Pass on the value of x.

B2 *T is the number that you will receive.*

Let $a * b = ab - 1$ for all a and b.

Pass on the value of $5 * (T * 2)$.

B3 *T is the number that you will receive.*

Suppose

$$a : b = 2 : 3$$
$$b : c = 4 : 5 \text{ and}$$
$$a + c - T = 15.$$

Pass on the value of $\frac{1}{3}(c - a)$.

B4 *T is the number that you will receive.*

The diagram shows a right-angled triangle with its inscribed circle.

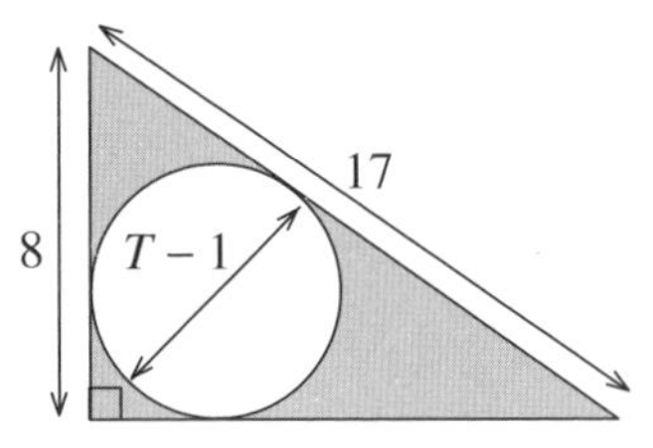

The area of the shaded region can be expressed in the form $a - b\pi$, where a and b are integers.
Write down the value of $\frac{1}{3}(a - b)$.

C1 The network below shows the different routes from A to B.

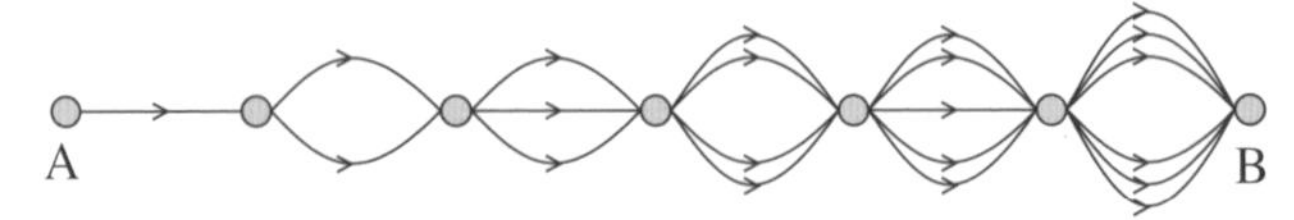

Pass on one more than one thirty-sixth of the number of different possible routes from A to B.

C2 *T is the number that you will receive.*

The cross-sectional area of a triangular prism of length 48 cm is $T - 1$ cm^2.

A similar triangular prism has a cross-sectional area of 5 cm^2 and a volume of V cm^3.
Pass on the value of $\frac{1}{10}V$.

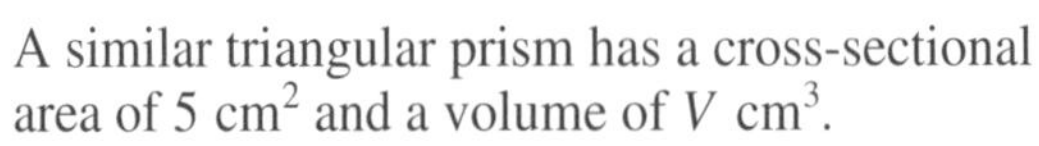

C3 *T is the number that you will receive.*

Felix the fly is sitting at one vertex of a cuboid of length $T - 2$ cm, width 5 cm and height 2 cm.

Felix travels along each edge of the cuboid at least once, returning to the starting vertex.

The shortest route he can take is of length l.

Pass on the value of $l + 4$.

C4 *T is the number that you will receive.*

Simplify

$$\frac{T(3 + \sqrt{5})}{3 - \sqrt{5}}.$$

Express your answer in the form $b + c\sqrt{5}$, where b and c are integers.

Write down the value of $b - c$.

D1 Five boys have the same total weight as eight girls.
Twelve girls have the same total weight as five sheep.
Eight sheep have the same total weight as six deer.
x boys have the same total weight as eleven deer.

You can assume that all boys are identical in weight, all girls are identical in weight, all sheep are identical in weight and all deer are identical in weight.

Pass on the value of x.

D2 *T is the number that you will receive.*

The equations

$$x^2 - Tx + 120 = 0$$

$$x^2 - 14x + T = 2$$

have solutions $x = a$ and $x = b$, $x = c$ and $x = d$ respectively.

Pass on the value of $\dfrac{a + b + c + d}{3}$.

D3 *T is the number that you will receive.*

The area, A, enclosed between the lines
$x + y = T - 2$,
$x + 2y = T + 3$ and
$2x + y = T$
is represented by the shaded
region as shown in the diagram.

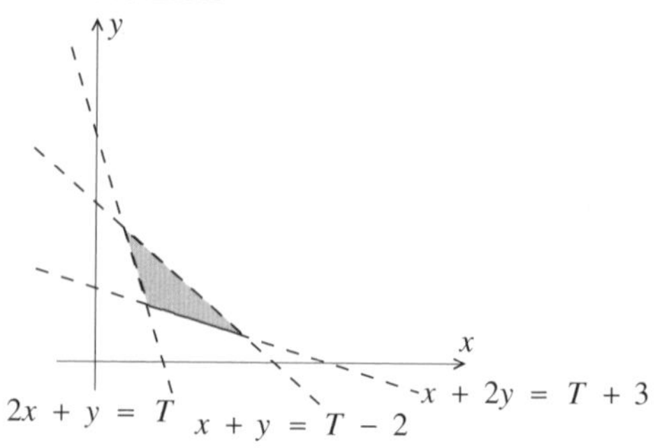

Pass on the value of 4A.

D4 *T is the number that you will receive.*

Five integers have

a mean of 6,
a median of $T - 1$ and
a mode of 4.

Write down the largest possible range of the five numbers.

Group Round answers

1.	Number of powers	4
2.	Value of x	-15
3.	Position of 2014	(61, 3)
4.	Value of m	$2 - \sqrt{3}$
5.	First term	513
6.	Length of path	16 cm
7.	Height of frustrum : radius of base	8 : 7
8.	Value of R	$\frac{25}{4}$ cm
9.	Value of x	$\frac{1 + \sqrt{5}}{2}$
10.	Area of octagon $ABCDEFGH$	52 cm^2

Crossnumber: Completed grid

[1] 1		[2] 3		[3] 9		[4] 4		[5] 2	1
[6] 2	0	5	3	3		6		6	
8		0		[7] 1	1	7		1	
				4		[8] 8	4	3	[9] 1
[10] 1	0	0		[11] 2	[12] 7	9			9
4			[13] 2	6	1		[14] 2	5	6
[15] 4	[16] 6	7	5		5				
	9		[17] 2	7	5		[18] 6		[19] 2
	1		9		[20] 1	1	2	2	2
[21] 1	2		3		7		5		1

Mini-Relay answers

	1	2	3	4
A	23	16	66	33
B	6	54	7	17
C	21	12	80	160
D	22	12	6	7

Other aspects of the UKMT

As well as the Maths Challenges, the UKMT is involved in other events and activities.

Enriching Mathematical Thinking
UKMT Teacher Meetings 2014

Five meetings were held this year: Brighton (University of Sussex), Bristol (University of Bristol), Edinburgh (University of Edinburgh), Greenwich (University of Greenwich) and Leicester (University of Leicester).

Around 280 teachers attended the one-day events. Each meeting featured four sessions with lunch and refreshment breaks and delegates received a resource pack to take back to the classroom.

NRICH (www.nrich.maths.org.uk) gave sessions at all five meetings and we are grateful to Charlie Gilderdale, Alison Kiddle and Lynne McLure for the quality of these sessions and the accompanying resources.

Rob Eastaway, author and Director of Maths Inspiration, gave inspiring talks on the subject of Mathematical Modelling at Brighton, Edinburgh and Leicester, Vinay Kathotia (Nuffield Foundation) engaged delegates at Greenwich with his interactive session on Mathematics and Story Telling, while Colin Wright entertained and enthused delegates with his talk/display on the Mathematics of Juggling at Bristol.

UKMT volunteers led a session at each event demonstrating the mathematical thinking behind the questions used in the UK Maths Challenges and the Team Maths Challenges, and how UKMT materials can be used to stimulate classroom interest. The 2014 speakers were David Crawford, Ceri Fiddes, Adam McBride and Stephen Power.

We are also grateful to our volunteers Dennis Pinshon, Sue Essex and Mary Teresa Fyfe who ran the fourth session on the Primary Team Maths Resources.

The delegate fee was £70, which included refreshments, lunch and a resources pack full of materials to take back to the classroom. Feedback was once again extremely positive.

Mathematical Circles

The Mathematical Circles are a new UKMT initiative which developed from two trial events in spring 2012. Following on from the success of these, a further two events were run in early 2013 in Glasgow and Leeds, and thanks to a grant from the Department for Education, we were able to expand these events from April 2013.

Local schools are invited to select two students from Year 10 (and equivalent) to send to the two-day events which are comprised of mathematically demanding work through topics such as geometry, proof and modular arithmetic. Students have the opportunity to discuss mathematics and make new friends from other schools around their region.

Our thanks go to the following people who ran the events, and to the schools who supported these:

Hull, University of Hull, run by John Slater

Wells, Wells Cathedral School, run by Susie Jameson

Manchester, University of Manchester, run by Alan Slomson

Cumbria, St Joseph's Catholic High School, Workington, run by Alan Slomson

Greenwich, University of Greenwich, run by Peter Neumann

Cambridge, University of Cambridge, run by Julian Gilbey

Exeter, University of Exeter, run by Nick Geere

Glasgow, Hutchesons' Grammar School, run by Steven O'Hagan

Warwick, Warwick School, run by Karl Hayward-Bradley

Gloucester, Wycliffe School, run by James Welham

St Albans, St Albans High School for Girls, run by Sue Cubbon

Oxford, University of Oxford, run by Peter Neumann

West London, St Paul's School, run by Dominic Rowland

Newcastle, Newcastle University, run by Anne Baker

Wakefield, Queen Elizabeth Grammar School, run by Dean Bunnell

A sample timetable is given below:

9.30	Arrival and registration	Arrival and mathematical activities
10.00	Divisibility and some total problems	Introduction to Fibonacci and proof
11.00	Break	Break
11.15	Continued fractions	Very big numbers
12.15	Lunch	Lunch
1.00	Geometry 1	Geometry 2
2.00	Break	Break

2.15	Coding and Compression	Combinatorics with Gauss, fun with Euclid
3.15	Close	Close

Thanks are also given to those people who ran sessions at these events (a list of which is given at in the Volunteers section of the Yearbook).

Mathematical Circles are being run throughout the next academic year. If you would like to find out more about how you can become involved in the Mathematical Circles, either through your school hosting an event or by supporting us in running a session, please do contact us at enquiry@ukmt.org.uk.

Primary Team Maths Resources

In recognition and support of the growing number of secondary schools organising and hosting local team maths events for their feeder schools, UKMT developed a set of Primary Team Maths Resources (PTMR) intended for use at such events, which was launched in spring 2012. A further set of materials was made available in January 2013, and in January 2014.

Schools may choose to use the materials in other ways, e.g. a primary school may use the materials to run a competition for their own Year 5 and 6 pupils (and equivalent), or a secondary school may use the materials as an end of term activity for their Year 7 pupils.

The PTMR included more materials than would be needed for any one competition, allowing schools to pick and choose those most appropriate for their purposes. Some of the rounds are familiar from the UKMT Team Challenges (the Group Round, Crossnumber, Relay and Mini Relay) and the material included some new rounds (the Logic Round, Make a Number, Open Ended Questions, and Speed Test).

The 2014 PTMR and full instructions for suggested use is available by contacting the UKMT via email at enquiry@ukmt.org.uk. Further details including sample materials can be found on our website at

http://www.ukmt.org.uk/team-challenges/primary-team-maths-resources/.

Best in School Events

Since 2007, the UKMT has partnered with the Royal Institution to invite top scoring IMC candidates to attend RI masterclass celebration events. These events give students from Year 9 (and equivalent) and sometimes Year 12 (and equivalent) the opportunity to attend inspiring lectures, meet mathematicians from their local area, and have a go at 'hands-on' mathematics.

In 2014, these events took place in Edinburgh, Liverpool, London (Year 9 and Year 12 events), and Plymouth.

Website – www.ukmt.org.uk

Visit the UKMT's website for information about all the UKMT's activities, including the Maths Challenges, team events, latest UKMT news and newsletters, contact details, and to purchase publications and past papers.

There are online resources featuring past questions from the Challenges, mentoring questions, and sample Primary Team Maths Challenge materials. There are also links to sponsors, supporters and other mathematical bodies providing further resources for young mathematicians.

Other similar bodies overseas

The UKMT has links of varying degrees of formality with several similar organisations in other countries. It is also a member of the World Federation of National Mathematics Competitions (WFNMC). What follows is a brief description of some of these other organisations. Some of the information is taken from the organisations' web sites but a UK slant has been applied.

"Kangourou des Mathématiques"

http://www.math-ksf.org/

The obvious question is: why Kangaroo? The name was given in tribute to the pioneering efforts of the Australian Mathematics Trust. The Kangaroo contest is run by local organisers in each country under the auspices of the 'Association Kangourou sans Frontières', which was founded by a small group of countries in 1991. There are now over 50 countries involved and more than six million participants throughout Europe and beyond, from the UK to Mongolia and from Norway to Cyprus.

In the UK in 2014, over 7000 children in the years equivalent to English Years 9, 10 and 11 took part in the 'Cadet' and 'Junior' levels of the Kangaroo competition, as a follow-up to the Intermediate Maths Challenge. Four representatives of the UK Mathematics Trust, Andrew Jobbings, Paul Murray, David Crawford and Rachel Greenhalgh, attended the meeting in Cyprus, at which the 2013 Kangaroo papers were constructed. In 2013, the annual meeting was held in the UK, see the next page for a report.

The main objective of the Kangaroo, like all the competitions described in this section, is to stimulate and motivate large numbers of pupils, as well as to contribute to the development of a mathematical culture which will be accessible to, and enjoyed by, many children and young people. The Association also encourages cross-cultural activities; in some countries, for example, prize-winners are invited to attend a mathematics 'camp' with similar participants from other nations.

Association Kangourou sans Frontières 2013

The Association Kangourou Sans Frontièrs (AKSF) is an independent international association which promotes mathematics among young people around the world through the annual Kangaroo mathematics contest

The annual meeting of AKSF takes place in a different country each year, and in 2013 this took place in Edinburgh from Tuesday 29th October – Sunday 3rd November, and was organised by the UKMT. The aim of the meeting is to select questions which will then form the six different Mathematical Kangaroo papers taken by around six million students aged 7 – 18 in schools worldwide, as a way of promoting mathematics to young people across the globe. These Mathematical Kangaroo competitions usually take place on the third Thursday in March each year, and the UKMT uses these competitions as follow-on rounds to its Maths Challenges.

As well as setting the papers, the AKSF meeting gives around 150 delegates the opportunity to meet people (mainly teachers of mathematics and academics) from more than 50 other nations worldwide and share their ideas and experiences in mathematics and mathematical competitions.

An AKSF conference has been held every year since 1993, and 2013 was the first time the UK has hosted the event. AKSF2014 will be held in Puerto Rico.

Our thanks go to our supporters of AKSF2013: to the Edinburgh Mathematical Society, London Mathematical Society, James Clerk Maxwell Foundation, Dean's of Scotland, Walkers, Edinburgh tourist office, and the Edinburgh Conference Centre. Our thanks also go to the Bailie of Edinburgh who attended the opening ceremony, to Colin Wright who provided excellent evening entertainment with his mathematical juggling performance, and to the Edinburgh Marriott Hotel.

The conference was organised by Rachel Greenhalgh and Andrew Jobbings, with huge assistance from Bev Detoeuf and other members of the KSF2013 Organising Committee: David Crawford, Howard Groves, Adam McBride, Paul Murray, Bill Richardson and Alan Slomson.

Final thanks go to the fabulous and invaluable UKMT volunteer support at the event, from Andrew Bell, Madeleine Copin, Karen Fogden, Mary Teresa Fyfe, Howard Groves, Adam McBride, Steven O'Hagan, Bill Richardson and Mary Roberts. David Crawford, Andrew Jobbings and Paul Murray were the UK representatives at the meeting itself.

AKSF2013 Conference, Programme.

Wednesday, October 30th

9 - 12pm	Board Meeting
1pm onwards	Arrivals and registration
7.30 - 10pm	Welcome reception – welcome drink, soup and piper

Thursday, October 31st

9 – 10am	Opening meeting
10 – 10.30am	Morning refreshments served
10.30 – 11.30pm	Opening meeting continued
11.30 – 1pm	Working groups
1 – 1.45pm	Lunch
1.45 – 3.30pm	Working groups
3.15 – 4.00pm	Afternoon refreshments served
3.30 – 5.30pm	Working groups
5.30 – 6.30pm	Colin Wright
7.30pm	Board Meeting 2
8pm	Dinner
9.30pm	Plenary sessions

Friday, November 1st

8.30 – 10.30am	Working groups
10.15 – 11.am	Morning refreshments served
10.30 – 12.30pm	Working groups
12.30 – 1.30pm	Lunch, including exchange of prizes at 1pm
1.30 – 3.30pm	Working groups
3.30 – 3.45pm	Afternoon refreshments served
3.30 – 6.15pm	Working groups
7.30pm	Scottish evening – formal dinner and ceilidh

Saturday, November 2nd

8.30 – 10am	Working groups
10 – 10.15am	Morning refreshments served
10 – 12pm	Working groups
12.30 – 1.30pm	Lunch
1.45pm	Coach departs for Edinburgh tour
6.30pm	Evening out – informal dinner

Sunday, November 3rd

8.30 – 11am	AGM
11am onwards	Departure

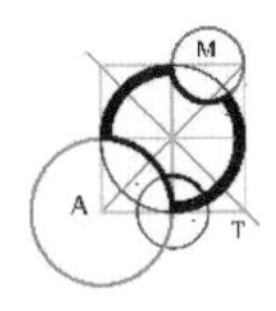

The Australian Mathematics Trust

www.amt.canberra.edu.au

For over twenty-five years, the Australian Mathematics Competition has been one of the major events on the Australian Education Calendar, with about one in three Australian secondary students entering each year to test their skills. That's over half a million participants a year.

The Competition commenced in 1978 under the leadership of the late Professor Peter O'Halloran, of the University of Canberra, after a successful pilot scheme had run in Canberra for two years.

The questions are multiple-choice and students have 75 minutes in which to answer 30 questions. There are follow-up rounds for high scorers.

In common with the other organisations described here, the AMC also extends its mathematical enrichment activities by publishing high quality material which can be used in the classroom.

Whilst the AMC provides students all over Australia with an opportunity to solve the same problems on the same day, it is also an international event, with most of the countries of the Pacific and South-East Asia participating, as well as a few schools from further afield. New Zealand and Singapore each enter a further 30,000 students to help give the Competition an international flavour.

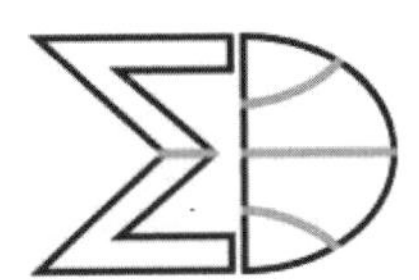

World Federation of National Mathematics Competitions – WFNMC

www.amt.canberra.edu.au/wfnmc.html

The Federation was created in 1984 during the Fifth International Congress for Mathematical Education.

The Federation aims to provide a focal point for those interested in, and concerned with, conducting national mathematics competitions for the purpose of stimulating the learning of mathematics. Its objectives include:

- Serving as a resource for the exchange of information and ideas on mathematics competitions through publications and conferences.
- Assisting with the development and improvement of mathematics competitions.

- Increasing public awareness of the role of mathematics competitions in the education of all students and ensuring that the importance of that role is properly recognised in academic circles.
- Creating and enhancing professional links between mathematicians involved in competitions around the world.

The World Federation of National Mathematics Competitions is an organisation of national mathematics competitions affiliated as a Special Interest Group of the International Commission for Mathematical Instruction (ICMI).

It administers a number of activities, including

- The Journal *Mathematics Competitions*
- An international conference every four years.
- David Hilbert and Paul Erdős Awards for mathematicians prominent on an international or national scale in mathematical enrichment activities.

The UKMT sent two delegates, Tony Gardiner and Bill Richardson, to the WFNMC conference in Zhong Shan in 1998 and provided support for several delegates who attended ICME 9 in Tokyo in August 2000, at which the WFNMC provided a strand.

In August 2002, the WFNMC held another conference, similar to the one in 1998. The venue for this was Melbourne, Victoria. On this occasion, the UKMT provided support for two delegates: Howard Groves and Bill Richardson.

In July 2006, WFNMC 5 was held in the UK at Robinson College, Cambridge. This event was a tremendous success with around 100 delegates from many parts of the world.

In July 2007, WFNMC had a strand at ICME 11 in Mexico. UKMT was represented by Bill Richardson.

In July 2010, WFNMC 6 was held in Riga. The UKMT was represented by Howard Groves, Dean Bunnell, David Crawford and James Welham.

In July 2014, WFNMC 7 was held in Colombia. The UKMT was represented by David Crawford.

Lists of volunteers involved in the UKMT's activities

UKMT officer bearers

Chair: Professor Frances Kirwan

Secretary: Dr Alan Eames-Jones
Treasurer: Prof. Adam McBride

The Council

Professor Frances Kirwan	
Mr Richard Atkins (to April 2014)	Mrs Anne Baker
Professor John Brindley	Professor Chris Budd
Dr Colin Campbell	Dr Katie Chicot
Dr James Cranch	Dr Diane Crann
Mr Alex Crews	Dr Ceri Fiddes
Mr Karl Hayward-Bradley	Professor Adam McBride
Mr Steve Mulligan (from April 2014)	Miss Jenny Ramsden
Mr Bill Richardson (Vice-Chair)	Professor Alastair Rucklidge
Dr John Silvester	Dr Geoff Smith (Vice-Chair)

Members of the Trust who are not on the Council or members of a Subtrust

The Mathematical Association	The Royal Institution	Mr Dennis Archer
Dr Roger Bray	Mr Dean Bunnell	Mrs Mary Teresa Fyfe
Dr Tony Gardiner	Mr Terry Heard	Mrs Margaret Jackson
Mrs Susie Jameson-Petvin	Dr Andrew Jobbings	Dr Vinay Kathotia
Mrs Patricia King	Professor Tom Körner	Dr Gerry Leversha
Mr Nick Lord	Mr Tony Mann	Mr Dennis Orton
Mrs Mary Read	Prof. Christopher Robson	Dr Adrian Sanders
Dr Sara Santos	Prof. Bernard Silverman	Mr Robert Smart
Dr Brian Stewart	Mr Peter Thomas	Mr Brian Wilson
Ms Mary Wimbury		

The Subtrusts

British Mathematical Olympiad Subtrust

Dr Geoff Smith (Chair)	Dr Don Collins (Treasurer)	
Dr James Cranch	Dr Ceri Fiddes	
Dr Vesna Kadelberg (Secretary)	Professor Imre Leader	Dr Joseph Myers
Dr Vicky Neale	Mr Dominic Yeo	

Team Maths Challenge Subtrust

Mr Steve Mulligan (Chair)
Mr Alex Crews
Mr Dusty de Sainte Croix
Mr Karl Hayward-Bradley
Miss Pam Hunt (Statistician)
Dr Peter Neumann (Secretary)
Mr Martin Perkins (Treasurer)

Challenges Subtrust

Mr Bill Richardson (Chair)
Ms Anne Baker
Professor John Brindley (Treasurer)
Dr David Crawford
Mrs Karen Fogden
Mr Howard Groves
Dr Calum Kilgour
Professor Adam McBride
Mr Paul Murray
Dr Steven O'Hagan
Mr Stephen Power
Miss Jenny Ramsden (Secretary)
Mr Peter Ransom
Professor Chris Robson
Dr Alan Slomson

Other Committees

Finance and General Purposes Committee

Dr Alan Eames-Jones
Professor Frances Kirwan
Professor Adam McBride
Mr Stephen Mulligan
Mr Bill Richardson
Dr Geoff Smith
Mrs Rachel Greenhalgh (UKMT Director)

Nominations Committee

Dr Katie Chicot (Chair)
Professor Chris Budd
Mrs Mary Teresa Fyfe
Mr Stephen Mulligan
Ms Mary Wimbury

Outreach Committee

Mr James Welham (Chair)
Professor John Brindley
Dr Katie Chicot
Mrs Mary Teresa Fyfe (Secretary)
Miss Pam Hunt
Mr Tony Mann
Miss Jenny Ramsden
Dr Alan Slomson
Mrs Rachel Greenhalgh
Mrs Shona Raffle-Edwards

Publications Committee

Dr Gerry Leversha (Chair)
Mr James Gazet
Mr Nick Lord
Mr Mark Strutt

Members of the BMOS Extended Committee

Robin Bhattacharyya (Loughborough GS)
Philip Coggins (ex Bedford School)
Mary Teresa Fyfe (Hutchesons' GS)
James Gazet (Eton College)
Ben Green (Trinity College, Cambridge)
Andrew Jobbings (Arbelos)
Jeremy King (Tonbridge School)
Patricia King (ex Benenden School, Kent)
Gerry Leversha (formerly St Paul's School)
Adam McBride (Uni. of Strathclyde)
David Monk (ex Edinburgh University)
Joseph Myers (CodeSourcery)
Peter Neumann (Queen's Coll., Oxford)
Alan Pears (ex King's College, London)
Adrian Sanders (ex Trinity College, Camb.)
Zhivko Stoyanov (University of Bath)
Alan West (ex Leeds University)
Brian Wilson (ex Royal Holloway, London)

BMOS Markers

Richard Atkins (Oundle School, Leader)
James Aaronson (Trinity Coll, Cambridge)
Ben Barrett (Trinity Coll, Cambridge)
Natalie Behague (Trinity Coll, Cambridge)
Alexander Betts (Trinity Coll, Cambridge)
Ilya Chevyrev (University of Oxford)
Philip Coggins (ex Bedford School)
James Cranch (University of Sheffield)
Tim Cross (KES, Birmingham)
Paul Fannon (Stephen Perse Foundation)
Mark Flanagan (University Coll, Dublin)
Richard Freeland (Trinity Coll, Cambridge)
James Gazet (Eton College)
Ed Godfrey (Trinity Coll, Cambridge)
Jo Harbour (Mayfield Pri. Sch, Cambridge)
Karl Hayward-Bradley (Warwick School)
John Haslegrave (University of Sheffield)
Tim Hennock (Trinity Coll, Cambridge)
Maria Holdcroft (Queen's Coll, Oxford)
Ina Hughes (University of Leeds)
Ian Jackson (Tonbridge School)
Andrew Jobbings (Arbelos)
Vesna Kadelburg (Stephen Perse Found.)
Jeremy King (Tonbridge Sch)
Gerry Leversha (formerly St Paul's School)
Sam Maltby (New Vision)
Matei Mandache (Trinity Coll, Cambridge)
David Mestel (Trinity Coll, Cambridge)
Joseph Myers (CodeSourcery, Inc)
Vicky Neale (Murray Edwards Coll., Cam.)
Peter Neumann (ex Queen's College, Oxford)
Sylvia Neumann (Oxford)
Craig Newbold (Trinity Coll, Cambridge)
Preeyan Parmar (Trinity Coll, Cambridge)
David Phillips (Trinity Coll, Cambridge)
Hannah Roberts (Trinity Coll, Cambridge)
Dominic Rowland (St Paul's School)
Jack Shotton (Imperial College, London)
Geoff Smith (Uni. of Bath)
Karthik Tadinada (St Paul's School, London)
Jerome Watson (Bedford School)
Dominic Yeo (University of Oxford)
Alison Zhu (KPMG UK Ltd)

MOG Markers

James Aaronson (Trinity Coll, Cambridge)	Ross Atkins (Oxford)
Ben Barrett (Trinity Coll, Cambridge)	Natalie Behague (Trinity Coll, Cambridge)
Andrew Carlotti (Trinity Coll, Cambridge)	Andrea Chlebikova (St Catharine's Cambridge)
Philip Coggins (ex Bedford Sch)	James Cranch (University of Sheffield)
Rosie Cretney (Oxford)	Sue Cubbon (St Albans, Herts)
Matthew Dawes (Bath)	Elena Dulskyte
Paul Fannon (The Stephen Perse Foundation)	Richard Freeland (Trinity Coll, Cambridge)
Adam Goucher (Trinity Coll, Cambridge)	Jo Harbour (Mayfield Pri. Sch., Cambridge)
Maria Holdcroft (Queen's Coll, Oxford)	Andrew Jobbings (Arbelos)
Vesna Kadelburg (Stephen Perse Foundation)	Josh Lam (Trinity Coll, Cambridge)
David Mestel (Trinity Coll, Cambridge)	Joseph Myers (CodeSourcery, Inc.)
Vicky Neale (Murray Edwards College)	Peter Neumann (ex Queen's Coll, Oxford)
Sylvia Neumann (Oxford)	Martin Orr (University College London)
Preeyan Parmar (Trinity Coll, Cambridge)	David Phillips (Trinity Coll, Cambridge)
Aled Walker (Trinity Coll, Cambridge)	Alison Zhu (KPMG UK Ltd)

Markers for IMOK and JMO

Anne Baker	(Conyers School, Stockton-on-Tees)	IMOK
Natalie Behague	(Trinity College, Cambridge)	IMOK
Chris Berry	(Winchester College)	IMOK
Dean Bunnell	(ex Queen Elizabeth GS, Wakefield)	IMOK / JMO
Valerie Chapman	(Northwich)	IMOK
Philip Coggins	(ex Bedford School)	IMOK / JMO
James Cranch	(University of Sheffield)	IMOK / JMO
David Crawford	(Leicester Grammar School)	IMOK / JMO
Tim Cross	(KES, Birmingham)	IMOK
Sue Cubbon	(St Albans, Herts)	IMOK
Wendy Dersley	(Southwold)	JMO
David Forster	(Oratory School)	IMOK
Mary Teresa Fyfe	(Hutchesons' Grammar School, Glasgow)	IMOK / JMO
Carol Gainlall	(Park House School, Newbury)	IMOK / JMO
Gwyn Gardiner	(King Edward's School, Birmingham)	IMOK
Tony Gardiner	(Birmingham)	IMOK
James Gazet	(Eton College)	IMOK
Michael Griffiths	(Warrington)	IMOK
Howard Groves	(ex RGS, Worcester)	IMOK
Peter Hall	(East Sussex)	IMOK
Hugh Hill	(Winchester College)	IMOK
Rita Holland	(Cambridge)	IMOK

Carl James	(Leicester Grammar School)	IMOK
Magdalena Jasicova	(Cambridge)	IMOK / JMO
Andrew Jobbings	(Arbelos, Shipley)	IMOK / JMO
David Knipe	(Cambridge)	IMOK
Gerry Leversha	(formerly St Paul's School)	IMOK
Aleksandar Lishkov	(Oxford)	IMOK
Nick Lord	(Tonbridge School)	IMOK
Sam Maltby	(Sheffield)	IMOK / JMO
Peter Neumann	(The Queen's College, Oxford)	IMOK / JMO
Sylvia Neumann	(Oxford)	IMOK / JMO
Steven O'Hagan	(Hutchesons' Grammar School,Glasgow)	IMOK / JMO
Andy Parkinson	(Brockhill Park Performing Arts College)	IMOK
Jenny Perkins	(Torbridge High School, Plymouth)	JMO
Stephen Power	(St Swithuns School, Winchester)	IMOK / JMO
Laurence Rackham	(King Edward's School, Birmingham)	JMO
Jenny Ramsden	(High Wycombe)	IMOK / JMO
Christine Randall	(Southampton)	IMOK
Alexandra Randolph	(St Paul's Girls School, London)	IMOK
Peter Ransom	(Southampton)	IMOK / JMO
Lionel Richard	(Frankfurt International School)	JMO
Jerome Ripp	(Marymount International School, London)	IMOK
Dominic Rowland	(St Paul's School, London)	IMOK
Paul Russell	(Churchill College, Cambridge)	JMO
Jenni Sambrook	(Uckfield)	IMOK
Fiona Shen	(Queen Ethelburga's College, York)	IMOK / JMO
John Slater	(Market Rasen)	IMOK / JMO
Alan Slomson	(University of Leeds)	JMO
Karthik Tadinada	(St Paul's School, London)	IMOK
Alex Voice	(Westminster Abbey Choir School, London)	JMO
Paul Walter	(Highgate School, London)	IMOK
Fran Watson	(Cambridge)	IMOK
Jerome Watson	(Bedford School)	IMOK
David Webber	(University of Glasgow)	IMOK / JMO
Michaela Weiserova	(Surrey)	IMOK
Brian Wilson	(University of London)	IMOK
Rosie Wiltshire	(Wootton Bassett School)	IMOK
Heather Yorston	(University of Strathclyde)	IMOK

Problems Groups

There are currently five groups. The first being the BMO Setting Committee.

Jeremy King	(Chair) (Tonbridge School)
Alexander Betts	(Merton College, Oxford)
Julian Gilbey	(London)
Paul Jefferys	(ex Trinity College, Cambridge)
Gerry Leversha	(formerly St Paul's School)
Jack Shotton	(Imperial College, London)
Geoff Smith	(University of Bath)

The other six groups have overlapping membership. There is one group for each and the chair is shown in []: the Senior Mathematical Challenge (S) [Howard Groves]; the Junior and Intermediate Mathematical Challenges (I&J) [Howard Groves]; the Junior Mathematical Olympiad (JMO) [Steven O'Hagan]; the IMOK Olympiad papers [Andrew Jobbings]; the Intermediate Kangaroo (IK) [David Crawford and Paul Murray]; Senior Kangaroo (SK) [Carl James and David Crawford]. Those involved are listed below.

Steve Barge	(Sacred Heart Catholic College)	S
Dean Bunnell	(Queen Elizabeth GS, Wakefield)	S / IMOK / JMO
Kerry Burnham	(Torquay Boys' Grammar School)	I&J
James Cranch	(University of Sheffield)	IMOK
David Crawford	(Leicester Grammar School)	SK / IK
Karen Fogden	(Henry Box School, Witney)	S / I&J / JMO
Mary Teresa Fyfe	(Hutchesons' GS, Glasgow)	S / IMOK / JMO
Carol Gainlall	(Park House School, Newbury)	I&J
Tony Gardiner	(Birmingham)	I&J / IMOK / JMO
Nick Geere	(Kelly College)	S
Michael Griffiths	(Warrington)	S / IMOK
Howard Groves	(ex RGS, Worcester)	S / I&J / IMOK / JMO
Jo Harbour	(Wolvercote Primary School)	JMO
Carl James	(Leicester Grammar School)	SK
Andrew Jobbings	(Arbelos, Shipley)	S / I&J / IMOK / JMO
Gerry Leversha	(formerly St Paul's School)	IMOK
Paul Murray	(Lord Williams School, Thame)	I&J / JMO / IK
Steven O'Hagan	(Hutchesons' GS, Glasgow)	JMO
Andy Parkinson	(Beckfoot School, Bingley)	IMOK
Stephen Power	(St. Swithun's School, Winchester)	I&J
Alexandra Randolph	(St Paul's School, London)	JMO
Peter Ransom	(Southampton)	I&J
Lionel Richard	(Hutchesons' GS, Glasgow)	S
Alan Slomson	(University of Leeds)	S / I&J
Ian Vanderburgh	(University of Waterloo, Canada)	I&J
Alex Voice	(Westminster Abbey Choir School)	I&J / JMO

It is appropriate at this stage to acknowledge and thank those who helped at various stages with the moderation and checking of these papers: Adam McBride, Peter Neumann, Stephen Power, Jenny Ramsden and Chris Robson. We are also grateful to Claire Hall in the MCO for all the checking she has done.

Summer School Staff

Summer School for Girls – August 2013

Natalie Behague
Victor Flynn
Sam Ford
Bob Gray
Howard Groves
Jo Harbour
Vesna Kadelburg
Vinay Kathotia
Zoe Kelly
Lizzie Kimber
Chloe Martindale
Helen McCartney
Claire Rebello
Hannah Roberts
Colva Roney-Dougal
Alan Slomson
Matthew Towers
Sophie Wragg

Oxford Week 1 – August 2013

Anne Andrews
Greg Andrews
Natalie Behague
Michael Bradley
Joshua Clark
Sue Cubbon
Richard Earl
Ben Green
Jo Harbour
Anna Hufton
Vesna Kadelburg
Vinay Kathotia
Frances Kirwan
Martin Lester
Peter Neumann
Martin Orr
Andrew Paverd
Alan Slomson
Geoff Smith

Oxford Week 2 – August 2013

Philip Coggins
David Crawford
Richard Freeland
Maria Holdcroft
Andrew Jobbings
Frances Kirwan
Vicky Neale
Florence Salter
Dan Schwarz
John Slater
Geoff Smith
Sophie Wragg
Dominic Yeo

Leeds Week 1 – July 2014

Sally-Anne Bennett
Dean Bunnell
Mary-Teresa Fyfe
Tony Gardiner
Magdalena Jasicova
Andrew Jobbings
Lizzie Kimber
Steven O'Hagan
Dominic Rowland
Alan Slomson
Karthik Tadinada

Leeds Week 2 – July 2014

Anne Andrews
Robin Bhattacharyya
Michael Bradley
Oliver Feng
James Gazet
Maria Holdcroft
Ina Hughes
Gerry Leversha
Paul Russell

TMC coordinators and regional helpers

[also involved in the writing (W) and checking (C) of materials where indicated]

Patricia Andrews
Beth Ashfield (C)
Ann Ault (W)
Martin Bailey
Anne Baker
Bridget Ballantyne
Andrew Bell
Elizabeth Bull
Dean Bunnell (W)
Kerry Burnham
Keith Cadman (W)
Madeleine Copin (C)
Elaine Corr
James Cranch
David Crawford (W)
Rosie Cretney
Alex Crews
Dusty de Sainte Croix (C)
Geoffrey Dolamore
Sue Essex (W)
Sally-Jane Fell
Sheldon Fernandes
Jackie Fox
Roy Fraser
Helen Gauld
Peter Hall
Karl Hayward-Bradley (W)
Terry Heard
Fraser Heywood (W)
Rita Holland
Sue Hughes
Sally Anne Huk
Pam Hunt
Andrina Inglis
Andrew Jobbings (W)
Tricia Lunel
Pat Lyden
Matthew Miller (W)
Hilary Monaghan
Steve Mulligan
Helen Mumby
Peter Neumann (W)
Pauline Noble
Andy Parkinson
Martin Perkins (C)
Dennis Pinshon
Valerie Pinto
Vivian Pinto
Stephen Power
Jenny Ramsden (C)
Peter Ransom (W)
Heather Reeve
Syra Saddique
Nikki Shepherd
John Slater
Alan Slomson
Graeme Spurr
Anne Strong
Penny Thompson (W)
James Welham
Ian Wiltshire
Rosie Wiltshire

Additional local helpers and organisers at TMC host venues

Anthony Alonzi
Morag Anderson
Emma Atkins
Sharon Austin
Ralph Barlow
David Bedford
Helena Benzinski
Rachel Blewett
Rhiannon Bourke
Frank Bray
Nigel Brookes
Paul Bruten
Helen Burton
Maxine Clapham
Kath Conway
Kevin Coxshall
Ian Craig
Barry Darling
Elin Dupasquier
Ceri Fiddes
Lucy Gill
Nick Hamshaw
Fiona Harding
Laura Harvey
Chyna Hulland-Rumley
Georgie Introna
Martin Kemp
George Kinnear
Claire Maher
Neil Maltman
Helen Martin
Lin McIntosh
Iain Mitchell
Marijke Molenaar
Heather Morgan
David Morrissey
Julie Mundy
Damian Murphy
Malcolm O'Donnell
Gareth O'Reilly
Viren Patel
Colin Reid
John Robinson
Amelia Rood
Paula Rowlands
Ann Rush
Amanda Smallwood
Dominic Soares
Richard Stakes
Gerard Telfer
Paul Thomas
Aaron Treagus
Sam Twinam
Danny Walker
Jo Walker
Liz Ward
Phillip Watson
Jake Wright

STMC coordinators and regional helpers

[also involved in the writing (W) and checking (C) of materials where indicated]

Anne Andrews
Patricia Andrews
Ann Ault
Matthew Baker (W)
Andrew Bell
Karl Hayward-Bradley
Elizabeth Bull
Kerry Burnham (W)
Tony Cheslett (W)
Antony Collieu (W)
David Crawford (W)
Rosie Cretney
Alex Crews (C)
Laura Daniels
Geoffrey Dolamore
Sue Essex
Karen Fogden (W)
Mary Teresa Fyfe
Helen Gauld
Andrew Ginty (W)
Peter Hall (W)
Mark Harwood (W)
Terry Heard
Alexandra Hewitt (W)
Rita Holland
Sue Hughes
Sally Anne Huk
Pam Hunt
Andrina Inglis
John Lardner
Pat Lyden
James Munro (W)
Peter Neumann
Charlie Oakley (W)
Martin Perkins (C)
Dennis Pinshon (W)
Stephen Power
Jenny Ramsden (C)
Alexandra Randolph (W)
Katie Ray (W)
Heather Reeve
Syra Saddique
Nikki Shepherd
John Silvester (C)
John Slater
Alan Slomson
Anne Strong
Penny Thompson
James Welham
Rosie Wiltshire

Maths Circles Speakers and Event Leaders

Pat Andrews
Anne Baker
Natalie Behague
John Berry
Abigail Bown
Dean Bunnell
Kerry Burnham
Katie Chicot
Philip Coggins
James Cranch
Yvonne Croasdaile
Sue Cubbon
Alan Eames-Jones
Mary Teresa Fyfe
Mark Fitzsimons
Nick Geere
Julian Gilbey
Kathryn Gillow
Susie Jameson-Petvin
Andrew Jobbings
Karl Hayward Bradley
Zoe Kelly
Tom Killick
Lizzy Kimber
Fiona Lawton
Gerry Leversha
Richard Lissaman
Kevin Lord
Tony Mann
Emily Maw
Adam McBride
Vicky Neale
Peter Neumann
Steven O'Hagan
Stephen Power
Alexandra Randolph
Peter Ransom
Montana Reid
Dominic Rowland
Jo Sibley
Geoff Smith
Jean Smith
John Slater
Alan Slomson
Frank Taylor
Barbara Thompson
James Welham
Cath Wilkins
Dominic Yeo

We thank the following schools and universities for hosting Maths Circles events

Hutchesons' Grammar School
Queen Elizabeth Gr. Sch., Wakefield
St Joseph's Catholic High Sch., Cumbria
University of Exeter
University of Manchester
University of Cambridge
Wells Cathedral School, Somerset
Newcastle University
St Albans High School for Girls
St Paul's School, London
University of Greenwich
University of Hull
Warwick School
Wycliffe College, Gloucestershire

BMOS Mentoring Schemes

James Cranch (Director)

Junior Scheme Coordinator: John Slater

Intermediate Scheme Coordinator: Richard Atkins

Intermediate external mentors:

Alice Ahn
Sally Anne Bennett
Neill Cooper
Andrew Jobbings
Zoe Kelly
Roger Kilby
Gordon Montgomery
Robbie Peck
David Phillips
Ian Slater
Alan Slomson
Pavel Stroev
Alasdair Thorley

Senior Scheme Coordinator: Andre Rzym

Senior external mentors:

Anne Andrews
Katriona Barr
Benjamin Barrett
Natalie Behague
Don Berry
Sam Cappleman-Lynes
Nicholas Chee
Andrea Chlebikova
Xenatasha Cologne-Brookes
Samuel Crew
John Cullen
Pawel Czerniawski
Natasha Davey
Chris Ellingham
Robin Elliott
Oliver Feng
John Fernley
Mary Teresa Fyfe
Simon Game
James Gazet
Julian Gilbey
James Hall
Matthew Haughton
Paul Healey
Fraser Heywood
Maria Holdcroft
Rosanna Holdsworth
Daniel Hu
Ina Hughes
Michael Illing
Susie Jameson-Petvin
Sahl Khan
Robert Lasenby
Jonathan Lee
Gerry Leversha
Michael Lipton
Daniel Low
Chris Luke
Matei Mandache
David Marti-Pete
Gareth McCaugham
David Mestel
Jan Mikolajczak
Lewis Morgan
Vicky Neale
Peter Neumann
Samuel Porritt
Keith Porteous

Hannah Pothecary
Jerome Ripp
Cicely Robinson
Julia Robson
Roberto Rubio
Florence Salter
Peter Scott
Jack Shotton
Ben Spells
Stephen Tate
Oliver Thomas
Matthew Towers
Federica Vian
Paul Voutier
Paul Walter
Perry Wang
Mark Wildon
Daniel Wilson
Dorothy Winn
Dominic Yeo
Michael Yiasemides
Fabian Ying

Advanced Scheme Coordinator: Richard Freeland

Advanced external mentors:

James Aaronson
Andrew Carlotti
Richard Freeland
Adam Goucher
Tim Hennock
Paul Jefferys
Henry Liu
Jordan Millar
Joseph Myers
Preeyan Parmar

UKMT Publications

The books published by the UK Mathematics Trust are grouped into series.

The *YEARBOOKS* series documents all the UKMT activities, including details of all the challenge papers and solutions, lists of high scorers, accounts of the IMO and Olympiad training camps, and other information about the Trust's work during each year.

1. 2013-2014 Yearbook

This is our 16th Yearbook, having published one a year since 1998-1999. Edited by Bill Richardson, the Yearbook documents all the UKMT activities from that particular year. They include all the challenge papers and solutions at every level; list of high scorers; tales from the IMO and Olympiad training camps; details of the UKMT's other activities; and a round-up of global mathematical associations.

Previous Yearbooks are available to purchase. Please contact the UKMT for further details.

PAST PAPERS

1. *Ten Years of Mathematical Challenges 1997 to 2006*

Edited by Bill Richardson, this book was published to celebrate the tenth anniversary of the founding of UKMT. This 188-page book contains question papers and solutions for nine Senior Challenges, ten Intermediate Challenges, and ten Junior Challenges.

2. *Past Paper Booklets and electronic pdfs – Junior, Intermediate, Senior Challenges and follow-on rounds.*

We sell Junior, Intermediate and Senior past paper booklets and electronic pdfs. These contain the Mathematics Challenge question papers, solutions, and a summary chart of all the answers.

The JMO booklet contains four years' papers and solutions for the Junior Mathematical Olympiad, the follow up to the JMC.

The 2013 IMOK booklet contains the papers and solutions for the suite of Intermediate follow-on rounds – the Grey Kangaroo, the Pink Kangaroo, Cayley, Hamilton and Maclaurin. Electronic versions of the IMOK Olympiad rounds and the JMO are also available.

BMO booklets containing material for the British Mathematical Olympiad Round 1 or 2 are also available.

The *HANDBOOK* series is aimed particularly at students at secondary school who are interested in acquiring the knowledge and skills which are useful for tackling challenging problems, such as those posed in the competitions administered by the UKMT.

1. *Plane Euclidean Geometry: Theory and Problems*,
   AD Gardiner and CJ Bradley

An excellent book for students aged 15-18 and teachers who want to learn how to solve problems in elementary Euclidean geometry. The book follows the development of Euclid; contents include Pythagoras, trigonometry, circle theorems, and Ceva and Menelaus. The book contains hundreds of problems, many with hints and solutions.

2. *Introduction to Inequalities*, CJ Bradley

Introduction to Inequalities is a thoroughly revised and extended edition of a book which was initially published as part of the composite volume 'Introductions to Number Theory and Inequalities'. This accessible text aims to show students how to select and apply the correct sort of inequality to solve a given problem.

3. *A Mathematical Olympiad Primer*, Geoff C Smith

This UKMT publication provides an excellent guide for young mathematicians preparing for competitions such as the British Mathematical Olympiad. The book has recently been updated and extended and contains theory including algebra, combinatorics and geometry, and BMO1 problems and solutions from 1996 onwards.

4. *Introduction to Number Theory*, CJ Bradley

This book for students aged 15 upwards aims to show how to tackle the sort of problems on number theory which are set in mathematics competitions. Topics include primes and divisibility, congruence arithmetic and the representation of real numbers by decimals.

5. *A Problem Solver's Handbook*, Andrew Jobbings

This recently published book is an informal guide to Intermediate Olympiads, not only for potential candidates, but for anyone wishing to tackle more challenging problems. The discussions of sample questions aim to show how to attack a problem which may be quite unlike anything seen before.

The *EXCURSIONS IN MATHEMATICS* series consists of monographs which focus on a particular topic of interest and investigate it in some detail, using a wide range of ideas and techniques. They are aimed at high school students, undergraduates, and others who are prepared to pursue a subject in some depth, but do not require specialised knowledge.

1. *The Backbone of Pascal's Triangle*, Martin Griffiths

Everything covered in this book is connected to the sequence of numbers: 2, 6, 20, 70, 252, 924, 3432, ... Some readers might recognize this list straight away, while others will not have seen it before. Either way, students and teachers alike may well be astounded at both the variety and the depth of mathematical ideas that it can lead to.

2. *A Prime Puzzle*, Martin Griffiths

The prime numbers 2, 3, 5, 7, ... are the building blocks of our number system. Under certain conditions, any arithmetic progression of positive integers contains infinitely many primes, as proved by Gustave Dirichlet. This book seeks to provide a complete proof which is accessible to school students possessing post-16 mathematical knowledge. All the techniques needed are carefully developed and explained.

The *PATHWAYS* series aims to provide classroom teaching material for use in secondary school. Each title develops a subject in more depth and detail than is normally required by public examinations or national curricula.

1. *Crossing the Bridge*, Gerry Leversha

This book provides a course on geometry for use in the classroom, re-emphasising some traditional features of geometrical education. The bulk of the text is devoted to carefully constructed exercises for classroom discussion or individual study. It is suitable for students aged 13 and upwards.

2. *The Geometry of the Triangle*, Gerry Leversha

The basic geometry of the triangle is widely known, but readers of this book will find that there are many more delights to discover. The book is full of stimulating results and careful exposition, and thus forms a trustworthy guide. Recommended for ages 16+.

The *PROBLEMS* series consists of collections of high-quality and original problems of Olympiad standard.

1. *New Problems in Euclidean Geometry*, David Monk

This book should appeal to anyone aged 16+ who enjoys solving the kind of challenging and attractive geometry problems that have virtually vanished from the school curriculum, but which still play a central role in national and international mathematics competitions. It is a treasure trove of wonderful geometrical problems, with hints for their solutions.

We also sell:

1. *The First 25 Years of the Superbrain*, Diarmuid Early & Des MacHale

This is an extraordinary collection of mathematical problems laced with some puzzles. This book will be of interest to those preparing for senior Olympiad examinations, to teachers of mathematics, and to all those who enjoy solving problems in mathematics.

2. *The Algebra of Geometry*, Christopher J Bradley

In the 19th century, the algebra of the plane was part of the armoury of every serious mathematician. In recent times the major fronts of research mathematics have moved elsewhere. However, those skills and methods are alive and well, and can be found in this book. The Algebra of Geometry deserves a place on the shelf of every enthusiast for Euclidean Geometry, amateur or professional, and is certainly valuable reading for students wishing to compete in senior Mathematical Olympiads. For age 16+ mathematicians.

3. The UKMT is the European agent for a large number of books published by the Art of Problem Solving (http://www.artofproblemsolving.com/).

To find out more about these publications and to order copies, please go to the UKMT website at www.publications.ukmt.org.uk.

In addition to the books above, UKMT continues to publish its termly Newsletter, giving the latest news from the Trust, mathematical articles, examples from Challenge papers and occasional posters for the classroom wall. This is sent free to all schools participating in the UKMT Maths Challenges.